Reminiscences of

Captain John Vavasour Noel, Jr.

U.S. Navy (Retired)

U.S. Naval Institute

Annapolis, Maryland

1987

Preface

A generation of naval officers has benefited from Captain John Vavasour Noel's interest in naval science and dedication to the service. This prolific author is responsible for such standard texts as Division Officer's Guide, Naval Terms Dictionary, The Bluejackets' Manual, and The VNR Dictionary of Ships and the Sea and various articles in Proceedings.

Several main threads run through Captain Noel's oral history, the strongest being devotion to his wife, Mary Hess Noel. She has been an enthusiastic and gracious partner in a life that has taken them across the globe.

Captain Noel's pride in his successful sea commands is evident and justified. During World War II, he commanded the light minelayer Sicard (DM-21), in which he served at Pearl Harbor when the Japanese attacked. From May 1944 through the rest of the war, he commanded the Lamson (DD-367), leading that ship during the Leyte Gulf and Ormoc Bay landings of October-December 1944 and when she served as fighter-director to Army planes that launched raids on the mainland of Japan from Iwo Jima in 1945. During bombardments for the Ormoc landings, a Japanese kamikaze plane carrying a bomb caused a gasoline fire to sweep the Lamson bridge, resulting in many deaths and a precarious leap from the bridge for Noel and other survivors. Postwar commands included the stores ship Altair (AKS-32), in which he pioneered the use of helicopters for underway replenishment in the late 1950s, and command of the light cruiser Springfield (CLG-7), flagship of Commander Sixth Fleet and two future CNOs, Admirals George Anderson and David McDonald.

Another thread is his professional writing. Captain Noel was persuaded to become involved with the Naval Institute Press while an instructor at the Naval Academy in the early 1950s, and this 35-year association has continued to produce standard works that can be found in virtually every wardroom library.

Still another theme in this oral history is tennis and Captain Noel's skill and lifelong love for the game that has been demonstrated as captain of the Naval Academy tennis team in the mid-1930s, and at exotic locations around the world.

After graduating from the Academy in 1936, cruiser duty followed in Indianapolis (CA-35) and Astoria (CA-34). Among postwar tours were duties as assistant chief of naval personnel for special projects in the mid-1950s, where he implemented a new, Navy-wide moral leadership program, postgraduate studies at Stanford University and the Industrial College of the Armed Forces, and service as naval aide to the Assistant Secretary of the Navy (Personnel and Reserve Force), where he got caught up in civilian-versus-military debate over the Judge Advocate General Corps in the early 1960s.

Credit for this volume is shared with Commander Etta-Belle Kitchen, U.S. Navy (Retired), who conducted the interviews at the Noels' home in Sante Fe. The transcription was done by Mrs. Deborah Reid of the Naval Institute staff.

Susan B. Sweeney
Oral History Department
U.S. Naval Institute
June 1987

CAPTAIN JOHN VAVASOUR NOEL, JR., UNITED STATES NAVY (RETIRED)

John Vavasour Noel, Jr., son of John V. and Eda Anderson Noel, was born on 2 June 1912, in Lima, Peru, where his father was founder and owner of several publications in English, among them the West Coast Leader. He lived in Valley Cottage, New York, most of his childhood, except for a year in Mexico City, and for five years prior to his naval service, lived in Charleston, South Carolina, where he attended Mount Hermon (preparatory) School and the College of Charleston.

On 3 March 1931, he enlisted in the U.S. Naval Reserve, and on 15 June 1932, he was honorably discharged to enter the U.S. Naval Academy, Annapolis, Maryland. As a midshipman he participated in athletics, being captain of the tennis team for one year and Naval Academy squash racquets champion for two years, 1935, 1936. Graduated and commissioned ensign on 4 June 1936, he subsequently advanced in rank, attaining that of captain to date from 1 March 1955.

From June 1936 until November 1938 he served as a junior officer on board the USS Astoria (CA-34), operating on the East and West Coasts. He then had communication duty on the staff of Commander Scouting Force, U.S. Fleet, attached to the USS Indianapolis (CA-35), flagship. In July 1940 he was transferred to the USS Sicard (DM-21), and in that light minelayer participated in action at Pearl Harbor on 7 December 1941, and the occupation and defense of Cape Torokina in November and December 1943. He received a letter of commendation with ribbon and "V" from Commander South Pacific Force, "For skillful and effective performance of duty under adverse circumstances while serving as Commanding Officer of a light mine layer operating in enemy-controlled waters of the Solomon Islands are during the period from November 1 to 8, 1943..."

Detached from the Sicard in March 1944, he attended West Coast Sound School at San Diego, California, for a month, and in May of that year assumed command of the USS Lamson (DD-367), which he commanded throughout the remainder of the war. Under his command, the Lamson took part in the Leyte landings in October and November 1944, and in the Ormoc Bay landings in December of that year. He was awarded the Bronze Star Medal with Combat "V" and a letter of commendation with star and "V" for his commendation ribbon from the Commander in Chief Pacific Fleet, for services in that command. The citations follow in part:

Bronze Star Medal: "For heroic achievement as Commanding Officer of the USS LAMSON, in action against enemy Japanese forces at Ormoc Bay, Leyte, Philippine Islands, on December 7,

1944. [He] directed a highly accurate and sustained bombardment of enemy-held shore in support of our invading troops despite the constant threat of aircraft attack and fire from Japanese land batteries [and] turned his ship to help defend the retiring convoy against enemy bombers and suicide planes which repeatedly attempted to penetrate the screen provided by warships. Under his inspiring command the LAMSON sent up a deadly and accurate fire, materially assisting in repulsing the attackers and in destroying fourteen aircraft..."

Letter of Commendation: "For meritorious conduct in the performance of outstanding service as Commanding Officer of the USS LAMSON from May 1944 to August 1945, while on anti-submarine patrols and escort duty, and also for a short time as a fighter-director ship on picket duty. His outstanding seamanship and professional skill contributed materially to the LAMSON's operations..."

Upon his return to the United States in August 1945, he was ordered to report in September to the Office of the Chief of Naval Operations, Navy Department, Washington, D.C. He served there until May 1947, and in June reported to Stanford University, California, to earn a master's degree in personnel administration. In September 1948 he again went to sea, this time as operations and plans officer on the staff of Commander Amphibious Group One, attached to the USS Mount McKinley (AGC-7), flagship.

When detached from staff duty in August 1950, he returned to the Naval Academy to serve for three years as an instructor in the Department of Seamanship and Navigation. From July 1953 until July 1954, he had duty afloat as executive officer of the USS Rochester (CA-124), after which he attended the Industrial College of the Armed Forces, Washington, D.C., in 1954-1955. In June 1955 he reported for duty as head of the Personnel Plans Branch, Bureau of Naval Personnel, Navy Department, and in March 1958 was ordered to sea as commanding officer of the USS Altair (AKS-32).

He served for two years as naval aide to the Assistant Secretary of the Navy (Personnel and Reserve Forces), and left the Navy Department in March 1961 to be commanding officer of the USS Springfield (CLG-7). On 17 January 1962 he was ordered detached for duty as U.S. naval attache and U.S. naval attache for air, Paris, France. He retired from active duty on 4 June 1965.

In addition to the Bronze Star with Combat "V" and the Commendation Ribbon with star and "V," Captain Noel has the

American Defense Service Medal, Fleet Clasp; Asiatic-Pacific Campaign Medal with four stars; American Campaign Medal; World War II Victory Medal; Navy Occupation Service Medal, Asia Clasp; National Defense Service Medal; the Korean Service Medal; United Nations Service Medal; and the Philippine Liberation Ribbon with star.

Married to the former Mary Hess of Bremerton, Washington, Captain Noel has three children: Carol Vavasour Noel Stephens, John Vavasour Noel III, and Joyeux Vavasour Noel.

Authorization

The U.S. Naval Institute is hereby authorized to make available to individuals, libraries and other repositories of its choosing the transcripts of two oral history interviews concerning the life and career of the undersigned. The interviews were recorded on 8 and 9 August 1984 in collaboration with Commander Etta-Belle Kitchen, U.S. Navy (Retired), for the U.S. Naval Institute.

The undersigned does hereby release and assign to the U.S. Naval Institute all right, title, restriction, and interest in the interviews. The copyright in both the oral and transcribed versions shall be the sole property of the U.S. Naval Institute. The tape recordings of the interviews are and will remain the property of the U.S. Naval Institute.

Signed and sealed this _____12th_____ day of __June__ 1987.

John Vavasour Noel
Captain, U.S. Navy (Retired)

Interview Number 1 with Captain John Vavasour Noel, Jr.,
U.S. Navy (Retired)

Place: Captain Noel's home in Santa Fe, New Mexico

Date: 8 August 1984

Subject: Biography

Interviewer: Commander Etta-Belle Kitchen, U.S. Navy (Retired)

Q: Good morning, Captain. Thank you for your time. The Navy appreciates your doing the background research which you have done and giving your time for the interview.

Captain Noel: It's an honor, of course, to be interviewed for this program. When I see the distinguished people who have already been interviewed, I sense that now you're getting down perhaps to those who had a worm's eye-view of the war.

Q: Not true. I have to deny that right now. The first thing that I think anyone looking at your biography would wonder is the origin or the meaning of your middle name. That's a very interesting name.

Captain Noel: The word "Vavasour" means "vassal of the vassals" in archaic French. It's a term that one encounters in Chaucer, but it is, in fact, an obsolete and very old minor title.* My family's name before they left the Isle of Jersey about 1800 was Vavasour Dit Noel, "the Vavasours who were called Noel." This is a custom on the Isle of Jersey. The family originally, of course, came from France; they were French Huguenots. My great-great-grandfather, who came to Canada from the Isle of Jersey, called himself Jean le Vavasour Dit Noel. Then he anglicized it when he got married, to John Vavasour Noel.

Q: That's very interesting. Not only is your name interesting, but as I've familiarized myself somewhat with your life, I find that we should begin at the beginning. Your early years to me I find very unusual. So it would be nice if we began with those.

Captain Noel: I was born in Lima, Peru, because my father had started a newspaper there, the first English newspaper in Peru. A few years after he started, in 1912, I was born. The newspaper was a success at first and then when the war broke out in Europe in 1914, there were economic troubles. He gave up the newspaper business, and the family, my mother, originally Swedish, and one sister, moved to Richfield, Connecticut.

I grew up in the vicinity of New York, out on Rockland Lake,

---

*Geoffrey Chaucer (1340-1400), an English poet of the Middle Ages, is probably best known for The Canterbury Tales, representing the stories of 23 pilgrims at an inn.

as a matter of fact, in a town called Valley Cottage, within commuting distance of New York City, where I went to school at times. I also went to school for a year in Mexico City, where my father was doing some work with the Mexican Government. My father was one of the founders of the Pan American Union and had devoted his life mostly to working in Latin America.

After going to school in Valley Cottage and at the Walden School in New York City, I went to Mount Herman Preparatory School. Then, since my family had moved to Charleston, South Carolina, my father then doing some work in Cuba with the tobacco commission and the Bacardi Brothers, I went to high school in Charleston. I lived in Charleston until I went off to the Naval Academy. After graduating from high school, I went to the College of Charleston for two years and then was able to go to the Naval Academy through the Naval Reserve. The Naval Reserve is allowed 25 candidates to the Naval Academy. In those days all you had to do was to go to sea, be recommended by your commanding officer in the Naval Reserve unit, pass the entrance examinations, and you were in. Since we had no political connections in South Carolina, this seemed to be a simple way and an easy way to get to the Naval Academy.

Q: I presume you wanted to go to the Naval Academy. What was your impelling reason behind that?

Captain Noel: I had met in Charleston, while I was a college boy, some of the young officers who came through Charleston every year in destroyers on their way to the Caribbean. Admiral Halsey was the squadron commander, and in one particular ship I had two or three good friends.* I thought their life was so interesting, and I was already aware of the fact that my family could not afford to send me north to school. I was spending most of my time at the College of Charleston making home brew in the fraternity house. I thought it was a good move to get off and work my way through college.

Q: That's unusual preparation for the Naval Academy. Tell me about some of your experiences in the Academy. Do you have any recollections that you'd like to include in your biography?

Captain Noel: I don't know how pertinent or how important they are. I had a great time at the Academy. I was 20 when I went in. I didn't take the school too seriously. I just barely passed a few courses; I got good marks in others. I stood about in the middle of my class.** I devoted myself at times to chasing girls and drinking beer and playing tennis and squash

---
*Captain William F. Halsey, Jr., USN, Commander Destroyer Squadron Fourteen, 1930-1932. Halsey, who eventually reached the rank of fleet admiral, is best known for his service as Commander South Pacific and Commander Third Fleet during World War II.
**Noel stood number 151 of the 262 graduates in the Naval Academy class of 1936.

racquets. I thought it was a great place. It was more, looking back on it, a training institution than an educational one. In those days it was not particularly stimulating intellectually, but it was a great life, prepared me for my profession, and fortunately I was able to get a more formal education later, when the Navy sent me to Stanford to get a master's degree in personnel administration.

Q: But you went through the Academy and you did graduate as an ensign in . . .

Captain Noel: 1936. Commissioned an ensign after perhaps an undistinguished career at the Naval Academy, and was ordered to the USS Astoria, a heavy cruiser. Again tennis had an influence on my life. The Assistant Chief of the Bureau of Navigation, who in those days handled personnel, was Admiral Chester Nimitz, who had a great interest in tennis and who had a son in my class, whom I know very well to this day.*

Q: What is that son's name?

Captain Noel: Chester Nimitz, Jr., who's been a very successful

---

*Captain Chester W. Nimitz, USN, served as Assistant Chief of the Bureau of Navigation from 1935 to 1938; as a rear admiral, he was chief of the bureau from June 1939 until December 1941. As a four-star admiral he commanded the U.S. Pacific Fleet through almost all of World War II.

executive. There were four of us from the tennis team ordered to two cruisers because for years our cruisers, spending part of the summer in New England, had been pretty much required to enter a naval tennis tournament at Bar Harbor. The people up there had arranged the tennis tournament between the British and the American navies. The American Navy was usually caught aback and had no really good contestants, so this time Chester Nimitz was determined that we would have at least some fair players up there. Two of us in the Astoria and two in the New Orleans had a marvelous summer; our only duty was to play tennis. We went ashore in Newport and Portland and Bar Harbor and had a great time playing tennis. Ironically, it turned out that that summer the British didn't turn up in Bar Harbor, so none of this drill succeeded in defeating any British tennis players, but in those days before the great fire at Bar Harbor, it was a very, very glossy, luxurious resort and rather a new experience for a small-time fellow from the Naval Academy.*

Q: It reminds me of the ad, they say, "Join the Navy and see the world." In your case it was really appropriate.

Captain Noel: We saw the world. I remember a dinner at the Dorrance house outside of Bar Harbor, where there was a footman

---
*Bar Harbor, Maine, was a summer resort town, greatly damaged by fire in 1947.

Noel #1 - 7

behind every chair, and there must have been a dozen people for dinner.

Q: Then you stayed in the Atlantic, I believe, for only a year. Then your ship was ordered out to the Pacific?

Captain Noel: Yes, the winter of 1936-37, after a shipyard overhaul. I must mention that our new skipper that came aboard in the fall, Pop Gill, was a well-known character in the sense that he was a superb naval officer but also a very enthusiastic tennis player. So you can imagine how arduous my duties were when Pop Gill came aboard.* When in port, I was accustomed to being aroused by his steward and told to be on the quarterdeck ready to play tennis within an hour. This was the sort of a life we had for a while. My shipmates in the Astoria were not delighted with my exemption from many duties, but we got along. I had the good fortune to have a good division and have a good gunnery score, so nobody thought really ill of me. But it was a very stimulating life. We went to the West Coast where they had not seen many naval ships. This was the beginning of our period of being very concerned about the Japanese. We deployed a large part of the Navy to the Pacific. So we had the pleasure of being based in Long Beach and going into San Francisco and Portland,

---

*Captain Charles C. Gill, USN.

Oregon, as almost the first large naval units. Of course, we were greeted with tremendous hospitality.

Q: I remember that ship coming into Portland, Oregon. I lived there in those days.

Captain Noel: It was 1937, as I recall. They had the Tournament of Roses, so we made fast along the waterfront, and every sailor who went down that accommodation ladder had his choice of a rosy-cheeked girl who wanted to show him the town. We officers were greeted on the street by strangers who introduced themselves and said that this was the name and address of their club and would we please make ourselves at home. In those days in Portland you could only buy a drink in a private club. This was hospitality with a capital H. We had a division commander who was also a well-known tennis player, Admiral Walter S. Anderson, and he would pick us up and take us out to the tennis club.* Life still was mild duties aboard ship, a lot of good tennis and a lot of good liberty ashore.

Q: I have a thought that about that time your skipper was Kelly Turner.

---
*Rear Admiral Walter S. Anderson, USN, Commander Cruiser Division Four.

Captain Noel: Afterwards. Just after Pop Gill, Kelly Turner came aboard, and there was an impressive man.* He would call the chief engineer up on the bridge. I was assistant navigator and spent all my time on the bridge when we were under way, so I could observe the heads of departments being called up for a conference, which really wasn't much of a conference. They were lectured by Kelly Turner on how to run their departments, and he knew everything about engineering and gunnery and communications. He was a very tough fellow who later earned the name "Terrible Turner," as an amphibious commander, but a good officer to work for. I was his general quarters officer of the deck. I was his officer of the deck when we made our Cast recovery of the float seaplanes.** You didn't make a single mistake of a degree or a half a knot when you were doing things for Kelly Turner. You could find yourself under hack if you didn't have the colors exactly two-blocked as you came into port.*** It didn't happen

---

*Captain Richmond Kelly Turner, USN, commanded the Astoria (CA-34) from 1938 to 1940. Turner eventually reached four-star rank after highly successful service as an amphibious force commander during World War II.

**"Cast" was used for the letter C in the phonetic alphabet of the time. The recovery involved the cruiser making a turn in order to create a slick on which the floatplane could land. The plane then taxied onto a sea sled and was hoisted back aboard by one of the ship's cranes.

***Under hack meant an officer was suspended from duty for a period of time and confined to his stateroom for whatever infraction he had committed. Having the colors two-blocked meant that the top of the flag was all the way up to the top of the flagstaff.

to me, but most of my contemporaries had some slight problem of this kind. But on the other hand, he knew his profession, and he was fair.

Q: That's the kind of person that you learn from. You had your usual tour there on the Astoria, and then you, as usual, were transferred to another ship, I presume?

Captain Noel: Yes, I was transferred from the Astoria to the staff of Commander Scouting Force, Vice Admiral Adolphus Andrews, as one of his communication watch officers. I did have a wonderful tour on the Astoria, because in those days the routine for freshly assigned ensigns was to have them serve six months in each department, so I got a good background in engineering and gunnery. As assistant navigator I gained a great deal of experience.

After I left the Astoria, she took the Japanese ambassador's body back to Japan, and that was a trip that I'm sorry I missed.* But I did have an interesting tour in the Indianapolis, which was the flagship. My job there was, as the name implies, communication watch officer. The four of us stood watches

---

*On 26 February 1939, Hiroshi Saito, a recent Japanese ambassador to the United States, died in Washington, D.C. As a gesture of international goodwill, the U.S. Government sent his ashes to Japan on board the Astoria, which arrived in Yokohama Harbor on 17 April.

Noel #1 - 11

monitoring all the rather elaborate communications, many of them coded, that came in and out of major commands.

Q: Where was it actually?

Captain Noel: The Indianapolis was with the Pacific Fleet, based in Long Beach. We made one trip to the Caribbean through the Panama Canal, went into Galveston, where I had the good luck to have a week's leave and flew down to Mexico, where Mary had gone during my absence to stay with my mother and father. She hadn't met them before. I should interpose here that I'd been married in 1938 when the Astoria came into Bremerton for a major overhaul.*

We were in the Caribbean when relations with Japan continued to deteriorate, and we were suddenly ordered from the Caribbean back through the canal to the Pacific, instead of the cruise that had been planned, which was north to New York. I had some leave in Galveston, as I mentioned, and got down to Mexico City to spend a week with Mary, and I had the good fortune of coming back on the airplane with Josephus Daniels, who was our ambassador

---
*The overhaul was at the Puget Sound Navy Yard, Bremerton, Washington.

there.* He was famous in the Navy, as most people know, for having made us dry; he forbade any alcohol being consumed aboard ship, one of the wisest things that anybody has ever done and one in which I've always rejoiced. The commanding officer has enough problems aboard ship without worrying about his people getting drunk or his officer of the deck at night being a bit woozy.

We came back to the Pacific, and then at that time they formed the Hawaiian detachment, of which Admiral Adolphus Andrews, Commander Scouting Force, was in command. This detachment was sent out to Pearl Harbor to reinforce the few ships that we had there. This, again, was in response to our growing problems with Japan.

We went in the Indianpolis to Hawaii in 1939. Mary followed. We found a tiny apartment on Waikiki. It was marvelous living on the beach, didn't even have glass in the windows. I joined the old Outrigger Canoe Club and surfed with the Kahanamoku brothers. Of course, we were only in port 25 or 30% of the time, but when we were in port it was glorious living in the Hawaiian Islands and enjoying the traditional sports. Surfing then was only known

---

*Josephus Daniels was Secretary of the Navy from 1913 to 1921. As of 1 July 1914, Daniels issued an order ending the practice of having officers' wine messes on board ships, and the ships of the U.S. Navy have been officially dry since then. The Assistant Secretary of the Navy during Daniels's tenure was Franklin D. Roosevelt. When Roosevelt became President in 1933, he named Daniels ambassador to Mexico. Daniels held the post for eight years.

Noel #1 - 13

really in the islands, and it was done in the Hawaiian fashion with big, solid 90-pound boards. It took a lot of skill and strength to learn surfing then, but within a year the California lifeguards had invented a hollow plywood board that was very much easier for novices like us to learn on.

Q: I'd like to go back, because I know that Mary, Mrs. Noel, has been a vital part of your life. You said you met her in Bremerton, but I think we ought to review a little bit more of that.

Captain Noel: Yes, I should elaborate on that a bit. The Astoria, at the end of 1937, was sent to Bremerton for a shipyard overhaul.

Q: I presume you went right up there after you'd been to Portland, after you'd had these coastal visits.

Captain Noel: Yes. There I had the great good fortune at a dinner party, to which I'd been invited as a spare man, to meet Mary. We were immediately attracted to each other, but her date in those days was a friend off the Ranger, so I had to wait a few days until Ranger left port, and then I asked her for a date. Anyway, I borrowed $65 from my dear roommate and doubles partner and tennis-playing friend Hoyt Mann and bought a leaky old car which was enough to get me out to where Mary lived on Marine Drive.* The ship went back to Long Beach in the spring and then suddenly was ordered up to Kodiak by way of Bremerton, and returned to Bremerton after the visit to Kodiak. I don't remember the military purpose of this visit. I do remember we caught an awful lot of trout up there. We all went fishing, but I don't remember anything very substantive about it.

On our return to Bremerton, Mary and I were married quietly, with no one there except two friends who sort of crashed the wedding, because Mary's stepfather had just died and we were married by the chaplain in the garden of his house on Marine Drive, and set up housekeeping then in Long Beach.

My marriage to Mary Hess of Bremerton, at 18 a sophomore at the University of Washington, was the most important event of my life and seems to gain in significance with time. When I met her, I had no thoughts of marriage, but this extraordinary woman captured my heart and mind instantly. In a demanding, often impoverished and adventurous life, Mary has been a superb mother, hostess, companion, and friend. She has a far-reaching, enquiring mind and an immense sympathy and compassion for all. What success I had as naval attache in Paris and country director for the International Executive Service Corps in Morocco and Iran, for example, can be attributed to her sure touch in dealing

---

*Ensign Hoyt D. Mann, USN.

Noel #1 - 15

with foreigners and Americans alike.

Q: That would have been 1937 you were married?

Captain Noel: 1938. You couldn't marry in those days until you had been graduated for two years. So I met her in the first part of '38, and we were married in June of 1938 and went to Long Beach, where we found a little apartment on the beach and took up a wonderful life, going to sea for a week or ten days, coming in for a week or ten days. It was almost an ideal life. Being out a week gave the wives time to get the household in order, and when we came in we had a brand-new party.

We're back now, I think, to our stay in Hawaii before the war.

Q: Yes.

Captain Noel: While we were in Hawaii, I was transferred from the Indianapolis, from the staff of ComScoFor to the USS Sicard (DM-21), an old World War I four-piper destroyer, almost the last of her class, built in Bath, Maine. She had been converted to a minelayer, which meant that the torpedo tubes were removed and mine tracks were put on each side of the deck aft. But otherwise she had all the characteristics of a destroyer.

Mine Division One had been homeported in Hawaii for many

years, and we hadn't done any real mining, of course, but we had mining practices and we had gunnery practices. I was ordered as the gunnery officer, and I was also the first lieutenant. These ships were undermanned and under-officered, and the life aboard ship was increasingly demanding, because we had more and more exercises, more and more things to do, more and more communications. And not many more people, since the Navy was expanding in those days. But it was still a great life to live in Hawaii and go to sea a moderate amount of the time and enjoy the delights of Hawaii when we were ashore.

Q: Was the condition of the world or of the Pacific an alarming one at that time?

Captain Noel: I'm afraid I wasn't that concerned about it. I am amazed now that I didn't follow events in Europe more carefully, but I don't seem to have much recollection of being concerned. Of course, I was a newlywed. Our first child, Carol, was born in the islands while we were there. I think I was too much wrapped up in being an impoverished but very happy young ensign and lieutenant (junior grade), starting a family, working hard at my profession, playing hard when the surf was up, to be much concerned about international events. I will say this, that the night before Pearl Harbor, a group of us old friends had gotten together. We were drinking champagne, and I made the unequivocal statement that the Japanese would never be insane enough to commit national suicide by attacking us without warning. You can imagine that about five hours later when I woke up and all hell had broken loose, I was convinced that this was about the silliest thing I had ever said. The reason the subject came up was we all had a great deal of intelligence, none of it particularly secret, that the Japanese were on the move. But we never thought they had either the courage or the professional ability to reach Pearl Harbor and hit us there. We knew they were going to hit something, probably the Philippines.

Q: I think we're now at the point of your experiences at Pearl Harbor, and I think you've aptly called it one man's viewpoint of Pearl Harbor.

Captain Noel: When Mary found out that she was to have Carol there, we had to leave our apartment in Waikiki because no babies were allowed there, and we found a wonderful, small, modern house up on Halawa Heights, overlooking part of Pearl Harbor and particularly the channel. It was in this house that we were introduced to World War II. We had a Japanese nurse for the baby, but this was Sunday, of course, and on Sundays we used to take turns getting up and heating a bottle for Carol, who was then some six-eight months old. This morning of December seventh was my turn. As I walked into the kitchen which adjoined the

Noel #1 - 18

little dining room with big glass windows overlooking Pearl Harbor, I was a bit foggy, but I couldn't help but observe all the splashes and smoke and the uproar that seemed to be going on in the direction of Pearl Harbor. My first thought was that the Army must be having a Sunday morning exercise that I didn't know about, until my skipper, who was a keen communicator and always had a radio turned on, called me from Waikiki, where he couldn't see anything. But he said, "Jack, I hear that the Japanese are bombing Pearl Harbor."

I said, "Captain, you must be right. That's just what I'm looking at. I'll join you at the ship."*

At this time our Sicard was at one of the Baker Six berths in the shipyard right next to Ten Ten Dock, where the Pennsylvania was moored. Ahead of the Pennsylvania were the Cassin and Downes in dry dock. The Japanese intelligence was so good that after they missed the Pennsylvania with their torpedoes and high altitude bombing in the first attack at 8:00 o'clock on the battleships moored along Ford Island, they went after the Pennsylvania. We were the recipient of no direct attack, because we were too minor to be their major target, but we did receive many of the bombs, the shorts, that missed the Pennsylvania.

At any rate, I jumped into my clothes and roared out to Pearl Harbor. I remember I went through the gate at high speed. The

---

*Commander William C. Schultz, USN, was the commanding officer of the Sicard (DD-346) in December 1941.

Marines had manned their antiaircraft guns and were firing furiously. We went to the ship where we found we really had nothing to do but help other ships around us, because we had no armament aboard. We had been stripped down for a shipyard overhaul. My chief gunner's mate, a wonderful fellow named Case, and my right-hand man for shooting some great gunnery scores, had found somewhere an old World War I Lewis .30-caliber machine gun and was cradling it in his arms and shooting at the Japanese dive bombers as they pulled out over us and the Pennsylvania, with tears running out of his eyes from frustration. You could see that his tracers were hitting the armored bottoms of these Japanese planes and doing no harm at all.

Anyway, when I came aboard, the skipper was there and trying to put his tin hat together. We had been provided with World War I steel helmets, sort of the flat dish-shaped ones that you're all familiar with that had a leather strap arrangement that you fitted over your head that had to be screwed in to the steel hat. They were issued unassembled, and we had all assembled our hats because we had to wear them at general quarters, but he, being the captain, had his hat stuck in a drawer somewhere. He came out in the wardroom and said, "Jack, will you put this hat together for me?" So I was forced to sit down at the wardroom table and adjust these screws in his hat while the ship rose out of the water every once in a while a couple of feet when a near-miss would land in the water alongside. Incidentally, we were not hit, but we did lose our motor whaleboat, which was made fast at the stern. This little test of nerve, I suppose, was good for me. I didn't want to show the skipper I was scared and nervous, which, of course, I was. But I put his tin hat together.

All we could do was to send some of our people to the ships down the dock and help them load their guns, and we sent a group of men over to the Pennsylvania. We lost some on the Pennsylvania when she was hit. I noticed that right alongside of us the captain of the destroyer was acting as his own number one loader. He had a couple of people pointing and training, and he was throwing the shells in while they were shooting. It was a rather every-man-for-himself morning with ships backing clear of the slip and the guns going off and the whistles blowing. No damage done to the Sicard.

Q: You said the captain of the destroyer was loading ammunition. It's an event worthy of note, I think.

Captain Noel: It sort of expressed the flavor of that morning. Then, as the last Japanese attack had been made--as everyone probably knows, the Japanese only attacked Pearl Harbor once, which was a very grave mistake. They should have, of course, come in again and destroyed the fuel tanks and the shipyard repair facilities, which would have given them an immense

Noel #1 - 21

advantage.

Q: Did you ever evaluate why they didn't?

Captain Noel: Yes. I've read Japanese accounts of it. The commander of the Japanese air group almost got himself court-martialed and shot for waving his hands in front of the admiral insisting they go back, because the defenses had been destroyed. There were no defenses left, and it would have been a very easy affair. But the senior admiral was an old chap, non-aviator, as I recall, and he had had a great success and he was going to retire.* I think they were still afraid of our B-17 bombers. A flight had flown in that morning, and I think this concerned the admiral. It needn't have, because those B-17s never hit anything, including the Battle of Midway, but that's because it was early in the war and they really weren't suited to that kind of warfare.

When the Japanese attack was over, we heard a radio report that the Japanese were landing at Barbers Point. This was one of the radio broadcasts made by the many Japanese that had come into the Japanese consulate. We'd been stupid enough, we Americans, to let the Japanese consulate have diplomatic immunity for about 200 real bad types, and they were the ones who committed the

---
*The commander of the Pearl Harbor striking force was Vice Admiral Chuichi Nagumo, Imperial Japanese Navy.

sabotage and the disinformation. There wasn't a single Japanese of American citizenship who was disloyal. This was a fact that was not brought out immediately. Our Japanese neighbors were, of course, loyal and friendly and took Mary under their wing during the attack.

To get back to the word that the Japanese were landing at Barbers Point, which, of course, wasn't true at all, we were all concerned then that we might have to fight in another fashion, and we had no guns, machine guns. We had enough ammunition for a few .45 pistols, which were sort of the decorative thing that an officer of the deck wore when he was on duty. Stewards came in the wardroom and asked if they could have the decorative sabers that we had--we called them cutlases, but they were really old cavalry sabers that were decoration on the wardroom wall--if they could have those sabers, which they carried off and sharpened up. Everybody was quite serious about defending themselves at that point, because we were convinced the Japanese were ashore.

Everything was quiet. In the afternoon, the commodore of MineDiv One said that we minelayers might as well give liberty to our people who had families ashore and who were worried about them, since there wasn't a darn thing we could do. We had nothing to shoot. This was a great thing for us. I went home to find Mary in some apprehension. The Japanese grandmother had come over to hold her hand and had said to her--this was interpreted by the Japanese neighbor--that she was completely confused by what was going on. Here the people of her old country were killing the children of her new country, and she was going to go home and turn in. I stayed at home for a few hours. I had to report back after dark. That was a very hairy experience, because I wanted to leave the car with Mary. So I called the Red Cross, who had broadcast over the radio that they would provide transportation out to Pearl Harbor. The car that the Red Cross sent was manned by two very inebriated Hawaiians who, of course, had never driven in a blackout and who staggered out to Pearl Harbor. I was more concerned for my life during that half hour than I had been all day.

We spent a rather restless night with the whole harbor erupting in gunfire every time a dog barked. You can tell that some people were nervous. I should say that some of the planes from the Enterprise came in that night looking for the field at Ford Island and were fired upon. We didn't have anything to shoot at them with, so we were guiltless, but Fighting Six was shot at when they made a pass at Pearl Harbor. Otherwise, the night had no terrors.

We got up at dawn. This was when we had expected another Japanese attack, and it was a very unhappy feeling to be there with nothing to shoot with and expecting another massive bombing. Of course, there was no such bombing, and December the seventh passed into history.

I don't have to describe the damage in Pearl Harbor, but I'd like to observe that it was really, all in all, one of the most fortunate things that happened to the country as a whole. It solidified the Americans behind the war effort. It forced us into a war against Germany which we had to go into to preserve Western Europe. The tragedy of losing 2,000 or 3,000 lives, of course, is very real. We didn't lose many ships that were very useful. Those old battleships were repaired in time to be useful in the amphibious landings two and three years later. At the time, if they hadn't been damaged and sunk in Pearl Harbor, they would have gone out in deep water and been sunk permanently. So we did lose three or four destroyers and a few other ships, but the damage to the Navy, except for personnel, was rather light.

I'd also like to observe that I had the greatest respect and sympathy for Admiral Kimmel, who was exercising us at top speed before December the seventh.* We were working about as hard as people can work at their profession. The ships had to come into Pearl Harbor for logistic support. When we were at sea, we were firing guns and running at high speed at night. I saw four destroyers collide one night in a mock torpedo attack with all ships darkened.

Q: You saw this?

---
*Admiral Husband E. Kimmel, USN, Commander in Chief Pacific Fleet from February through December 1941.

Captain Noel: Yes. Admiral Kimmel passed the word down through the senior officers. Admiral Anderson, my tennis-playing friend, who was then Commander Battleships, told me, "Pass the word along, Jack, that Admiral Kimmel is very concerned that he has to push you people as hard as he's pushing you."* Because we'd go to sea during the week and would be working, really, around the clock. But he said it was necessary. Admiral Kimmel did not have the means to patrol all the waters around Pearl Harbor, around the Hawaiian Islands. There were just not enough patrol planes. I sat in at meetings where I heard this stated. The Army had the responsibility under the joint Army-Navy plans for defending the Hawaiian Islands. Admiral Kimmel, I think, did everything a reasonable man would do and was a victim, of course, of the old naval axiom, "When your ship runs aground, the captain gets court-martialed."

Q: Then after the horror of Pearl Harbor, your ship finished in overhaul. Let's go on from there.

Captain Noel: I should say that life was quite different in the islands after Pearl Harbor. I knew that Mary would have to leave

---

*Rear Admiral Walter Stratton, USN, Commander Battleships Battle Force. For Anderson's memories of the attack on Pearl Harbor, see Air Raid: Pearl Harbor! Recollections of a Day of Infamy (Annapolis: U.S. Naval Institute Press, 1981), pages 127-133.

with Carol, so we moved down to a lovely old beach hotel which no longer exists, called the Niumalo, next to the Halekulani, which does still exist. We gave up the house on the hill. Mary applied for a flight back to San Francisco in a Pan American Clipper, but it turned out when I checked on this just before the Battle of Midway, when things began to get tense, that they'd lost her name somewhere, so I had the great pleasure of having Mary in the islands for at least a few months.

When our overhaul was completed, we mostly were sent out on ten-day and two-week patrols, patrolling offshore at eight knots. During this period we did lay a mine field at French Frigate Shoal, one of the long Hawaiian chain that goes out to Midway and beyond. French Frigate Shoal is not inhabited; it has a sheltered harbor where it appeared that the Japanese were keeping a submarine or two to refuel their huge, long-range flying boats. After Pearl Harbor, one of these flying boats did make a pass over Oahu at night. This was a matter, of course, of concern, so we laid a mine field in this harbor at French Frigate Shoal, which we hoped would inhibit the submarines from coming in there and having the sheltered waters they needed to refuel the flying boat. I understand that this was an effective means and that the flying boats did not return, and it was fortunate that they didn't because it would have been a very serious matter just before Midway for the Japanese intelligence to observe the carriers and ships that we were assembling out there based on the superb intelligence in breaking the Japanese codes that had been gained, mostly due to the efforts of Commander Joe Rochefort.* This assembling of ships would have sort of blown the whole ball game, because it would have revealed to the Japanese that we knew about their plans at Midway. Our only hope at defeating them at Midway was to have them think that all we had was one carrier in the Pacific, which is all we would have had if Joe Rochefort and his associates had not broken the code and if Admiral Nimitz had not had the guts to believe in what Joe was deducing. If we'd only had one carrier to defend us against the Japanese at Midway, they would have certainly captured the Hawaiian Islands and probably would have been able to attack the West Coast.

Suffice it to say that we laid the mine field, and just before the Battle of Midway we did escort an aircraft transport that brought some more fighter planes out to Midway. As we were docked there, we asked permission of the island commander if we could go for a swim.** He said, "Yes, but you'll have to lay some barbed wire out on those beaches for me if you're going to go swimming." So we did.

Upon my return to Pearl Harbor, as I've said before, I checked on the Pan American list, because we knew something was going to break. We got Mary out in the Clipper, quite an

---
*Commander Joseph J. Rochefort, USN, was officer in charge of the Fleet Radio Unit at Pearl Harbor. His oral history is in the Naval Institute collection.
**The atoll commander was Captain Cyril T. Simard, USN.

adventurous trip in those days, 15 pounds of baggage in a pillowcase for both of them. Of course, when they landed at San Francisco, it's a good thing that we had some friends to meet them, because baby Carol had never had shoes on and I don't think she owned many clothes, and Mary had lived in the tropics for years, so they were received by friends. It was very difficult going into Pearl Harbor every once in a while during the war and not finding her there. I think if I'd had it to do all over again, I'd have found some way that she could have gotten a job there and stayed, because I went in and out of Pearl Harbor for the rest of the war.

Q: Wasn't the Clipper only a matter of a few years of operation at that point?

Captain Noel: Yes. It had been operating a very short time. It operated from Pearl City, where later on the destroyers built a big destroyer base.

Q: So it was kind of nerve-racking, just the flight itself, I would suspect.

Captain Noel: It was quite an adventure, Mary reported, but it was a much more pleasant way to go back with a small child than to wrestle with a transport ship.

So much for the preparations for the Battle of Midway. Of course, the Battle of Midway was one of the great battles of history, somewhat, I believe, still unrecognized as such. It never received the publicity we thought it should have had, but I think historians will eventually put it in its correct perspective. It was a great feat of arms.

Q: I didn't realize that, that it hadn't been considered as great as it is entitled to.

Captain Noel: Unfortunately, the naval ships that took part were under radio silence for about four days. The Army planes returning from Midway had claimed quite sincerely that they had hit dozens of ships and sunk dozens of carriers. As far as the press was concerned, by the time the Navy got back to Pearl Harbor, the Battle of Midway had already been won by the B-17s, which, of course, never got a single hit. But the near-misses to somebody at 15,000 feet looked close enough to be hits.

At any rate, the whole battle was a feat of arms that started with the great work of Joe Rochefort and his people in breaking the Japanese code. The whole battle really depended on us having just barely enough forces to accomplish what we did.

The next interesting thing is that by great good fortune Admiral Halsey was taken down with a skin disease and had to be hospitalized just as he was about to be sent out in command of all the ships. Admiral Spruance, a non-aviator, a quiet and unassuming chap whose real story has never been written because he permitted no interviews and kept no journals.* But Admiral Spruance was the real tactical genius of the Pacific and was told off by Admiral Nimitz to take charge, even though he was junior to Admiral Fletcher.** But Halsey knew Spruance and recommended that he be put in charge. Halsey didn't have the temperament for this sort of a battle and would have been drawn off by the Japanese as they attempted to draw Spruance west after the Japanese had lost their carriers. Admiral Spruance was almost openly insulted by the aviators on his flagship for being "chicken" and not going after the Japanese. Of course, they had those very fast battleships which would have destroyed our carriers. It was the genius of Spruance that he knew just exactly what he had to do and what he could do, that after destroying the carriers and essentially breaking the back of Japanese sea power, that he followed his orders from Nimitz, which were to preserve, if he could, his own carriers, because that's all we had in the whole damn Pacific. He had the great good sense to retreat when he had to.

The _Sicard_ played no part at all in the Battle of Midway. We

---

*Rear Admiral Raymond A. Spruance, USN. His biography is Thomas B. Buell's _The Quiet Warrior_ (Boston: Little, Brown and Company, 1974).
**Rear Admiral Frank Jack Fletcher, USN, Commander Task Force 17 during the Battle of Midway.

were at our familiar berth in Pearl Harbor, the Baker 6 berth, right alongside a salvage tug. The skipper was over in the wardroom and we were playing poker. It wasn't a very serious poker game, because out of the coding machine, which was in the captain's cabin near the wardroom, because there was no other room for it, came a single tape. All the secret stuff in those days was on one channel, so even little people like us could listen in on Admiral Nimitz and all his commands.

Q: Could everybody?

Captain Noel: Anybody who had an ECM, which is a decoding machine. All the major fleet units had it. I think we were at the bottom of the list of major fleet units, but still we had one. Here as we passed it, the tape came out of the captain's cabin and, unbroken, was just passed right around the wardroom table and everybody read all the reports of the sightings and what was going on, the ships reported sunk and the damage to the Yorktown. When we heard the Yorktown had been torpedoed, the skipper of the salvage tug got up and cashed in his chips and said, "Well, I'm getting under way because I know I'm going to get orders to do so." Sure enough, before he'd had a chance to get out of the harbor, his orders came through to go to meet the Yorktown and try to save her. They did put out the fires on the Yorktown, but she was torpedoed finally by a Japanese submarine and lost.

As this battle unfolded, of course, it was tremendously interesting. One of the more ridiculous aspects, however, was the commander of a patrol wing up in Kodiak, whose name was Gehres.* He was later skipper of the Franklin when she was damaged. He insisted on not only giving the results of his action and all the things he was doing, his naval planes found the Japanese up in the Aleutians and told the Army Air Corps up there, that they'd found the Japanese in the fog. They told the Air Corps bombers up there that they would stay over the Japanese force and send out MOs. This, of course, is the radio signal on which aircraft can home. The answer they got--this is just gossip, of course--was, "What is an MO?" But at any rate, Admiral Gehres's people were doing a fine job up there, but he insisted on composing citations for medals at the same time as they were doing all these great feats of arms. He insisted on sending this stuff in on this one secret circuit until finally Admiral Nimitz told him to stop sending in such extraneous stuff, that first class mail would do.

In June of 1942, shortly after Midway, Mine Division One, which was Sicard, Flusser, Preble, and Tracy, sailed for Indian Island mine depot near Seattle, actually at Port Townsend. Our job was to load some Mark 6 World War I mines. The mines had to

---
*Captain Leslie E. Gehres, USN.

be overhauled by our own minemen before we could take them aboard, so we had a marvelous two weeks there, those of us who were lucky enough to have our families join us, and we stayed at a country inn called Chevy Chase. After the Hawaiian Islands, a sunny summer in the northwest was gorgeous.

We headed north and laid our mine field off Kodiak to protect the anchorage there, which was used as a base by our naval forces that were protecting the Aleutians.

After laying our mines and a few days to see the town that had a Russian church and to do a little fishing that I'd remembered was so good in Woman's Bay, where we again caught almost a boat full of Dolly Varden trout, we went back to the Hawaiian Islands, where we took up our routine patrolling.*

We sailed again, this time with mines aboard, for Adak in the Aleutians. This we were establishing as an American base. There was an airfield there and an anchorage. Our job was to lay mines in the narrow passages on both sides of Adak and between the other Aleutian islands to deny their passage to Japanese forces. This was an interesting exercise, in that the visibility was generally poor, we had no navigational radar, the currents were strong, and we had to do some very precise and difficult navigating to put our mines in position where they really did

---

*Dolly Varden trout are very common in Alaska where they feed on salmon eggs, at one time to an extent that the state put a bounty on them.

inhibit the passage of any Japanese ships or submarines.

Winter operations in the Bering Sea in a little old ship like the Sicard were rather wearing. We really didn't have many good cold-weather clothes. This World War I destroyer was essentially unheated, and the weather was indescribably bad. These ferocious gales would periodically sweep across the whole chain, and during this period both the Japanese and the Americans would give up any thought of the war and just hang on to survive.

Q: Equally miserable. What time of year was this?

Captain Noel: November and December. We patrolled back and forth. We once started to train for a mission which was to tow some PT boats into Attu and attack Japanese shipping there. But this, fortunately, was aborted by some fellow who had some common sense, because I doubt whether there would be any sort of a rig you could get around a PT boat that would permit a towing cable that wouldn't tear out.

At any rate, we patrolled and survived the weather and occasionally went into Dutch Harbor. We were three months under way. I think we got mail once and food not at all. They sent a tanker to Adak so we were able to go alongside the tanker.

Our last trip into Dutch Harbor before we headed south was marked by another one of these howling gales that parted us from our mooring. Our anchor chain, which we had looped through the ring on this great big mooring, pulled out of a pelican hook on deck. We, in the middle of the night, went coasting down the harbor. Of course, we had steam at the throttle and we managed to get out through the gate and wait out there until daylight, where we were due to pick up a tanker, the Kaskaskia, and escort her south. When the Kaskaskia came out and saw the huge seas that were running from the north, she asked us what our maximum safe speed was. We said, "Twelve knots." She immediately sent us a signal to make 15 knots. This resulted in a tremendous beating. We lost fuel oil suction, we were pitching so badly, and our deck plates on the main deck started to crack from the engine room hatches outboard. We remembered that the Wasmuth, one of our class, although she was a minesweeper, had broken up in the Aleutians, because the depth charges had gone off.* There was little we could do until the crack really threatened the ship. Before the crack had extended itself more than 6 or 8 inches and we had regained fuel suction, we received our signal to turn south and go through Unimak Pass. I'll never forget the tremendous relief, not only in having the ship survive, but in seeing these huge mountainous swells rolling down from us, from the north, and knowing that we were going with them as we surfed down their slopes.

---

* On 27 December 1942, while the USS Wasmuth (DMS-15) was escorting a convoy through a heavy Alaskan storm, heavy seas wrenched depth charges from her deck, and they exploded nearby. Part of her stern was lost, so her officers and crew were transferred to the oiler Ramapo (AO-12). The Wasmuth sank on 29 December.

Q: It seems to me that the winter spent there as you have described it is truly indescribable in its misery and unimaginable for anyone who wasn't there with you. I am sure you were grateful to be leaving that part of the world.

Captain Noel: It was a great pleasure to leave that part of the world, and actually we were on our way to San Diego, where we became a control vessel for amphibious landings. Around San Diego they were rehearsing amphibious landings, including the one on Attu. Our job as a control vessel was to take the first wave of assault boats to the line of departure exactly on time. This had to be coordinated, of course, with the aircraft strikes and the shore bombardment that went along with the landing. We had many practice landings off California.

Mary and Carol joined me in San Diego. We found a furnished house and had a very rare and wonderful time with some family life and were lucky enough to be able to entertain the officers of the ship for a mint julep party. This was a historic event decided upon almost *in extremis*, because we had such a mixed bag of young reserve officers that came to the ship--an Indian, an intellectual from Antioch, and a deep water Baptist from Tennessee, among others. We decided a mint julep party was the way to get this wardroom all on the same frequency. Well, I got so tired of making mint juleps that night that I just had a couple of beers. We had a lot of soft drinks for the deep water

Baptists, but they apparently didn't know what mint juleps were, and they said they'd drink them and they did. They got falling-down drunk. There wasn't a glass left in the house. Everybody was pitching glasses into the fireplace after making patriotic toasts. But at any rate, it was a great party. The police did not bother us. Nobody really disgraced themselves other than just getting drunk and uproarious. And we did have a little more cohesion in the wardroom.

After we had been to San Diego and had trained for the landing at Attu, we returned to the Aleutians. We had a collision en route to Attu, which put us out of business for a while, and I took over command. We had been ordered to keep station in a dense fog off the Komandorski Islands, and the skipper was due to be relieved and he wasn't relieved as any punishment. There was no fault in this collision. We did not have navigational radar; we didn't have any kind of radar. We were trying to keep station by using sound gear on the wakes of the other ships, but we did hit another destroyer amidships and crumpled in our bow.* A salvage tug took the destroyer back to port. She had a flooded fireroom, but we suffered no casualties. The bow was bent back to the chiefs' quarters. And we got ourselves back to Adak. It was at that time in Adak with

---

*On 10 May 1943, just before the landings were scheduled at Attu, the Sicard collided in fog with the USS Macdonough (DD-351). The repairs to the Sicard at San Francisco were completed at the end of July.

the full concurrence of the skipper that we spliced the main brace. We had some medicinal whiskey aboard and we thought that this was an emergency, and we all had a stiff drink.

We went from the Aleutians to Mare Island, where we had a major overhaul and received some new guns.* This was the second time we'd been into Mare Island, and I knew enough to keep everybody off the ship until we had some boxcars alongside and had offloaded all the storerooms, in fact, taking everything personal off the ship and anything that could be stolen. The first time we'd gone into Mare Island, we had been naive enough to welcome all the shipyard workers aboard in the afternoon. We all went ashore that night, almost all, and the next morning when we came aboard, there was very little left that was liftable on the Sicard. This was nobody's fault in particular, except the fact that in the tremendous rush to build up the manpower of the shipyards, they hired any fellow that knew a screwdriver from a hammer, and they really didn't check his police record.

Q: Were they able to repair the damage done to the bow of the ship? I presume so.

Captain Noel: Yes. We got a new bow, we got some new guns that theoretically were antiaircraft guns, 3-inch/50s, to replace our

---
*Mare Island Navy Yard, Vallejo, California.

old 4-inch/50s, with which we were very accurate and fast firing. This was the decision of some idiot ashore, really, who never had to take these ships out in the forward area, because they gave us dual-purpose guns, 3-inch/50s, but didn't provide any central fire control system for them. So everything was sort of local control and was thoroughly unsatisfactory. But our job from then on was to lay mines, and this we could still do.

After getting repaired at the shipyard, we were ordered to the South Pacific, Mine Division One, to lay mines again. This should have been done, looking back on it, much sooner, because if they had been able to lay a small mine field near Savo Island, I don't think the Tokyo Express would have been able to cause the tremendous damage that they did when they attacked our ships that were supporting the landings at Guadalcanal. There was one battle there called the Battle of Savo Island where we lost three or four cruisers, including the Astoria.*

Q: That was devastating.

Captain Noel: This could have been prevented, I believe, if we'd have had a mine field out there.

---

*The Tokyo Express was a nickname given to the Japanese warships which periodically approached Guadalcanal at night from the north to attack American ships and to bombard American positions ashore. On the night of 8-9 August 1942, the Japanese force sank the USS Astoria (CA-34), USS Quincy (CA-39), USS Vincinnes (CA-44), and the Australian cruiser Canberra.

But anyhow, we went through Pearl Harbor where I called on Admiral Nimitz, as was his custom. All commanding officers from fleet units called on Admiral Nimitz every time they came through Pearl Harbor. This way this great man who had the Nelson touch kept in contact with his ships, even down to the lowliest destroyer.

In the South Pacific, we roamed from Noumea in New Caledonia north to the vicinity of Bougainville, still under Jap control. We patrolled, escorted, and laid mines up the Slot.

On one of these expeditions, our main feed pumps failed, and we were limited to the ten knots we could make with the auxiliary feed pumps. In these old ships, spares were not available for many parts of the machinery, and we had to make our own. This took six or eight hours. During this time, we were still in waters controlled by the Japanese and under Japanese air surveillance, and it was a rather unhappy feeling to be restricted to ten knots and knowing that we could be spotted and attacked. We were under radio silence, of course. I think this period lasted a little longer, because when Admiral Halsey finally sent us a message congratulating us on doing our job and saying he was glad to hear from us, he indicated that he'd been worried because we were a bit overdue.

One of our last minelaying expeditions was off Empress Augusta Bay, Cape Torokina, in which we laid a mine field off the cape to prevent the Japanese cruisers and destroyers from coming down and supporting their troops who were being attacked by the Army that had landed at Empress Augusta Bay, our Army. This was a use of moored mines, which we felt should have been used earlier in the war, particularly off Savo Island, and would have prevented that disastrous defeat we suffered when we were supporting with our cruisers the assault on Guadalcanal. This was an interesting operation because after we laid our mine field we retired at full speed and were able to witness a naval battle between the Japanese forces that had indeed come south to do just what we were trying to prevent and the American forces, some of them under Captain Arleigh Burke, that engaged them.* We could see the high trajectory 6-inch cruiser gunfire from the light cruisers and then the flatter trajectory of the 8-inch projectiles, and all of this on a clear night was quite a sight to see.

We did other odd jobs around the South Pacific. On one occasion when they were establishing an officers' club at Tulagi, we were told off to bring the initial supply of liquor up from Espiritu Santo. We had our magazines full of liquor and an armed guard sitting on it; nevertheless, our people did their best to drop a hogshead of British rum, hoping the thing would break and they could salvage some. All in a spirit of good fun.

---
*Captain Arleigh A. Burke, USN, was Commander Destroyer Squadron 23 during the Battle of Empress Augusta Bay in November 1943. As an admiral, Burke served as Chief of Naval Operations from 1955 to 1961.

It was not a happy situation, however, when the officers could go ashore in these places and get plastered, and the men had no recreation at all unless we organized it. That we did, even before it was legal. We carried beer aboard ship and then found someplace--once it was just a sand spit that was two feet underwater--for the men to go and get away from the ship and have a couple of cans of beer. Usually we could find a beach where we could sit under some palm trees. Of course, the officers joined the men and this was our total recreation for months on end. It was much harder on the men than the officers, and I think these officers' clubs with unlimited liquor were quite unnecessary.

The morale, however, of our people was very good, and if anybody wants a description of what life as like on one of these old four-pipers in the South Pacific, all they have to do is read The Caine Mutiny. Ensign Wouk was on one of the four-pipers down there.* As a matter of fact, I knew his skipper, who was a little punchy from having been a Naval Academy boxer, but he was not a Queeg by any means.** Queeg was a dramatic creature of fiction and really didn't follow any one particular officer. The Caine Mutiny is unique; it's the only book in which I've read a description of how life really was on the steel ships in the boiling tropics, and particularly a steel box that was built on

---
*Herman Wouk, a Naval Reserve officer, served in the destroyer minesweeper Southard (DMS-10).
**Commander Frederick R. Matthews, USN, is the officer being referred to.

the main deck to house a new piece of equipment to decode messages. It was originally built as a clipping room for 20-millimeter ammunition, but as soon as we got this new decoding and encoding equipment, we had to use it as a decoding room. You can imagine what life was like for the most junior ensign on the ship who was told off to operate this machine in a steel box on top of a steel deck.

Q: And the temperatures were running . . .

Captain Noel: Very high and a lot of humidity. But at least the weather was good down there. It was hot, but the Solomons are an area that rarely has bad weather. The seas were generally calm, and going by these islands early in the morning and sniffing the offshore breeze, one could smell the genuine smell of the jungle and the flowers and so on.

While anchored in Tulagi, I was relieved of command of the Sicard and ordered back to the United States, it turned out for 30 days' leave and command of the destroyer Lamson. It was a little interesting getting back from Tulagi, which is right across the water from Guadalcanal. Fortunately, the chief in charge of air transportation at Guadalcanal had been Admiral Anderson's writer in his last command and knew me from my tennis-playing relationship with Admiral Anderson. So the minute I showed up, I was assured of whatever priority I needed to get an airplane out of Henderson Field. It turned out that the last plane down was a big R4D which had initiated a new one-stop flight from Hawaii via Johnston Island to Gaudalcanal, but they had damaged their landing gear on landing on a mat there at Henderson Field, and we had to wait until they flew down a new wheel.

Q: Where is Henderson Field?

Captain Noel: On Guadalcanal.

I had fortified my seabag with many bottles of tax-free liquor that we carried on board, perfectly legally, for consumption ashore, knowing that nothing will get you faster across the face of the earth during wartime than a couple of good bottles of liquor. So I was made welcome immediately at sort of a VIP Quonset hut where the pilot, copilot, and crew of this R4D were awaiting this spare wheel. Since they had brought down some fresh milk and some lettuce from Hawaii, something we hadn't seen for months on end, it was a fair swap and we all lived high. They drank my liquor, and I ate their fresh food.

Eventually the airplane was fixed. We landed at Johnston Island to refuel. Somehow somebody left the top off one of the gas tanks, because as soon as we were airborne, we found ourselves sitting in two inches of gasoline, sloshing around the cabin floor. Everybody was advised not to light a cigarette. We told the field we were coming back. We did, got the gasoline out of there, topped off again and went to Hawaii. There I was put on the Matsonia which was now a troop carrier and had a rather luxurious, for a troop carrier, trip back to the United States.

I had found that Mary was in Palo Alto. I thought all this time she was still with her mother in Bremerton, and it was very fortunate that I stopped in, as I always did in San Francisco, at Newbegin's Bookstore to see our dear friend Chardie Bridget, whose husband was lost in the Philippines.* He was the great guy on Bataan who organized the Navy contingent as a Navy infantry and fought until he was captured and he was lost after that. Chardie Bridget said, "You know that Mary is in Palo Alto?" This was a blessing, because I was just about to try to work my way up to Bremerton. I went to Palo Alto and saw for the first time my son, who then was a few months old. We decided that we would go to Mexico on leave to visit my father and mother and my sister Jane. We took Carol, who was then about three, and Jackson. We had a marvelous holiday in Mexico City, then flew back to San Diego.

Before taking command of the Lamson in Mare Island, I was sent to San Diego to sonar school, where I was supposed to learn all about the latest methods of antisubmarine warfare, since that was a major chore of a destroyer. This time I had a much more

―――――――――
*Commander Francis J. Bridget, USN. He was later killed in an attack on the prisoner of war ship Oryoko Maru while en route to Japan.

modern destroyer that had rather advanced sound gear.

We had an interesting time and, of course, a wonderful time together in Coronado. Fortunately we were taken in off the street while we were walking back and forth looking for any sort of accommodations by Mary and Mac Jones, whom we had met the last time we were in Coronado. He was an intelligence officer with the amphibious Navy assigned to the Marines. This was a couple that we knew later in Europe, whose daughter and son-in-law we still know, and who stayed in our apartment in Paris for long periods of time when we were in our house in Spain. At any rate, we blessed the Joneses for taking us in literally off the street, because Coronado was jammed to the hilt at that time.

We suffered mildly a month of instruction, and then had the great good fortune to be assigned a Quonset hut in Mare Island. Although far from being a new destroyer, the Lamson was one of the 1,500-tonners and, as a matter of fact, was the class that followed the old four-pipers. Taking over a relatively modern destroyer was a great joy, tempered by the fact that I soon found that none of my officers were really qualified for the job that my predecessor had qualified them for so he could relieve their superiors in gunnery officer, engineer officer, communication officer, etc. This was nothing that couldn't be corrected by many months at sea, but it made our shipyard overhaul reasonably disastrous. The routine in a shipyard overhaul is that the ship's officers, under the commanding officer, are responsible by law and by custom for all the work the navy yard does. It's their responsibility to inspect each job and be hard-boiled before signing it off. My young heroes were not only ignorant, but they weren't very hard-boiled. They accepted in my name all sorts of jobs, from the fire control system to overhauling machinery that were done poorly or not done at all. When I say "done poorly," it's no reflection on the shipyard which was working for us and had been expanded by a factor of 100, and was struggling on its own to get things done.

We more or less stumbled out of Mare Island. I found that when we posted the first watch under way after securing from special sea detail that I didn't have a single trained helmsman in the deck force. I coached one of the boatswain's mates as we went out under the Golden Gate and soon qualified him as an instructor, and then he, on the way to Hawaii, instructed enough sailors from the deck force so we had a good, experienced watch. Of course, none of them had worked in close quarters or alongside ships fueling and that sort of thing, so we still didn't have a very well trained crew.

On the way to the Hawaiian Islands, I found that my navigator was a casual sort of relaxed fellow who transcribed his plotting sheets onto the big chart incorrectly and gave me a course to the Hawaiian Islands which was not the 268° that I remembered. The course from San Francisco to Pearl Harbor is a rhumbline; you don't change course at all, you don't follow a Great Circle course. You have one course. When he gave me something rather wild like 233°, I got him out of his bunk and we went over his work and we found out where we really were. I don't think we'd have missed the Hawaiian Islands, though, because we did have a good air search radar and when we spotted a great number of planes all disappearing beneath the horizon in a certain direction, and that would have told us something. But this was the only officer that was really not much good, and I had to fire him when we got to the islands.

Q: You're talking exclusively about reserve officers, aren't you?

Captain Noel: I only had one Naval Academy officer in the Lamson, and he was superb, and he was the one who was qualified for his job. But I must hasten to add that there was no essential difference to me between a reserve officer and a Naval Academy officer; it was a question of having them trained and having them experienced. The reserve officers were basically just the same sort of youngsters and just as smart and just as dedicated. Later on when I had the Rochester in 1953, the two best officers on the ship were a Naval Academy officer on one hand and a black officer from Los Angeles who was a graduate of the Merchant Marine Academy. I'd like to make it a matter of record that the reserve officers in large part fought and won the war at sea. There were very few of us regulars. My class only graduated 262 people. So the reserve officers, many of them had been through NROTC, had quite a good naval background. Others had come in straight from civilian life, and they had to learn it the hard way.

To go back to the Lamson, we stumbled into Pearl Harbor. I called first on Commander Destroyers Pacific, Admiral Kauffman, known as Stormy Kauffman, and I encountered a good deal of a hurricane when I told him that I was not fit to proceed to the forward area, that my guns wouldn't shoot and I had lots of engineering work to do, and that this was just a fact of life which I regretted.* After all the huffing and puffing was finished, he recognized the fact that I had just taken over the ship and had a few problems, and we were given time to put ourselves back together properly in Pearl Harbor, although it wouldn't have been necessary if my officers had done their job properly in Mare Island.

Q: Did this reflect badly on your record?

Captain Noel: No, not in the slightest. I continued to get good reports. It didn't reflect on me because it was obvious that we were making great progress in retraining or training a crew that

---

*Rear Admiral James L. Kauffman, USN, Commander Cruisers and Destroyers Pacific Fleet.

was very new. We had a lot of new officers, a lot of new men.

We were sent out to the forward area, first to Majuro for shakedown and then on to Hollandia. Finally they sent us to Leyte Gulf. We had missed the assault landings and the big battles in Surigao Strait off Leyte, but we were still very active in supporting the landing and expansion of the beach. We lost half of our squadron of eight ships in the six weeks in which we were there. We were under constant air attack, usually by kamikazes. This was under the most unfavorable conditions, because we were working around islands and our radar didn't protect us, because very often these aircraft could approach from behind a land mass, in the radar shadow of this land. We were a fighter director destroyer, we'd been so equipped. In other words, we had special electronic equipment when we were last in the shipyard. In supporting these small landings and these patrols, we would be given the fighter planes. The Army Air Corps pilots who were out there were quite inexperienced; very brave, of course, but they just didn't have the hours to make them as reliable as they could be. At dawn and at dusk we had Marine Corps fighter pilots, because the Air Corps chaps were not qualified to land and take off in the dark.

It was a very intense and difficult experience for all of us--on the alert, perhaps, around the clock, except when these ferocious typhoons would sweep through. It was almost a relief to know during the typhoon that at least you didn't have to be

Noel #1 - 51

looking for aircraft. The typhoons, however, were in their own way even more terrifying than enemy aircraft, because the typhoon would last days and you'd be struggling to save your ship, to survive. In the kamikaze attack, the kamikaze, if he made a run on you, would either hit you or miss you in a matter of 20 or 30 seconds, so it was, let us say, a brief period of terror.

Q: Was it during this period that Halsey's destroyers were lost?*

Captain Noel: No. That was a little later. That was actually about the middle of December when we left Leyte as one of the cripples after being hit by a kamikaze.** I guess I can mention now that as we left in this big convoy of cripples and amphibious ships, we passed within 90 miles of the center of that typhoon.

Q: That was a terrible, terrible experience. The words one says now can't describe what was a fact then.

Captain Noel: The experience that we all had with typhoons was

---
   *The Third Fleet destroyers, the Hull (DD-350), Spence (DD-512), and Monaghan (DD-354) sank as a result of being caught in a typhoon in the vicinity of the Philippines in mid-December 1944.
   **On 7 December 1944, while the Lamson (DD-367) was supporting a landing at Ormoc Bay on Leyte, she was hit by a plane which crashed forward of the superstructure. As a result, 21 crew members were killed and another 50 wounded.

interesting, because very few of us in the Navy had ever suffered a typhoon. By an alleged unspoken agreement with the Japanese, our ships operated east of 180 and the Japanese west of 180, so since most of the typhoons are west of 180, it was not a common practice for Navy ships to encounter typhoons. In the Caribbean, of course, we could encounter comparable storms, actually the same thing, except they're called hurricanes in the Caribbean. But the Navy made a practice of not operating in the Caribbean during the hurricane season.

Q: That's interesting and I never heard that before, that actually Navy ships weren't trained to know what to do in the practice of handling or operating in hurricanes or typhoons.

Captain Noel: That's true. As far as a formation of ships that had to periodically refuel, we had never had that experience in a typhoon. It was this aspect of that great disaster in which we lost those destroyers. It was the fact that they had been told to prepare to take on fuel, because this was standard routine. The carrier task force only had the endurance of its destroyers. The destroyers had to refuel frequently, because they used a lot of fuel at high speed. Refueling was a very simple operation when the weather wasn't too bad, but in a typhoon the ships that were preparing to fuel would be deballasted, they'd have to get the ballasting water out of the tanks, and therefore their stability would be very bad.

This was really a failure in command to start with, because Admiral Halsey never should have maintained his formation; he should have let the ships steer their own courses and survive. But he kept the ships in formation and had ordered refueling, which required ships to deballast. Now some of the skippers had the guts and were seamen enough to know what was coming up, who refused to deballast, and they saved their ships. The others who believed, perhaps a little too strongly, in always obeying orders deballasted and some of those lost their ships.

Q: Has that ever been a matter of record or written about? It's the first time I've heard about it as you're telling me.

Captain Noel: Yes, there's a book written on this subject.* This was a familiar experience in the Pacific; it was a familiar dilemma for commanders who had to get their destroyers refueled and yet didn't want to risk typhoons. But it took this particular incident that we're talking about to bring home to the high command, particularly to people like Admiral Halsey, although he had been a destroyer sailor and should have been aware of it, how dangerous it was to deballast your destroyers before you could be sure of refueling them.

---

*See Captain Charles R. Calhoun, USN(Ret.), <u>Typhoon: The Other Enemy</u> (Annapolis: Naval Institute Press, 1981).

The period in Leyte Gulf that we were supporting the Army was a very difficult one because we had trouble not only with the fighter planes, but we had trouble with communications. The flagship of Admiral Kinkaid, who was the senior Navy man--he commanded MacArthur's Navy--was McKinley.* I can never forget the voice call of the McKinley, which was "Warhorse," and how dramatic and emotional it was sometimes to be in a dilemma or be in danger and have old Warhorse come up on the circuit and relay whatever messages we needed to the right people.

Admiral Kinkaid himself was a remarkable man. Admiral Kinkaid was an admirals' admiral, who fought the war at sea, he was at ComNorPac, where I knew him slightly, up in the Aleutians, and then he had the most difficult job of being MacArthur's naval commander.** He called me in one night. We came in very late to our anchorage, about 2:00 o'clock. He asked me to come over, and he said he wanted to express General MacArthur's regrets and concerns. The way he was employing his naval units was very tough on the Navy, but this job had to be done, and he hoped that we would all recognize it, that was nothing abnormal or, let us say, naive in the way we were being used. We had to support the Army and we had to operate close to islands under this kamikaze attack.

---
*Admiral Thomas C. Kinkaid, USN, Commander Seventh Fleet.
**ComNorPac--Commander North Pacific Force; General Douglas MacArthur, U.S. Army.

Q: That helps somewhat, doesn't it, to have someone that you know is sympathetic to the problem?

Captain Noel: It sure does. This is the Nelson touch that Nimitz had and Kinkaid had. All the great commanders try to put themselves in the position of their subordinates. It goes right down to the captain of the ship, who has got to make people do things that are dangerous and uncomfortable, but he also makes it plain that these men have his sympathy and understanding.

Q: Did you ever have any personal contact with General MacArthur?

Captain Noel: No. I worked at his headquarters, saw him come and go. I worked with his subordinates. He was a great man in the Korean War, and I think he was a great man in every war, except that I hoped that Roosevelt would have had the political courage to reject his advice to attack in the Philippines and had followed Nimitz's strategy, which was to bypass the Philippines. There was no need to go into the Philippines at all. MacArthur had what he considered a moral debt to the Filipinos and perhaps we, as their colonial master, had a debt to them, but we should have bypassed them and saved lots of lives, and gone direct for the empire.

Q: That's interesting.

Captain Noel: The climax of the campaign for us started on 5 December when we escorted an Army force in LSMs around to the other side of Leyte Island to a place called Baybay. Our action report follows.* This is an interesting and somewhat significant action report in that it gives a detailed yet brief account of a typical operation in the Philippines by Army forces transported and supported by the Navy.

On December the sixth we departed San Pedro in support of a landing at Ormoc Bay on the west coast of Leyte. The landing at Ormoc was made successfully and our mission was accomplished. The Lamson's job was in shore bombardment, and we fired all our guns, including machine guns, at the enemy, who were in a town called Albuera. We were actually seeing the enemy and doing him much obvious damage, and it was a unique experience to be 1,000 yards off the beach and shooting at the Japanese soldiers who had fortified themselves in this town.

A tremendous air battle developed later in the morning and we could see our fighters shooting down enemy planes. We, as fighter director ship, of course, had control of many of the planes, and it was a real melee over the assault landing beach. A few of the planes we fired at turned out to be our own Army planes, but they soon understood our firm instructions never to

---

*The report is included as an appendix to this volume.

come at us head-on, because then we couldn't tell who they were.

We intercepted a message reporting that a force of Japanese destroyers was coming down from the north to attack our convoy. The Army sent out bombers and the ships were attacked both by the Army bombers and by Navy planes the following night.

In this melee we were officially credited with helping shoot down 14 planes. A Japanese plane suddenly appeared astern without radar warning. It was low on the water and we could see its guns blinking as it came in from the port quarter and hit us just below the bridge. We were doing nearly 30 knots and we were turning to port, to the left. Standing just forward of the director trunk behind the helmsman, I was one of the very few unwounded as bomb fragments swept the bridge and burning gasoline torched over the main top. I should say one of the few not killed or wounded, because I did lose a good many people on the bridge, including my executive officer. It was soon apparent that this gasoline fire, whipped by the wind, was making the bridge untenable, and the only exits from the bridge aft were covered with flame. A couple of us on the wing of the bridge on the starboard side took refuge from the flame. At this time I checked my executive officer, whom I found slumped over the flag bag, and he was dead. We had decided to go over the side because there was no other way to go. I dove over the side about 57 feet above the water, with the realization that I was going to pass very close to the propeller, because the ship was still making

Noel #1 - 58

about 27 knots and was turning to the left.

Q: You were diving on the opposite side?

Captain Noel: Yes. As I came up, I saw the propeller guard pass over my head. I was not concerned with being caught in the screws because actually there is no downward suction. If you're at the level under the water that the propellers are, you'll be chopped up by them as it passes through you, but if you're above the propellers, there's no particular reason why you should be hit by them. But I knew I was going to be in the wake, a very turbulent wake, so I took a deep breath, doubled up, and as I tumbled around in the wake of the ship, I knew from my experience in surfing at sea that there was no use trying to find the surface, because you very often didn't know in which direction it was, and the safest and surest thing was to just maintain your equilibrium and hold your breath and think of other things, which I did. I thought of home, family, and all the great things that I would see some day. Sure enough, I saw a glimmer of light; there was the surface of the water.

Q: Did you ever figure out how long you were below?

Captain Noel: No, probably a minute. You can hold your breath for a long time if you have to. To take part in these big surf competitions, you have to be able to hold your breath for three minutes. I found out in surfing once when I lost my board and thought that I could swim to the surface, I touched sand with my fingertips when I had only a few seconds of air left, and it scared me very badly. I kicked up from the bottom and managed to get up through 15 or 20 feet of water. But that experience taught me very profoundly, don't try to swim underwater and look for the surface. Let your natural buoyancy bring you up.

So everything worked out well. As I came to the surface, we were some thousands of yards from the Lamson, which had stopped. Other destroyers were circling around at 30 knots, shooting all over the place. My steward Jackson was a great favorite of the family's because he would occasionally be kind to us and sit with our children when we wanted to go out. Jackson came up sputtering and said, "Well, Captain, you can't say I ain't had a bath today, sir." Of course, we laughed. This stemmed from my occasional rebuke to him when he brought me my meals on the bridge that he could stand a shower.

At any rate, the water was warm and quiet, and we just stayed there until the Japanese planes had left for the moment. The shooting stopped, and the Flusser came alongside. I have a painting by Dwight Shepler which shows the Flusser coming alongside the life raft on which we had a very badly wounded man with the bottom of his leg shot off, and some of us swimming around the life raft. Flusser took us aboard. Just as I went up on the bridge and reported to the commodore and the skipper of the Flusser, the skipper of the Flusser said, "Go down to my cabin [fortunately he was my size] and pick out some of my clothes." Because all I had on was a pair of shorts. I had discarded my clothes in the water. So I put on some of his khakis and went up on the bridge.* Just then the Japanese planes came back, and we had another high-speed dodging round my ship, the Lamson, which was burning then, with a salvage tug alongside pouring water into her. I sat on the flag bag with a General London, an English observer, who told me about warfare in the desert with tanks, and we pretended to be very relaxed. Neither of us had anything to do. The poor chap was later killed in a kamikaze attack on a cruiser in which he was sailing.

As the afternoon progressed and the Japanese plane left again, the commodore ordered the salvage tug to keep clear and he would have the Flusser sink the Lamson so we could get on our way and get home and get out of there.** The salvage tug reported that the ship was not badly damaged, despite the apparent damage and the bridge being burned out. She had one fireroom flooded, the other intact, the engine room intact, and that he could get her back to Leyte Gulf, which he did. He lashed his ship to her side and we started back to Leyte Gulf.

---
*The commanding officer of the Flusser (DD-368) was Commander Theodore R. Vogeley, USN.
**The commodore embarked in the Flusser was Captain William M. Cole, USN, Commander Destroyer Squadron Five.

As soon as it was dark, I asked the <u>Flusser</u> to put me back on board with a couple of my men because we could still see remnants of some fire, and we wanted to get the rudder amidships because it was making it hard for the tug to push the <u>Lamson</u> back to port with the rudder hard over left. This we did. We went back aboard ship. The deck was covered with bodies and smoldering fired. We had three or four men, as I remember, and they got the rudder amidships. Then we had nothing to do but be passengers. We dragged out some mattresses from below and put them topside so we could sleep. I went to my safe in my room which had been pretty throughly blackened by smoke, but it was fairly intact. I opened my safe, got a bottle of whiskey, went back, and all of us had a stiff drink. Then we looked for some food. We found some canned food of some description somewhere. We hadn't eaten since before dawn. With that very necessary, rather illegal, drink . . .

Q: Who cared at that time?

Captain Noel: We were able to have a little appetite, had a little supper, and turned in. The next morning we were back in Leyte Gulf.

Q: What did you do with the men who had been killed?

Noel #1 - 62

Captain Noel: Didn't pay any attention to them.

Q: You just left them there?

Captain Noel: We made sure none of them were alive. But a grave detail from the Army came out the next day and took care of the bodies.

Q: But at that time you simply left them.

Captain Noel: Yes. We were worried about the people alive.

Q: Was that the most dreadful experience of your time in the Navy?

Captain Noel: It was a little gruesome stumbling around your own dead men, but I was concentrating then on saving the ship. Actually, the ship was not in such bad shape. We took the flooded fireroom all the way back to Bremerton, but one fireroom gave us plenty of steam. The engineers in the one engine room had secured everything very well before they abandoned ship, so the engine room was intact. We had no bridge and no methods of controlling the engine or the rudder, but we met that problem by putting up a very small platform forward of the burned-out bridge structure and installing there a gyro repeater. Our gyro compass was all right. We had a repeater from back aft put on this platform and ran a set of telephones, split phones, down to the engine room and to steering aft, where men were stationed to do the steering from the steering engine room. The other phone to the engine room went to the man on the throttles, so that's the way we went back to Bremerton. It was a lot simpler than it looked. All you had to do was to talk into your phone and you could change your speed or you could bring the ship right or left. We went alongside the *Iowa* for fuel later on, made our approach, stayed there and fueled, and made our departure, all with a set of phones to the engine room and to steering aft.

By that time we had a marvelous crew. The men in the steering aft never even told me of the steering casualty they had when we were alongside the battleship fueling. I did notice that we were moving away from the battleship and our hoses were being extended, but I didn't pay it too much attention because I had no report of any problems. They fixed the casualty and got us back alongside without any further ado and without even telling me that they were having any problems.

Q: How many men did you lose in this?

Captain Noel: About 50 men.

There was a seaplane tender that was anchored in Leyte Gulf at San Pedro Bay, the inner bay there, near Tacloban. We got it to use its crane and help us remove our heavy gun director, which was useless and all burned out. We were able to stick the director down in the socket of number one stack, and that was the stack leading to the forward fireroom that was flooded, so we didn't need it. I'm sorry I went to all this trouble, because as it turned out, they just scrapped this director. We should have just thrown it over the side. But it was of great help to get it down lower, from the viewpoint of stability.

With these preparations, within a few days we were ready for sea, and we left Leyte Gulf for Hollandia in a convoy of damaged ships and LSMs. As I said before, although we missed the center of that huge typhoon in which we lost so many ships, the weather where we were was not too bad. We were under air attack several times by the Japanese as we left, and they were met by a huge volume of fire from all these LSMs who had apparently been trading some of their food to the Army for machine guns. The LSMs just bristled with guns all over their welldecks and provided a huge salvo of antiaircraft fire for any Japanese planes that came near us.

Q: You went back safely, then, to Pearl?

Captain Noel: We went back to Hollandia, where some of my men had been sent to the hospital. There I had a couple of very good men who were not badly injured, and I waited a couple of days

Noel #1 - 65

until I could get them out of the hospital. Then we went back to Pearl.

Q: How long did it take you to get from Hollandia to Pearl?

Captain Noel: I would estimate two weeks. We fell in with some other ships. We fueled alongside the Iowa. I had a couple of very good friends and classmates on there, and we were provided with things like oranges and ice cream, which were a great novelty, because our food situation in the Philippines was very bad indeed. We were down to beans and biscuits practically. But we went to Pearl.

Q: You have done a separate study called "Homeward Bound," and I would like to have this next section labeled "Homeward Bound," and have you take excerpts out of that study which haven't been put in before. It's excellent.

Captain Noel: That I will do.

"For the Lamson, a battle-scarred destroyer badly damaged in the battle for the Philippines off Ormoc, there remained only the last leg of her journey home to be repaired. We could look forward to 2,500 miles of wet, cold, and probably stormy winter passage. We would lose the northeast trades the second day out of Pearl Harbor and the mild tradewind weather would become cold and gray with bruising westerly winds. At this time of year, January, we could expect the series of gales that moved east near the 40th parallel. This prospect did not really concern us as we moved up the channel in Pearl Harbor after a weary passage from the forward area. Not many ships had been given a beer party upon their return by Commander Destroyers Pacific, now Admiral Ainsworth.* The Lamson was assigned a berth normally reserved for flagships, a stone's throw from the pier at the destroyer base at Pearl City. The crew could almost talk to the crowds ashore who were gazing at this rusty burned wreck whose colors were still flying. In half an hour, most of the crew were ashore under the palm trees, drinking all the beer they could hold, and no worry about the shore patrol. This was a destroyer family affair.

"While the crew was being refreshed and the shipyard engineers swarmed over the ship making plans and estimates for needed voyage repairs to get us back to Bremerton, I lost no time in going ashore with my old friend, the gunnery officer on ComDesPac's staff, Commander Hal Bowen.** First, however, was a traditional call on CinCPac, Admiral Nimitz, who expected all his commanding officers to call on him. This was much more than a courtesy call, however. Admiral Nimitz and everyone else who

---
*Rear Admiral Walden L. Ainsworth, USN.
**ComDesPac--Commander Destroyers Pacific Fleet; Commander Harold G. Bowen, USN.

knew about the effectiveness of the desperate Japanese kamikaze attacks were very worried. We were losing ships and men at a high rate. These losses were being carefully concealed from the public, however, a fact that had considerable bearing on the orders the Lamson was to receive when we entered Puget Sound. In other words, the people in Puget Sound didn't really know we were that badly damaged.

"The final event that day for me was a gaudy party at the destroyer officers' club. It was a special, long-planned fiesta with Admiral Halsey and all the other notable flag and general officers there with Hilo Hattie and Eddie Duchin among the entertainers. Fortunately my white service dress uniform, stored away in my cabin, had escaped the fire and smoke. I noticed as I sat at a convivial table with old friends that my drinks were being lined up in front of me at least six deep. No one at that table was exactly dying of thirst, but no one else seemed to have such generous reserves. The key to this minor mystery was soon observed to be a squat, cheerful, little steward's mate Wilson, a Lamson man who had been so chronically and hopelessly seasick that I had transferred him months before to the staff on the beach.

"To prepare for the trip home to Bremerton, the Lamson's only major need was a better makeshift bridge. The canvas and angle iron jury rig on a machine gun platform contrived in Leyte Gulf and improved in Hollandia was sufficient shelter in the tropics.

For cruising in the North Pacific winter a more substantial enclosure was needed, including a plexiglas windshield. The gyro compass repeater and the split telephone to the engine room and steering room were still all the bridge instruments available. Seaman's eye had to substitute for compass bearings. But we had done our job so far, maneuvering under air attack off the Philippines, entering and leaving Hollandia, and screening a formation of cripples, and fueling under way from the battleship Iowa.

"We were all in a much more relaxed mood as we nursed the battered Lamson out through the reef-guarded channel from Pearl Harbor. As the sea watch was set, all hands thought of home, as only ten days or so away. North Pacific gales and making a landfall on the foggy coast of the northwest presented no major obstacles. The Lamson had weathered three typhoons on this cruise, and the cold of the North Pacific winter was less trying than the heat of the tropics in a steel ship. Except for those few who stood watch topside, the crew lived and worked belowdecks in well-heated compartments. The quartermasters, signalmen, and lookouts had heavy foul weather clothing and only stood a watch in four. There was no need to stand any gun watches since there were no enemy east of Hawaii. The quartermasters and signalmen manned a semi-portable emergency radar that had been installed in the wreckage of the old bridge. Our radio communications consisted of a borrowed portable Army set powered by storage batteries. The heftiest radioman, known as Striker, had to carry these 60-pound batteries periodically up from the engine room, no easy job on a lively ship in a seaway.*

"Soon the flying fish weather of the trades was behind us as the long North Pacific storm swells came rolling out of the west. The resulting deep, quick roll was in some contrast to the Lamson's normal slow roll, and it reassured the captain as an evidence of great stability useful if we suffered storm damage. Two hundred miles off Cape Destruction, we fell in with the USS Haraden, who was to be our somewhat elusive guide into Puget Sound, then up the channel to the shipyard at Bremerton. The Haraden was another cripple from the Philippines but had her bridge and all radars, etc., intact. Landfall was made on Victoria Island, and as we went up through the straits of Juan de Fuca, we received orders from Com 13 to put into the ammunition depot at Indian Island near Port Townsend to unload our depth charges.** Ships scheduled for major shipyard repairs did not carry depth charges or torpedoes into the yard. We learned later that our old depth charges would be barged out to sea and jettisoned in deep water. If we had known this, we could have deep-sixed them ourselves offshore.

"The pier at Indian Island was not difficult to reach in daylight even in the Lamson's condition, but no one relished the

---
*Radioman Frank Satterwhite, USNR.
**Com 13--Commander Thirteenth Naval District

thought of working our way back into Puget Sound that evening. Without normal piloting gear such as compass repeaters to take bearings and a lighted table for our charts and the necessary plotting, close work in restricted waters with strong winds and currents was an exhilarating exercise in shiphandling during daylight. To do this in the dark, however, in waters full of shipping and ferries, was another matter. None of us in the Lamson had been south of Indian Island in years, long before wartime nets, booms, and gate vessels. It was with some dismay, then, that the two ships received curt orders to proceed at once to the shipyard at Bremerton 40 miles away at the head of a narrow winding channel. After some consulation and a hearty damnation for all stateside shore-bound operations officers who had undoubtedly lost their wits, the two captains decided there must be some urgent military reason for this caper. There seemed no alternative. We would have to go.

"The night was clear and moonless with a moderate northwest wind. One reassuring factor was that the Haraden had aboard a supply officer who had been an active yachtsman in Puget Sound and knew the waters very well." As an aside, I have since met and talked to him. He's on the national board of the Audubon Society and was here not long ago.

"The Haraden was the first to clear the pier at Indian Island and took the lead as we passed an aircraft carrier anchored off Port Townsend. The Haraden's skipper was senior and her bridge was intact. In theory, the Haraden would lead the Lamson into the shipyard, but in fact she proved a poor and erratic guide, speeding up when traffic permitted but not slowing to permit the Lamson to catch up. We were both in a hurry to get to Bremerton before the usual early morning fog set in. Most of the trip had been made by midnight. There remained only narrow Rich Passage before the shipyard would be in sight. It was in this right-angle turn in Rich Passage that the Lamson barely escaped an ignominious grounding. The gate vessels had been passed at high speed. The Haraden was nowhere to be seen when suddenly the Lamson was in the turn of the channel and no obvious course to take to follow the channel. I knew that strong ebbing currents were to be expected, but I underestimated their strength and as I stopped engines to reduce speed while looking for the channel ahead, I could feel that the current had taken charge of us. We lost steerageway in this seven-knot current, and the Lamson was drifting into an eddy close to the bank. The navigator, Lieutenant Bob Apple, lost his composure for the first time on the cruise and declared that this was a hell of a way to end his career.* As the only other career officer, he had never so much as changed the tone of his voice when, as combat information officer, he had advised the captain of all enemy contacts, air, surface, or submarine, and all the tight places

---

*Lieutenant (junior grade) Robert E. Apple, USN.

we'd been. As a career officer, as the captain and as the navigator, running a ship aground was the ultimate disgrace. As we struggled to claw off the beach by going to full speed ahead, there were 10 or 15 seconds that seemed like centuries as the turbines came up to speed. Finally, as the propellers bit and full left rudder took hold, the dark mass of the trees ashore seemed to loom over the ship and a dog barked, I directed by telephone to the chief engineer "all engines ahead emergency." Then I added with some fervor, "Pour on the coal, Jim. For chrissake, don't spare the horses." These mixed metaphors were well-understood below and as the eddy had scoured a deep channel close to the beach, the Lamson did not touch.

"As the ship came out of her dark hole in the forest, the lights of Bremerton shone ahead and speed was reduced to ten knots while the crew topside made ready to go alongside a pier. But we reckoned without the morning fog, invisible and thick, showing its presence only by the lights ahead that went out as if someone had pulled a switch. There was no hope now of reaching that snug berth alongside that we all yearned for. We would have to anchor until daylight.

"We anchored off Bremerton and set the port watch. Almost immediately a message was received from Com 13: 'Lamson, get under way at daylight and proceed to the torpedo station at Keyport to offload torpedoes.' This was standard procedure to avoid the risks of explosives on board ships going into the yard for repairs. To the harassed skipper, me, sleepless now for several days, this order seemed to be the work of lunatics. Didn't they know how badly the Lamson was damaged? Our torpedo tubes were riddled with bomb fragments. It was soon obvious that the local authorities did not know about the recent and serious losses and damages suffered by the fleet in the Philippines. In a curt reply, we declined to go anywhere except alongside the dock in the shipyard for two reasons: we had only a rudimentary ship control jury rig unsuitable for piloting in restricted waters, and in addition the removal of her torpedoes was a complicated shipyard job and not just a routine removal."

Q: You mean Com 13 in Seattle?

Captain Noel: Yes.

"The berthing of the ship that morning attracted a large crowd. Here was the sort of evidence about the realities of war that the mainland rarely saw. The Lamson was ashambles above the main deck with the blackened shell of her top hamper looming over the stub of her forward stack in which nestled her main battery director, securely lashed down.

I put on my best khaki uniform, complete with long-handle winter underwear issued in Pearl for the trip home. My blues had all been ruined in the fire that swept my cabin after the hit. This gray woolen underwear persisted in creeping down over

Noel #1 - 74

my wrists for several inches. Thus attired, I sought Com 13's office to make an appointment the next day for the official call required. A surprised aide in the outer office informed the admiral that commanding officer of Lamson was there, and the admiral replied, 'Show him in.'"

Q: To clarify exactly where you made your report, you believe that it was in Bremerton rather than Seattle?

Captain Noel: It was in Bremerton. I thought at the time that this admiral was Com 13. I've forgotten his name, but I remember him with great pleasure, because he was a very understanding fellow. "I hadn't meant to call on anybody in the shape I was in, but the aide sent me in to see the admiral. I was furious at the jackasses on his staff and did not hide this feeling at all. I told the admiral with some heat that I had risked my ship more in Puget Sound in the last 12 hours than in bringing her halfway around the world. The admiral, who obviously was not well informed about the condition of the Lamson, took all of this with surprising calmness and even good humor. He could see that I was worn down to a raw edge, and he put me off gracefully.

"We had come home. We had struck our homeward bound pennant and could look forward to several months' respite from the boredom and occasional horror of war at sea. The glorious cool, wet wind of the Pacific northwest was balm, indeed, after months of blinding sun and the heat of a steel ship. Even the stirring sign hung over the quarterdeck the next day by the shipyard workers disturbed us little. This well-meaning but tactless message declared that 'The shipyard workers salute the brave men of the Lamson and pledge their utmost efforts day and night to get you back into the battle again quickly.'

"'Take your time,' we all prayed silently. 'There really is not that much of a hurry.'"

Q: At the end of your years in the Pacific, I want to refer to several commendations which you received, one being when you were on the Sicard, a letter of commendation with ribbon, and V from Commander South Pacific Force. It quotes, "With skillful and effective performance of duty under adverse circumstances while serving as commanding officer of a light minelayer operating in enemy-controlled waters of the Solomon Islands area during the period from November 1 to 8 1943," and then continues on.

For your duty as commanding officer of the Lamson, you received for the Leyte landings in October and November of '44 and the Ormoc Bay landings in December of that year, the Bronze Star Medal with combat V and a letter of commendation with Star and V from Commander in Chief Pacific Fleet for serving in that command.

Then in addition you received a letter of commendation, which says, "for meritorious conduct in the performance of outstanding service as commanding officer of the USS Lamson from May '44 to August '45 while on antisubmarine patrols and escort duty and also for a short time as a fighter director ship on picket duty. His outstanding seamanship and professional skill contributed materially to the Lamson's operations."

To continue on with some of the comments from the citation for the Bronze Star, I'm going to quote some more: "For heroic achievement as commanding officer of the USS Lamson in action, against enemy Japanese forces at Ormoc Bay, Leyte, Philippine Islands, on December 7, 1944. He directed a highly accurate and sustained bombardment of enemy-held shore in support of our invading troops despite a constant threat of aircraft attack and fire from Japanese land batteries, and turned his ship to help defend the retiring convoy against enemy bombers and suicide planes which repeatedly attempted to penetrate the screen provided by warships. Under his inspiring command the Lamson set up a deadly and accurate fire materially assisting and repulsing the attackers and in destroying 14 aircraft."

I know you have other commendations and medals. It depends on the circumstances as to which is the lesser or more important for you. I think only your philosophy would tell it.

Captain Noel: These citations you've just quoted are pretty routine and really don't amount to very much. They were pretty much standard. I had the philosophy during the war, as far as my people were concerned, that shooting and getting shot at was what we were paid for, and there was no need to pin medals on each other. Everybody used to comment about Mickey Rooney and some pet dog both getting Bronze Stars by the Army as entertainers in Europe, and we thought this was just about what decorations were worth.* However, perhaps at the end of this spiel, I have a few decorations I'd like to put in the record, such as a little note written to me by the laundry crew of the Springfield and a few letters written to me by men that served under me. These to me are much more worth being proud of than something sort of hammered out in large quantities to everybody who survived the war.

Q: Nevertheless, they do put into writing some of the things which surely should be said and probably there's many others that should be said and haven't been.

In Bremerton where the engineers are working fast to get the Lamson back into the war, you have comments about that period.

Captain Noel: To round out the picture, of course, as soon as I got ashore I called Mary's mother, who lived in Bremerton, found out where she was and went out to Mary's mother's house and had a night's sleep and a hot bath. I called Mary, who was in a little

---
*Mickey Rooney was one of the many movie stars in the stable of Metro-Goldwyn-Mayer studio.

Noel #1 - 78

house in Oakland, and told her to do her best to get up there on the train. The best she could do was get as far as Portland, so I used my allowance of gasoline. All of us who had leave during the war were given an allowance of gasoline. I used that allowance of gasoline to drive down to Portland and pick her up. It seemed to me at the time it was a sad commentary on our society that people who really needed transportation had such a hell of a time, when any racehorse or baseball player could go across the country first class on any train at any time. However, we were reunited at Mary's house on Marine Drive, and I managed to scrounge enough gasoline by repeated requisitions for gasoline to run the handy billies, which are little gasoline motor-driven emergency pumps.

Q: Did you have to apply for those to the shipyard?

Captain Noel: Yes.

Q: That's probably where I was.

Captain Noel: Nobody really commented on the fact that we must have run those handy billies all day and night, all the time.

Q: What were they?

Captain Noel: These were little portable pumps to pump water for fire. They were pumps that would draw water out of a ship, or you could use it to put water on a fire. We called them handy billies.

Another incident in the yard that was sort of amusing was that I had a very enterprising first lieutenant and he went over to salvage and found a lovely little clinker-built wherry, a little boat we could put an outboard motor on and use to go fishing in. He made what we used to call a midnight requisition; in other words, he took some of his men and went over and stole it. He didn't realize that as he was walking up the brow carrying this boat that pictures were being taken of the ship in the shipyard, and when we got them at sea much later, here was the first lieutenant and his thieving crew carrying a boat up the accommodation ladder, and nobody said anything.

The engineers worked well, and it was a much better <u>Lamson</u> when we sailed for Pearl after having this rest, with a lot of new people. This time we needed no availability in the shipyard at Pearl, and we were sent west immediately. Our troops had landed on Okinawa and the last bloody battles of the war against Japan were going to be fought. We were assigned to birddog duty between the Marianas and Iwo, which had just been captured, and the mainland of Japan. Being a birddog consisted in monitoring flights of B-29s and fighter planes that they flew from the Marianas to the empire. Our job was to be in radio contact with anybody who had any trouble and provide them any navigational or any other kind of assistance.

On the flight north we had nothing to do but observe. When they returned, particularly the fighters who very often couldn't find their Dumbo plane, their B-29 that was their guide on the return, would start out for Iwo Jima by themselves. A submarine just off the coast would pick them up and give them a course to steer to where we could pick them up on our radar, and we would give them a steer either to the next destroyer down the line or to Iwo Jima itself. In this way we would pass our lost fighter down to where he could land at Iwo. With the big B-29s, when they had to ditch, as they did occasionally, we would pick up the people. Usually they would set the pilot on automatic and they would all jump out in parachutes; then they were easy to pick up. It was striking to see the large number of planes, perhaps 30 or 40 damaged B-29s, all circling Iwo, claiming that they needed to get in the landing pattern first. But everybody, almost, made it and they got down, and we saved these hundreds of pilots who would have otherwise fallen in the ocean. This really made the taking of Iwo Jima worthwhile.

This duty was fairly routine except for the few times when we would have 24 or 48 hours between strikes, and then we would make a high-speed run to some of the islands such as Chichi Jima, still owned by the Japanese, where we might have the good fortune of intercepting some merchant ships supplying these islands or people trying to escape. This was not part of our authorized duty and we never reported what we did; we just shut down our radios and made for the nearest Japanese-held island as fast as we could, hoping to be able to use our guns. We never had any success; all we did was use a lot of fuel. But it broke the monotony.

Q: It gave people the sense of doing something worthwhile, I'd think.

Captain Noel: Sure, the men loved it.

We survived a few typhoons. On one occasion I took the station tanker under escort out of Iwo Jima, and during the middle of the typhoon the tanker reported to me that she was damaged and taking water and was going to sink. All I could do, really, was just to acknowledge the message, but fortunately she survived. This was an unusual typhoon in that it had two centers. It was a double typhoon.

On another mission, we were given some P-38s and sent out east of Iwo Jima to intercept a Japanese aircraft carrying some important admirals and generals up from Truk. Our intelligence had told us about this and we were hoping to intercept this airplane and shoot it down, but we never did.

All of this ended one morning, when anchored off Iwo Jima, we got Halsey's message: "The Japanese have surrendered. The war is

Noel #1 - 82

over, but there may be kamikazes in the air. If so, shoot them down in a friendly fashion."

My relief had come aboard the day before, so I was detached that day and caught a ride from Iwo to Saipan with a USO troupe of entertainers.* From Saipan I flew home to Oakland, and what a great event that was!

Q: It seems to me that according to the record, from your graduation from the Academy in 1936 until August of '45, you were continuously at sea.

Captain Noel: I had been. It had been no great hardship, but I was a rather odd bird when I came ashore finally. I'd been living on the bridge of two destroyers for three years and I was really undomesticated. To come back to a household with two children and get accustomed to sleeping at night and being alert during the day was an adjustment. I'd gotten used to a life where the tough times were generally at night. The easier times when I could afford to doze for hours at a time in my reclining chair were quite pleasant. At night, particularly in the Solomons and in the Philippines, it was when the moon was bright that the Japanese were a big threat. And I couldn't for years stand the sight of a full moon without worrying about when planes

---
*USO--United Services Organization

were going to come over.

Q: I would guess that Mary must have helped a great deal in helping with this adjustment, because I have observed in not only one or two couples that this was a difficulty they weren't able to overcome.

Captain Noel: Mary is wonderful. She had seen me bring in all these damaged ships, and as a result she knew exactly what I was doing. She was living by herself with a couple of small children, and she wasn't in too good shape herself. She lost a lot of weight. But we made the adjustment.

Going across the country from Oakland to Washington was a comedy of errors that seemed very difficult at the time. I suppose we can look back at it and laugh, but we elected to drive to Washington. This was a week or so after gas rationing had been lifted. There were very few accommodations along the road. It was very hard to find a square meal in some of these places like South Dakota. We took off and drove straight through and got to Reno looking for a hotel. But we couldn't find any place to sleep. In Reno my son threw his only pair of shoes out the window and we gave up and drove on. I was so tired I began to see double, so I asked Mary to drive and she sprained her ankle as she came round to get behind the wheel. By the time we got somewhere where we could wait in a motel for the people there to get out so we could have a bed, our son had broken out into chicken pox. The doctor we called said, "I can't tell you what this is or I would have to quarantine you, so go along with my blessings." So with a boy full of chicken pox and a car that persisted in overheating, a rather ill-matched pair for a husband and wife at that point, we went on. It got better. I figured out that if I stopped every few hours and used my daughter's rubber boot to fill the radiator from a nearby stream, we didn't overheat too badly.

Q: What kind of a car was it?

Captain Noel: A 1939 Ford.

Q: Did you have good luck when you arrived in Washington?

Captain Noel: We had a bad time, because I was still in uniform and we went into the Wardman Park where I had made reservations. But it turned out that after a rather long and indignant argument at the desk that I wasn't in the Wardman Park at all; I was in another hotel that looked very much like it. So I had to retreat in confusion, clutching a baby under one arm and a potty seat under the other.

We did finally find our Wardman Park with our reservations, and then had the good fortune to find a rent-controlled house in

Silver Spring. I suppose it was good fortune. If we had been forced to buy or build a house, we'd probably have made some money. But nevertheless, we settled down in a comfortable house in Silver Spring, and I reported to the Navy Department where I had a desk job disposing of the Navy's surplus ships. This was the first duty I'd had ashore.

Q: In the Pentagon?

Captain Noel: I was in the Pentagon, yes. It was a great privilege to be home almost every night. Occasionally I would have to take the duty for the CNO, but this didn't amount to very much.*

Q: Were there any incidents during this tour of duty? It sounds interesting and vital, the legal disposal of surplus naval ships. Is there any way you want to expand on that?

Captain Noel: No, not particularly. I had to write off my old ship, the Lamson. She was lost in the nuclear explosions at Bikini. I had disposed of the Sicard. That was a rather sentimental effort. But in general it was a bit of the old bureaucracy, not a bad life, with squash at the YMCA a couple of

---
*CNO--Chief of Naval Operations

times a week. The summers were very pleasant.

Q: When you say write off, what do you mean? What did you do with them, send them to shipyards?

Captain Noel: Under legislation, they had to be surveyed and processed and the surveys approved. It was a formal, legalistic sort of procedure that really didn't take anything except a responsible clerk.

Q: You enjoyed the life then, but maybe not the duty. Is that a fair statement?

Captain Noel: It sure is. Commanders were a dime a dozen after the war, and some of them I knew spent most of their time playing the horses in the Pentagon.

After two years in this rather dull job but enjoyable life in Washington, the Navy sent me to Stanford to learn personnel administration, which was to be my specialty when ashore. It had dawned on the Navy after the war that the administration of personnel was somewhat of a science and couldn't be left to the vagaries of any old sea dog who came ashore and decided he could do it. This was a great experience. This was my first real education. The Naval Academy was essentially a training school, as I've mentioned. I took all the possible courses and read widely in human relations and management, and got my master's degree in education in 1948.

Q: I'm sure with your mind, as I observe it today and yesterday, that being able to have a challenge, which getting an M.A. is, you liked that, didn't you?

Captain Noel: It was a great experience. After my mediocre marks at the Naval Academy, it was nice to get nothing less than a "B" at Stanford, and that was a pretty good mark to get at the business school. Not in the school of education where anybody could get a "B", but in the business school, which was highly competitive and full of very bright guys, you really had to work for it. It was a marvelous 15 months at Stanford, living in Menlo Park. We bought a little house for which we did the landscaping. We enjoyed the best of California in a quiet way, but it was 15 months devoted to study.

I was then ordered to sea as the planning officer on the staff of Commander Amphibious Group One, which was the major operational command in the Pacific Fleet. Planning officer was probably the best job on the staff.

Q: Where was that located?

Captain Noel: The staff's headquarters ashore was at the

amphibious base at Coronado. I was responsible as coordinator and editor for the production of complex and voluminous operation orders, then had the pleasure under the operations officer of their implementation, and finally coordinated and edited the final report. Navigating the fleet when at sea was an enjoyable additional duty. This was a fairly high-pressure job but one which I thoroughly enjoyed. At sea I was very busy because as tactical officer and navigator I would no sooner write the admiral's night orders for him and plan the night's steaming than it would be time for me to get up and figure out where we were and start the next day before dawn. So it was altogether a splendid job.

We built a small house in Coronado, which was a major effort. In addition to a really intriguing job with the Navy, our building this modern house was another first, in the sense that I had to build some of the furniture, because we couldn't afford all the things we needed. Mary and I did the gardening and finally won a prize for first year garden. This involved on my part rigging lights and digging outside after dark. We took a trailer up into the mountains and brought back leaf mold, and we scrounged some free manure at some of the adjoining dairy farms, and we went after it full blower. It was a thoroughly satisfactory experience. Coronado is a very keen town about gardening. I even got talked into submitting a flower arrangement that Mary suggested in the men's section. I never thought I would be entering flower arrangement competitions, but Mary said, "Why don't you climb that flame eucalyptus and bring down some of those wonderful blossoms." Here we've got a monkey pod vase that we picked up in the islands. Following her instructions I won first prize.

Q: That was fun.

Captain Noel: It was. It was sort of doing something that you normally wouldn't think of doing.

But all of this idyllic life in Coronado came to an end when we were ordered out to Japan in the spring of 1950 to train MacArthur's Army forces out there in amphibious warfare. This was our mission. This was an amphibious group, and his Army was, as I suppose everybody knows, at the start of the Korean War not a very military outfit. Every soldier had a little Japanese girl to clean his rifle and keep his bed warm, so it wasn't exactly a hardship post for the Army. We carried with us in the Mount McKinley a troop training unit from the Marines, so we were prepared to set up the whole thing, set up these little exercises to train the troops. When the North Koreans invaded, we were in Sasebo, having just finished one of these operations.

At this time, we are attaching as an appendix an account of how the Korean War started, as far as I saw it, and some impressions of my stay there. I was sent back because I'd been in this job a long time and my relief was on board. It was also a good thing, because when I did get back I found out that I was a pretty sick man, and it was some sort of a meningitis. It was an unfamiliar Asian virus that does not always paralyze, and I managed to escape the naval hospital in time to reach Annapolis late in the summer of 1950. I had orders to teach at the USNA.* I was very weak for about six months but otherwise undamaged and happy to be home for the birth of Joyeux Noel on 24 December 1950.

My duties teaching seamanship to midshipmen and later being assistant head of department were light and demanded little preparation or study. Stanford had opened my mind, and my last sea duty had started a regime of writing and editing that I missed. When I started to write these professional texts at the Naval Academy, it appealed to me because I missed the writing that I had had to do and that I had learned so much about in my job as planning officer. In writing a voluminous operation order and in large part editing it, it's obvious that the writing had to be very clear and very simple, because a lot of people followed these orders and orders had to be made clear. There could be nothing confusing about how the orders were written because there was enough confusion thrown into an amphibious landing by the stress of weather and, in wartime, the enemy. Writing the reports of these exercises was a challenge, in

---
*USNA--U.S. Naval Academy

writing something concise and clear and so on.

So when at the Naval Academy, the head of the department of seamanship showed me a manuscript for The Watch Officer's Guide that had been done by one of my associates and said, "Jack, this won't do. Will you take a whack at it?" I said, "Sure." The Watch Officer's Guide had been in the Navy for 50 years at least. It was a standard work that a watch officer generally looked over before he took over his watch. He certainly referred to it when he wrote his log. It was an exercise that I enjoyed, because not only did I have a chance to write simply, but I had a chance to use some of the seamanship that I had picked up after many years at sea. I did this book for the Naval Institute for, as I recall, $1 an hour, but I was happy to do something useful.

Q: I think we should point out what the Naval Institute does with these. Does everyone get them automatically, or does the Academy buy them for the Institute?

Captain Noel: They buy them. The Naval Institute is essentially the university press of the Naval Academy, and these professional books are sold to the midshipmen. The $1 an hour can be explained by the fact that up until this point the market for books like this was rather limited. We had a very small Navy and very few midshipmen. But with a greatly expanded NROTC program, with tens of thousands of young officers, it was soon obvious that the Naval Institute would have to do a little better than paying $1 an hour to get good professional writing. Eventually, when I wrote my next book, I received standard royalties. It took a little struggling to do this, but it happened.

In the meantime, I filled in by writing the current version of The Bluejackets' Manual which is even older than The Watch Officer's Guide and I worked on the professional magazine as Professional Notes editor. This magazine is known as the Naval Institute Proceedings. After doing The Watch Officer's Guide, it occurred to me that a much greater need in the Navy was some sort of technical assistance for the division officer. The division officer is a key man in any naval organization. He leads the basic unit of men in the Navy, which is the division, similar to the company in the Army. His job was learned before the war at sea as an apprentice, as I learned it in the Astoria. I was a junior division officer for a year. After a year of seeing how it should be done, I was fairly competent in doing it.

If a junior officer learning his job as a division officer had a competent boss, which he generally did, he really learned how to lead a division, how to inspect his men, inspire them, keep them content, see that they did their work, help them in their personal problems, etc. What I am speaking about now is the obvious need in the Navy for The Division Officer's Guide. It turned out when we consulted the Bureau of Naval Personnel that they had wanted a Division Officer's Guide for years, and they had sent several talented reserve officers to do the job in BuPers. But every time they got under way, they would have had enough points and they'd go back to civilian life. My skipper, the head of the department, Mike Flaherty, had had the same enthusiasm about the need for a Division Officer's Guide when he came back ashore after the war.* So, to make a long story short, I wrote an outline that was taken up to the bureau, they approved it, and I wrote the book in three or four months, and it was immediately accepted because it filled a need. It exists today. It's in its eighth edition and is a standard text for the junior officers in the Navy. It's not only used at the academies and at the NROTC units, but the surface warfare school uses it as its major text.** This is a school that all surface warfare officers have to go through.

Another aspect of my desire to write this book was a recognition of the fact that leadership training, even in the abstract, was completely absent in 1950 from the curriculum at the Naval Academy. Ninety-six hours a year of leadership training were devoted to shooting the rifle and pistol, but leadership was focused on military justice. They had a short course in Rocks and Shoals, but not a single word was said about modern management or the basics of human relations.*** Since

---
*Captain Michael F. Flaherty, USN.
**NROTC--Naval Reserve Officers Training Corps
***"Rocks and Shoals" was the nickname for the Articles for the Government of the Navy, which were in force until the adoption of the Uniform Code of Military Justice in 1951.

these were the two things that I had been the most interested in at Stanford and had read the most about and thought the most about, I thought that if I could word this book in proper seamanlike language without offending the old chaps who ran the Navy, to whom a word like "psychology" smelled of Communism, if I could put it in non-social scientist terms, which I had to, because even the thought of a social scientist made most senior Navy types see red, and quite literally red, this book might go. This is what I did pretty well, I think. I wrote a very simple, small book that's since been expanded considerably, which put in rather basic naval terms some of the principles of human relations and management which a young officer should know when he dealt with his men.

Having started on this writing kick and having a very easy job teaching and administering in the seamanship department, I then had occasion to help revise Knight's Modern Seamanship. Dear old Commodore Wentworth came over and showed us his manuscript.* We were teaching from the book which the Naval Academy had had for 50 years. He wanted us to review his revision. Well, this we did rather extensively. My lieutenant instructors were happy to each take a chapter and sort of bring it up to date. To make a long story short, the next time

---

*Commodore Ralph S. Wentworth, USN(Ret.), who had been graduated from the Naval Academy in 1912 and retired in 1946. He as a longtime fixture in the Annapolis area until his death in 1980 at the age of 89.

Knight's came up for revision a couple of years later, the publishers asked me to do it, and I've done it to this day. We've just gotten out the 17th edition.

I proposed about the same time to Van Nostrand to either revise their terrible little naval dictionary that had been done by Commander Soule or to do a new one.[*] He was a real old-timer. Soule's dictionary was horribly out of date. It was a little glossary, really. I wound up by doing a Naval Terms Dictionary, which has gone to four editions and is now owned by the Naval Institute, who bought it from Van Nostrand.[**]

A shiphandling book came on the horizon when a gifted shiphandler, a good seaman, a classmate of mine, Ed King, came to me and said he had all the notes he'd taken on shiphandling during the war and afterwards, and why didn't we do a book. I did. Van Nostrand did the book.[***] It was a good book, but it aroused unhappiness at the Naval Institute who got their own people to write a book, and the Navy has bought more of their books than our book, and our book is out of print.

Q: That's a funny attitude for them to take. Were they jealous?

---
[*]Commander Charles C. Soule, USN, Naval Terms and Definitions (New York: D. Van Nostrand Company, Inc., 1922).
[**]Commander John V. Noel, Jr., USN, Naval Terms Dictionary (New York: D. Van Nostrand Company, Inc., 1952).
[***]Commander E.R. King, USN, and Commander J.V. Noel, Jr., USN, Ship Handling (New York: D. Van Nostrand Company, Inc., 1954).

Captain Noel: Very. Old Roy Horn, now dead, with whom I had a few quarrels because he didn't believe that naval officers should be paid for any writing, and he hated to pay me more than $1 an hour, and I finally persuaded him that he had to enter the 20th century and pay royalties.*

Q: He was over at the Institute?

Captain Noel: He was the editor-publisher of the Naval Institute. He took great umbrage at the shiphandling book and managed to persude the Navy not to buy any until he had produced his shiphandling book, which was a very good one, Naval Shiphandling, done by Crenshaw.** Our book faded, and when it went out of print, we just let it go.

Q: Could you revise it or review it and publish it through some other channel?

Captain Noel: Yes, conceivably it could have been republished, but if one publisher couldn't sell it, I don't think another one could. I've written a couple of dictionaries, a boating

---
*The managing editor of the Naval Institute was Commander Roy de S. Horn, USN(Ret.).
**Commander Russell S. Crenshaw, Jr., USN, Naval Shiphandling (Annapolis: U.S. Naval Institute, 1955). The book has subsequently been revised with the publication of later editions. Such updating is necessary as new ships with differing characteristics enter the fleet.

dictionary and a dictionary of ships and the sea, and neither of them is selling well. They are very carefully done, but there's just no great allure in a dictionary.

Also at the Naval Academy I had the opportunity to be the secretary to the board of visitors in which I met a great many distinguished educators such as Father Hesburgh of Notre Dame.*
I also helped set up the first Parents Day at the Naval Academy in which in the summer after the plebes have come in, they ask the parents of all the new midshipmen to meet and to discuss matters. I was sent up to the Naval War College to observe their course in international law, and I wrote a simplified version for the Naval Academy curriculum.

Q: Of international law?

Captain Noel: International law. So it established their course in international law.

Q: Had they had one before?

Captain Noel: No.

Q: I would think that would be absolutely critical.

---
*Father Theodore Hesburgh

Captain Noel: The concept of the Naval Academy was that if you needed things like international law, you were senior enough to have gotten them at the War College, that actually the junior officers, the young officers, didn't really need it. It became, however, apparent that they should have an introduction to the subject, so they knew that the things that they were concerned with as junior officers, like the rules of the road, were essentially international law and very effective international law.

Q: So since all good things must end, your Naval Academy tour of duty terminated by some orders.

Captain Noel: Actually, John Quinn, my new skipper, was a friend of my boss in the seamanship department, and I met him at the Academy.* He said, "Would you like to be my executive officer?" So again I was pretty much fortunate in being able to pick my job, and I couldn't have asked for a better one. The Rochester was to be the flagship of the Seventh Fleet, which was in the Pacific, in the Far East. John Quinn was an extraordinary man. Thus, three wonderful, creative, and happy years ended with orders to the Rochester as executive officer, then under overhaul in Mare Island.

---
*Captain John Quinn, USN

Under the magnificent commanding officer John Quinn, we were able to rewrite the ship's organization with the cooperation of all concerned officers and petty officers. They then trained every man in his duties, including the division officers, and laid the foundation for a very happy and efficient ship.

Before receiving the flag aboard in Japan, the Rochester was sent on a show-the-flag cruise to Manila, Singapore, Bangkok, Saigon, and Hong Kong. While the crew went on liberty, official calls would be made and returned, and it was an experience which I think is best described by an article called "Showing the Flag in Southeast Asia," which appeared in the Proceedings.*

There is a big difference between a ship with a flag aboard and others. The captain of a ship without a flag, that is, without an admiral and his staff embarked, is king of the rock, monarch of all he surveys. He does not have to bow to the possible quirks and idiosyncrasies of a senior officer--even a junior staff officer can cause trouble. There are compensations, of course. Flagships visit more interesting ports and always go alongside the dock while other ships must anchor in the stream and run boats.

When we took the flag aboard the Rochester in Yokosuka, Japan, the ship was well shaken down. We all knew our jobs and looked forward to a good cruise. If we had to be away from home

---

*Commander John V. Noel, Jr., "Showing the Flag in Southeast Asia," U.S. Naval Institute, February 1955, pages 179-191.

for eight months in peacetime, at least we would be seeing the world. However, we braced ourselves for a bit of stress and strain with the inevitable crowding when staff personnel must have working and living space. The key to a potentially troublesome situation like this is to persuade the crew that our major mission is to support the admiral and his staff and that there would be no "them" and "us." The first staff officer to arrive was Captain Andrew Hill, who toured the ship with me and then pointed out firmly what space the staff would need.

The Seventh Fleet was composed of all ships in the Western Pacific and was commanded by Vice Admiral Mel Pride, USN. He was that rarity of his time, not an Annapolis graduate, was thoroughly competent and was liked and respected by all. We were very fortunate. The admiral and his staff operated and administered the Seventh Fleet, and as long as we provided a happy and efficient home for them, all was well.

Most of our time with Vice Admiral Pride and his staff aboard was spent in showing the flag--the U.S. flag. In every port, of course, we had to entertain at luncheons and dinners and receptions and at least once an open house for the general public with ice cream for the children, etc. We made a big point of entertaining children, and the men seemed to enjoy it. The entertaining involved a good deal of extra work on the part of the crew, but we all knew that without the flag aboard, we would not have seen as much of the Orient as we did. As exec, my job was to manage the ship and its people to ensure maximum spit and polish and efficiency. Captain John Quinn was the ideal outside man; receiving all guests at the admiral's side and being host himself at a number of functions.

I have a few other remarks I would like to make about this cruise. It was a great personal and professional experience. We had a superbly smart ship and crew because this is what all hands wanted. The happy crew loved Genial John, as they called him. He was their father image, while I toiled in detail and could be the occasional bastard that enforced regulations to ensure that we all lived well. Great emphasis was placed on improving habitability by the ship's force, on good food in the general mess, on having maximum liberty consonant with security and the ship's work, and particularly on effective communications up and down the line. A major tool here was the suggestion box, wherein every serious message was answered, signed or not, in the plan of the day. As far as I know, we were the first major fleet unit to have a suggestion box. It is standard today. We had almost no disciplinary problems as soon as it was clear that these were the responsibility of the men's division officer and that only those which he could not handle were brought to the captain's mast. If men did not behave ashore, they were jolly well kept on the ship until they changed their viewpoint. This very simple device enabled us to have almost a perfect record ashore with the shore patrol.

At the end of the cruise in our home port of Long Beach, where most petty officers had wives or girls ashore, we were able to start liberty as soon as the daily planned work and training was finished. This was magic indeed, and we finally were able to start liberty at 11:30 a.m. On Sunday we had no reveille. Only those on duty had to get up, and breakfast was served a la carte all morning. These innovative and highly successful small details of running a ship were made possible because I had the complete trust and faith of the skipper, John Quinn. Although it sounds rather extraordinary to be able to start liberty before lunch, the fact was that when the petty officers and senior officers and more responsible people on board ship knew that by getting the work done quickly they could go shore, they rounded up all the stray sailors who were hanging out in the post office line or the ship's service line or sick bay line and put them to work. Everybody got their work done quickly and didn't just stay around ship because somebody's directive said that liberty should start at 4:30 in the afternoon.

Q: I want to comment. Maybe you will later. But in the publication you speak of having a black officer and one who spoke Chinese.

Captain Noel: Oh, yes.

Noel #1 - 103

Q: That they were so wonderful in the PR ashore.

Captain Noel: Of course, we made a great impression, and this is nothing that other ships don't do, but we made a great impression by always having our Chinese officer and our black officer highly visible on the beach, refuting the communist propaganda everywhere we went that, of course, the Americans oppressed their blacks and were very mean to all minorities. The Chinese officer, of course, was a Californian American Chinese, but he did have a little Chinese and he did look Chinese. It was a highly successful public relations stunt, I suppose, but it's for the same reason that Admiral Anderson and the Sixth Fleet, when we lined up our side boys for ceremonial occasions on the flagship, he always had a black among the six or eight side boys.*

Q: We have forgotten what your grade is now. I know the last mention we made of it was when you were a commander.

Captain Noel: I'm still a commander. I have no complaints. I was a commander eight years out of the Naval Academy, and I didn't stay a commander too long. I became a captain a little

---
*Vice Admiral George W. Anderson, Jr., USN, served as Commander Sixth Fleet from 1959 to 1961. During part of that period, his fleet flagship was the USS Springfield (CLG-7), commanded by Captain Noel.

later when I went to the Industrial College.

Going back to the Rochester--before we leave that, I have a few more wonderful memories of Genial John Quinn. He was an extraordinary man who was modest. His family farm in Texas near Big Bend had struck oil, and he had all the money he needed and more, but he was quiet about it. It turned out when we went out to the Seventh Fleet in the Rochester and went through Hawaii, he discovered that the ship had no silver punchbowl and no silver service. The first Rochester had given it away, I guess, to the city of Rochester, so when they had another Rochester, nobody gave them any silver. He just quietly went ashore and spent thousands of dollars on the proper silver that a modern flagship should have, including a great big punchbowl. It must have set him back a fortune. In every way he was considerate of people. He had a brilliant career in the Bureau of Ordnance, did a lot of the work on the proximity fuze, which was so important to us, and as a result he had spent most of the war in the Bureau of Ordnance. He needed sea duty, and he was not a happy, comfortable shiphandler, but he could do it. He had the guts to do it. But he had the great good sense not to try to run the nuts and bolts of the ship. He knew that I'd been at sea a very long time and the nuts and bolts of a ship were my meat and drink, and he trusted me and let me run the ship. If it came to a pinch and we had a bad type that had to come up to the captain to be punished, why, it was such an engaging spectacle that the master-at-arms who had to preside would flip coins to see whose privilege it could be to take the prisoner up before Genial John.

Q: That's certainly unusual.

Captain Noel: These young rascals who had persisted in coming back to the ship days late or had really done something that none of us could grapple with, they just had to be brought up with a round turn, as they say. We would bring them up before Captain Quinn, and Captain Quinn would speak to them just like their father. He would ask them all about their family and their mother and their father and where they were from and what their hobbies were, and you could see this rascal figured that he was going to flim-flam this old fellow. I never brought a man to mast that wasn't guilty and didn't need a lot of punishment, so Genial John would give this chap his sincere and genial treatment and then give him the maximum--ten days bread and water, or something like that. This chap would almost have a fit because he thought by that time Genial John was going to take him home on his next vacation. This was immensely effective and was a source of great amusement and pride to the crew, that they had a captain who was so understanding and such a nice guy and just slugged these fellows who stepped out of line that badly and brought a bad name on the ship.

He was one of the best .45 pistol shots in the Navy, and

there are lots of amusing stories about him when he was on somebody's staff and was told off to go and take pistol instruction from a Marine colonel, as everybody had to do. He said nothing, but when the Marine colonel called upon him to shoot, of course, Genial John would put a group in about a quarter, and with that the Marine colonel would dismiss him instantly from the class. But he did have a great enthusiasm about shooting. When we'd go into port, he would do his best to take me ashore and teach me a little bit about shooting. I detested shooting a pistol, and I would always make some excuse, but we did go ashore and go shopping. I would take $10 and John would take his unlimited checkbook. The scale of our purchases would be somewhat different, but we'd have a good time and would both find bargains in our price range.

I have one more sea story to tell about John Quinn. We knew he was coming up for admiral and we were determined on the ship to do everything we could for him, because he'd assumed full responsibility for extra pay days, taking the risk that the supply officer, the paymaster, could not take, but he as captain could take, and there wasn't any real risk, but legally if one of the sailors had died when he had been a little bit overpaid, the paymaster would have been responsible for that amount of money. So John Quinn signed the proper papers. When we were going from one great liberty port to another, like Hong Kong to Singapore, why, the paymaster would pay us a little bit ahead. Strictly illegal but marvelous.

Just before we went back, we were to be given our tough administrative inspection, and we knew pretty much what it covered--the appearance of the ship and the damage control perfection of all the compartments, the appearance of the men and their uniforms and their haircuts, and the state of training of the people as could best be determined. All the little details of ship's administration were looked at with a fine-toothed comb. We were determined that we were going to have a great mark for Captain Quinn. Of course, this was my ploy as the executive officer to get everybody enthusiastic, and believe me, they were. We knew that this particular admiral had a great fetish about the back of people's shoes, their heels. So we went to a great deal of trouble in seeing that every man on board had a perfect uniform, a perfect haircut, and perfectly shined shoes. This flabbergasted admiral, after he had inspected the crew, said, "For the first time in my life I've inspected all the men on a ship who are able to be inspected, and I can't find a single mistake." Of course, that gave us a great kick. The night before inspection, I went to bed about 2:00 o'clock, and as I roamed around in the middle of the night before I finally turned in, I found every storeroom and office on the ship was full of men shining their shoes and buffing up their uniform and cleaning their office and making sure that Genial John would get a good mark, and he did.

Noel #1 - 108

Q: That's a real tribute, though, isn't it?

Captain Noel: A real tribute. We did get a very good mark, and he did become promoted. He was such a kind man that even when somebody badgered us a bit, as some of the training commands did and they moved us around from here to there and didn't seem to be very considerate of our welfare, the worst that John Quinn would say about anybody like this was that he believed that they lacked a certain sense of humor.

Q: We're going to go now to the Industrial College of the Armed Forces. According to my recollection, that was in 1955, which meant you went back to Washington, D.C., again.

Captain Noel: Yes. From the <u>Rochester</u> I was ordered to the Industrial College of the Armed Forces. It was either that or the Naval War College at Newport. One didn't have a choice; you were just sent somewhere. I was very happy to go to this Industrial College of the Armed Forces. The curriculums were not too dissimilar, although on our trips we'd go out and see something like the Ford Motor Company in Detroit, and so on.

But this rather relaxed academic tour of a little over a year allowed us the time to build a house in Arlington. Housing in the Navy was always a major problem, and it had gotten so difficult that the only way you could stay afloat financially was

Noel #1 - 109

to own a house, sell it, and then build or buy another house where you went. There was a rising housing market and you could come out a little ahead. At least you'd come out even, instead of just pouring rent down the drain. We could never afford to rent the kind of house that we wanted to live in; we had to build it. We built a very attractive house in Arlington which we designed ourselves and supervised the construction and did the landscaping. It was the best thing I remember about this Industrial College. I hate to admit that I never could get very enthusiastic about the curriculum, which was, I suppose, important but not particularly inspiring.

Q: Were there things you had to pass, or did you just simply attend it, good or bad? Did anyone ever fail it?

Captain Noel: You never failed it if you stayed sober and presented a reasonable paper when you were asked to, which was not too often. It was a senior officers' course, a captains' course.

Q: You were then a captain?

Captain Noel: I had by that time made captain, or I did at the time. It was a gentlemanly instructive sort of life, but no one of our advanced years and wartime experience was about to go into

Noel #1 - 110

a tizzy academically.

Q: What did you write your paper on?

Captain Noel: Morale and discipline. This was the same subject that I had chosen to write on at Stanford, and I must confess that I used most of the same material in a somewhat more military vein for the Industrial College.

In 1956 I was ordered to the Bureau of Naval Personnel as future plans officer at first and then as Assistant Chief of Naval Personnel for Special Projects. This was a marvelous assignment. I knew I was going to the Bureau of Naval Personnel, because I was listed as a personnel postgraduate and I'd taken the course at Stanford. So there was no doubt that I would have to put in my time in the bureau. I had a horror of getting some job stuck behind a pillar counting sailors, so I was very lucky, perhaps because I had met Admiral Holloway at a party in Annapolis. This was just before he took over as Superintendent.* Mary met him, too, and said, "Oh, Mr. Holloway, what do you do?" He was just the new Superintendent, not to be addressed as "Mr." But anyway, we did have a speaking acquaintance.

When I went to the Bureau of Naval Personnel, I got a very

---
*Rear Admiral James L. Holloway, Jr., USN, was Superintendent of the Naval Academy from January 1947 to April 1950. As a vice admiral, he served as Chief of Naval Personnel from 1953 to 1958.

fine job as future plans officer. My job was to work on the future ways we would handle personnel and how we could administer personnel. This led to nothing spectacular, except I did have a major part in originating the NESEP program--Naval Enlisted Scientific Education Program. This was at the behest of Secretary of the Navy Gates, who was persuaded by one of his friends that we had a great many very talented people in the Navy who had not had the opportunity for a higher education.* This friend of Tom Gates was Admiral Luis de Florez, a very talented second-generation Spaniard who was a well-known inventor and had many ideas, almost all of them very good.** He had sold Tom Gates on the idea that we needed an educational program to produce some future great scientists. We in the Bureau of Naval Personnel were bleeding for good technicians, so we wanted to provide some way to uncover the engineering abilities of our men.

The program that was finally evolved and one in which I was overruled, together with Admiral Rickover, in our need for engineers, was a four-year college program.*** This turned out to be a very worthwhile operation. The first year we had an amazing group of men. Many of them had left high school and had gotten married. That ruled them out of most programs for

---
*Thomas S. Gates, Secretary of the Navy from April 1957 to June 1959.
**Rear Admiral Luis de Florez, USNR.
***Rear Admiral Hyman G. Rickover, USN, who was instrumental in the development of nuclear propulsion in the U.S. Navy.

advancement to officer. They had been badly adjusted perhaps at home or in school and had rushed into the Navy, but they all had one thing in common: they had tremendous IQs. We persuaded all 52 of the NROTC colleges with whom we'd had such success with our programs to take these enlisted men that we had selected on our say-so, without giving them any confirming examinations. We devised the tests and we uncovered for years--the program has ended now, but for years we sent to college highly gifted people from seaman first to chief petty officer. They could get promoted as they deserved while they were at college. We had a chief petty officer who two years later graduated from the University of North Carolina, Phi Beta Kappa, at the head of his class. We had extraordinarily good men. I occasionally run into officers who said, "Yes, I came into the Navy through the NESEP program." These men could all earn a commission, get promoted, whatever rating they had, and then apply for commission and eventually get it. This was one of the adventures of being a personnel planner. I don't remember many others. Most of it was a struggle to improve the utilization of men on ships. We built ships on the basis that you needed X number of men on deck to scrape and paint. Therefore, the gunners didn't care how many people they put in their turrets to fire the guns and load the ammunition by hand because they knew the ship had to have so many people to paint and scrape. On the other hand, the people who designed the bulkheads and the decks and designed the ship knew the guns required so many people to load them and fire them, that they had no great motivation for making economies in such things as putting Formica on the bulkheads below deck and letting the hard-working sailor just wipe them off rather than having to scrape it and paint it.

Interview Number 2 with Captain John .V. Noel, Jr.,
U.S. Navy (Retired)

Place: Captain Noel's home in Santa Fe, New Mexico

Date: 9 August 1984

Subject: Biography

Interviewer: Commander Etta-Belle Kitchen, U.S. Navy (Retired)

Q: You're on duty as Assistant Chief of Naval Personnel for Special Projects and some of your special duties.

Captain Noel: It was an interesting job, one of them that I had to persuade the technical bureaus that saving manpower was just as important as saving resources or saving money. While I saw no immediate success in this movement, all the trends, of course, since then have been to devise ships that are more automated and don't require as many men. Of course, the Navy found at the same time that industry did that men cost a great deal of money to recruit, train, and maintain, and retire.

As Assistant Chief for Special Projects for Admiral Holloway, who became a great friend, I was given a number of interesting special assignments, usually on loan to the Chief of Naval Operations, the Secretary of the Navy, or the Secretary of Defense. One job, which was fascinating, was implementing for the Secretary of Defense the first government-paid hospital plan for the military dependents on active duty. This involved speaking in the name of the Secretary of Defense to a specially called meeting of the American Medical Association and persuading them to cooperate on a program that involved payment on a fixed fee basis for medical care in civilian hospitals.

Q: That must have been something with the AMA.*

Captain Noel: To the AMA, particularly their lunatic right wing--this was extremely sensitive, but they had been forced, really, patriotically to support the law which merely said that the Secretary of Defense was authorized to implement such plans as he saw fit to provide medical care in civilian hospitals to military personnel and their dependents. In other words, the Congress passed the buck to the Secretary of Defense, and all I could do was go to Chicago, and speaking to the AMA, say, "This law gives both of us an opportunity. The Secretary of Defense, for whom I speak, can't make a foot of progress without your full support, so I hope that you will appoint some people to work with me and my two associates and that together we can agree on something that's good for the country, good for the military, and good for the medical profession."

Q: Would that have been both Navy and Army?

---
*AMA--American Medical Association

Captain Noel: All defense. This sort of disarmed the AMA. They admitted that who could quarrel with an appeal like that, and they did appoint an outstanding group, headed by a doctor in Washington, to work with me and my people in hammering out a medical plan. The key, of course, was, who was to decide how much was to be charged for the military dependent or military man in a civilian hospital. The government couldn't write an open ticket. There was no way it could be done at the pleasure of the doctor who was presiding as he would write out his bill for a private citizen. We had to work through the state medical societies, and most of them agreed to put together a schedule of fees. An appendectomy would be this much money. Of course, this tended to drive them up, because although an appendectomy was cheaper in Georgia than it was in New York, the people in Georgia hated to admit it and made every effort to ease the costs up a little bit. However, there were some states that were difficult to deal with, and in that case we would just ask the civilian doctor in that state to send his bill to the Department of the Army in Washington where a fair amount would be paid. It was paid, and the thing worked that way.

We had many sticky questions: How do you care and pay for mental illness? How long an illness? How do you prevent abuses? How do you keep old retired people from cluttering up the doctor's time in a place like Washington, when really there's nothing wrong with them? They just are lonely and want to talk to somebody? We were authorized by the law to charge a nominal amount for each visit, but we decided not to, that these little sessions had great therapeutic value. And how were you going to tell if a man really had something wrong with him or a woman or a child and when they didn't? You had to really see them. You couldn't charge them for every visit.

The program worked. It was a great adventure for me to be immersed in medicine for six months.

My only problems were with the very aggressive and conservative AMA lobby in Washington, who got spooked a few times about things we were doing and appealed to the White House. On one occasion they called a retired general, who was President Eisenhower's personal physician. I got a frantic call from the Secretary of Defense's office saying that the White House was calling, very upset. Of course, the White House and the Secretary of Defense's office were inclined to alarm each other. It's just some bureaucrat over there. But it turned out that the general did have some questions, and I asked him to lunch. He said he couldn't come, but he asked me to come over. We had a pleasant talk. I explained what we were doing and he couldn't have been friendlier. It helped that I knew his son, who was a contemporary of mine, and I'd played golf with him. But it was an example of the touchiness of the AMA, whose highly paid lobby was paid to fend off any real or possible damage to the prerogatives of the medical profession.

Q: At one time I understood that the medical profession had the highest paid lobbyists of any group in Washington.

Captain Noel: I think they still do. I had no particular problem with them, because the people who really ran the AMA were completely in support of their own task force that worked with my people. So after a very few hitches, we put a program together which apparently worked pretty well. This program was the beginning of CHAMPUS, which is working now.*

Other special projects I had involved devising and implementing a Navywide moral leadership program for the Secretary of the Navy, Tom Gates. This was based on traditional naval doctrine, modern management techniques, and moral responsibility.** It was very well received in the fleet, especially by junior personnel, and had a measurable success in improving discipline, but the word "moral" seemed to bother the bureaucrats, and the program evolved into the present leadership and management, education and training (LMET) program.

Q: I remember when that came out. I was up in Bainbridge then.

Captain Noel: You do?

---

*CHAMPUS--Civilian Health and Medical Program of the Uniformed Services.
**An article describing the program is included as an appendix to this volume.

Q: I just thought it was so wonderful.

Captain Noel: The man who worked with me on this program, two people, a civilian, Fred Dyer, Bureau of Naval Personnel, and a Navy chaplain, then a lieutenant, called John J. O'Connor, who was later the senior chaplain in the Navy and now is the archbishop in New York and a cardinal. O'Connor was and is a superb man and had conceived this concept of moral responsibility as being a key to naval leadership. The way that it got to the Secretary of the Navy's attention was through an Admiral Black Jack Reeves, who was a tough old bird who apparently had gotten religion and had been influenced enough by John O'Connor to persuade, as I understand it, Secretary of the Navy Tom Gates to tell the Chief of Naval Personnel that he wanted a leadership program devised for the Navy which would have a moral basis.* Admiral Holloway sort of hemmed and hawed on this for a while, but finally told me off to go and make the Secretary of the Navy happy, because if I didn't, the Secretary of the Navy was going to, according to my information, fire Admiral Holloway.

Q: Excuse me. I have to interrupt, because you've used this term several times: "told you off." Now my understanding of "told me off" was really to get rid of you, to tell you off. You

---

*Admiral John W. Reeves, Jr., USN(Ret.)

are using it, I think, as having you do a different job.

Captain Noel: I think you can use "to tell off"--a man is told off to clean up the head. You can say that in the Navy quite properly. He may be told off if he doesn't clean up the head properly, but he can be told off to do a certain job.

Q: Okay. So anyway, Admiral Holloway didn't want to have the Secretary of the Navy say, "Goodbye, Admiral Holloway."

Captain Noel: Right. Tom Gates's aide at the time was one of my oldest friends, Admiral Noel Gayler, and he said, "Jack, the Secretary is serious about this and you'd better come down with an answer."*

So to make a long story short, the chaplain concerned, John O'Connor and Fred Dyer and I sat down and worked out a leadership program. The interesting part about this--it's never been a matter of record, as far as I know--was that the origin of Admiral Reeves's conviction, there was a successful way to appeal to men on the basis of their moral responsibility to do a job, was a program that had been started at the aircraft repair facility at Pensacola. They were having a lot of problems getting these sailors in overhauling and putting together the

---
*Captain Noel M. Gayler, USN, whose recollections are in the Naval Institute oral history collection.

aircraft to be always sure to get the cotter pin in on top of the nut so the nut didn't fly off the bolt and we didn't lose a multi-million dollar aircraft and a multi-million dollar pilot.

Q: Apparently some people today haven't learned that lesson.

Captain Noel: That's true. But the thesis was that you could reach people in leadership by appealing to their abstract sense of morality. You didn't care whether they chased girls or drank liquor; you cared and they had to care how they did their job. This moral leadership program, unfortunately, really didn't stick in the Navy very long. It did, however, result in a program for missile and aircraft and armament production called Zero Defects, which some civilian outfit in Chicago got ahold of and, ironically enough, sold back to the Navy. The man who was selling it told me, without knowing any of my background in the moral leadership program, told me that the origin of all their programs, which they were selling for lots of money to all of industry, was based on our moral responsibility program of leadership in the Navy. The Pershing missiles that Martin Marietta started to make, and which they're still making with some problems, couldn't have gotten off the production lines if they hadn't adopted this program of Zero Defects, in which they persuaded everybody to talk to everybody else about how they could do their job better and not have any defects in the production line of a missile.

Q: I think that's astonishing.

Captain Noel: Isn't it? This fellow told me this in Paris. As a matter of fact, I tried to sell this program later to the French.

Another project I was involved in, less significant perhaps, was a survey of officers' clubs allegedly in a good deal of financial trouble. I put together a small team of food and drink and hotel experts. I recall that one of them was a reserve officer called back to active duty; he was a vice president of Schrafts in New York. We got a small airplane and, being winter, naturally we flew south, and we decided to look over officers' clubs and see what their problems were. Well, it was the most simple and obvious problem in the world. Where the admiral and particularly the admiral's wife got involved in the affairs of the officers' club and insisted that it be a refuge for the old fuds, where junior officers had to wear a coat at dinner, the club was generally in financial difficulties. If, as was true particularly at Little Creek, Virginia, at the amphibious base, there was a formal dining room and also a place below with candles and a piano and a bar, the young officers could come in off the beach in their shorts and carry on and have a sandwich if they wanted it instead of dinner, clubs like that were just coining money. It was just obvious and simple human relations.

I remember one shocking admiral's wife who took all the club's reserve money and built a four-holer woman's john complete with copper downspouts.

Q: It's hard for me to believe.

Captain Noel: I'm sure she had the best intentions in the world, but I don't think she understood that the junior officers, the bachelors, who really support a club, you have to make the ambiance happy for them.

Really the only thing that evolved from this expedition of any importance was that we learned that most officers' clubs were managed by civilians, and they weren't allowed to hire much more than a GS-8, which didn't give them men of the experience or quality or background necessary to really run an officers' club.

So we had graduates of the hotel management school at Cornell, who were graduating and joining the Navy for two years of active duty. We set up a special officers' club managers school for them at Patuxent. With three months of naval indoctrination, these chaps professionally trained in hotel and restauarant management, made very good officers' club managers.

Q: The story of the admiral's wife reminds me--it may be apocryphal, I hope it is--that the admiral's wife, when the ladies were in the ladies' room, suggested they line up by grade. That story really got around.

Captain Noel: There were a few, but I must say not very many.

Q: Did you ever hear that story before?

Captain Noel: No, never did. I met an admiral's wife when I'd been retired several years, at Sotogrande, a golf resort in Spain, where they were both visiting. We had a house there at the time. We were all at dinner on New Year's Eve and she took umbrage at my not shagging drinks for her and dancing with her and waiting attendance upon her because she was an admiral's wife. I just couldn't believe it, but she naturally assumed that anybody who was junior in rank to her husband was supposed to take care of her.

Q: I hate to know the end of that story.

Captain Noel: I didn't pay any attention to her. Mary and I went off to another party and left her to stew in her own juice. Her husband was sort of a bore, too.

Another project I had was very interesting. A good friend of mine in the Navy, a Jewish chaplain, Josh Goldberg, had been in New York for 17 years before he came to Washington; he was really the unofficial Jewish mayor of New York.* Everybody in New York knew him, and he was a very dynamic fellow married to a very successful executive. He persuaded the Secretary of the Navy, Mr. Thomas, that a very good thing for all concerned would be to hold a conference of all the chaplains of the NATO countries, that this conference should include a tour in the United States, a meeting with the President at the White House, and in general be something that would solidify the good spirit and morale of NATO.**

The Secretary of the Navy thought it was a great idea, gave me his own big airplane and $8,000 of very rare funds, the kind that don't have to be accounted for, and told me to go over to Paris and they'd send out some messages. In Paris I was to pick up all the NATO chaplains. Well, this was a great adventure, of course. I hadn't been to Paris. I started to contact the NATO chaplains that reported. There was a chaplain from the Netherlands, a rather mystical Protestant. Actually, he was confessor to the Queen. I think his name was Silvan. Anyway, he called and said he was at the hotel but didn't have any money, and would I come and pay his hotel bill and pick him up, which I was happy to do. That's what my funds were for, for just such eccentric men of the cloth. The Greek Orthodox chaplain was a

---
*Captain Joshua L. Goldberg, CHC, USNR, whose recollections are contained in the oral history program of the Navy's Chaplain Corps.
*NATO--North Atlantic Treaty Organization

bit of a problem. He needed complete privacy. He was horrified at the thought of sharing a room with anybody when we scheduled him to the BOQ. The Orthodox Jewish chaplain of the French was a very troublesome fellow who had agreed to fly with us on the date we were scheduled to take off, but then suddenly decided that this was some sort of a holy day and he couldn't fly that day, and he wanted a ticket to fly later. We had already gone to a great deal of trouble to provide him with his kosher food in all parts of the United States where this gang was to visit, and this was just too much. I told him very politely that if he couldn't travel with us, we would have to leave him behind, which we did.

This was a very successful expedition or conference, I understand. When we took off from Orly, I think probably the Lord was implored for safety in more languages than had happened before in one airplane. My communications were limited to very bad French and poor English, so the British Catholic chaplain volunteered to be my interpreter and passed out instructions, such as, "We will pass a bottle of Scotch down the aisle on the left side." Well-equipped with Scotch, brandy, and cigars, we had the usual long flight in those days from east to west across the Atlantic, stopping at the Azores.

A small vignette of this sort of thing. We had for the first time the Protestant and Catholic chaplains of the Netherlands meet each other socially.

Q: Interesting.

Captain Noel: So these things do some good. Josh Goldberg later, when he was retired, came to Paris, where I was the naval attache and busy trying to collect some intelligence, and said, "Why don't you get in bed with the Israel attaches here? They have the best intelligence on Russia that any group has, and you might do a little trading." He introduced me to two splendid officers who were the Israeli attaches, and before I left, there was every indication that we could find something the Israelis wanted and that they had lots that we wanted.

Q: What kind of a plane was it in that time?

Captain Noel: It was an R6D, as I recall. It was a propeller plane, but the biggest and the latest of the Douglas prop planes. It was very comfortable travel, particularly for the Secretary of the Navy. He had his own private quarters aft. All the staff members had bunks. That was really the way to cross the Atlantic. It didn't matter how long it took. You could climb into your bunk and snore away and have a good meal when you got up. You were not jammed into some little seat somewhere for an uncomfortable eight or nine hours.

Q: Sounds good.

Noel #2 - 128

Captain Noel: One final word about this interesting tour as Assistant Chief for Special Projects. I was on loan repeatedly to the Secretary of Defense and mostly to Carter Burgess, the Assistant Secretary of Defense for Personnel. He was a very interesting and dynamic fellow who believed in working around the clock. Sometimes we'd get home at 3:00 a.m. and be expected to be in the office at 7:00. But he did give us some interesting assignments. The Hoover Commission had met and had made a lot of mostly ill-advised recommendations for how we could save money and personnel and how the Department of Defense could be run more efficiently by civilians, in fact, how the whole military effort could be run more efficiently by civilians, which, of course, may be true in some instances.* Several times I was secretary to a hastily convened task force of senior officers who were gathered together to fight off some of these recommendations of the Hoover Commission, which looked wonderful on paper, very similar to the Grace Commission that is in this period now, making all sort of recommendations to save money, and which has been seized upon by Mr. Reagan as evidence that there's a great waste here and a great waste there.

Q: I wanted to ask if we had covered, referring now to the moral leadership program, have we covered the acceptance and reaction

---

*This commission was under the aegis of former President Herbert C. Hoover.

of the fleet to that program?

Captain Noel: I think probably we have covered most of that in the appendix. First I should say how it was implemented. I wrote a General Order 21, which was quickly approved by Secretary Gates. This set up the guidelines of this program and its general substance. Then an office was set up in the Bureau of Naval Personnel to make the study material available and to provide the specific guidance for holding the specific techniques, the discussion periods that were so important to establish good communication between the men and their officers. This was a rather obvious technique, the guided discussion, but it took a good deal of understanding and sometimes subtlety on the part of the leader, the division officer or the head of department, to bring his men and his people around to the viewpoint that he wanted them to. Instead of just getting up and saying, "This is what you'll do because you have to and because it's important," the trick was to start a discussion going in which the men would be brought around to see that this was the obvious and the wise course of action for them.

Q: It developed in their own thinking.

Captain Noel: Right. I think if they had had this leadership program in effect and in force, for example, in the Pueblo, we never would have had that disastrous turnover to the North Korean Navy of a whole ship without any damage done to it, with all that secret equipment on board.* In any discussion of the ship's mission and responsibilities, somebody, perhaps some very junior person, would have said, "But, Captain, what do we do if they try to capture us?" And the obvious thing, at least they could have had a hand grenade handy that they could have thrown down the engine room hatch. It's very hard to imagine a Navy ship without a scuttle-ship bill, but apparently they were unprepared.

Q: Is that usual to have a scuttle-ship bill?

Captain Noel: Every ship I've ever had heard of, I'm sure the regulations require it. Certainly all ship's organization books that are based on the type commander's organization book specify such a bill. Of course, this was an oddball intelligence-gathering ship and there are many people who are responsible for the state of unpreparedness, not the least of which was the National Security Agency, which really ran the ship.

To get back to the moral leadership program, it was very well received, particularly by the junior officers, because implied in this program was something that took effect later in the Navy

---

*The electronic intelligence ship Pueblo (AGER-2) was seized by North Korean forces on 23 January 1968. Her commanding officer, Commander Lloyd Bucher, USN, surrendered his ship without offering any resistance. The crew members were held as prisoners in North Korea until released on 22 December 1968.

under Admiral Zumwalt, which was to dissipate if possible all the vestiges of the ancient days of "do it as I say, damn it, and don't ask any questions."* All of the oppressive, minor things that caused our reenlistment rate to practically reach zero at one time, the harshness to intelligent young American men and women of being told arbitrarily to do things without being given a reason. Those matters were being eased by General Order 21, and it finally took Zumwalt to be tough enough to dissipate almost all of these unpleasant small practices which prevented our reenlistment rate from rising. Of course, under Zumwalt's regime, as much as he was disliked by some of the conventional senior officers, the reenlistment rate started to climb.

Q: Do you have some examples of those small matters that were the basis of lots of irritation?

Captain Noel: The onerous regulations in regard to uniform. The captain of a flagship who was so intimidated by having a flag aboard that he didn't let his deckhands paint the ship in dungarees. He made them wear blues, and that meant they had to have a set of blues to paint in and a set of blues to go ashore in.

---
*Admiral Elmo R. Zumwalt, Jr., USN, Chief of Naval Operations from 1970 to 1974.

Q: Which they had to pay for?

Captain Noel: Oh, yes, out of their own pocket. And arbitrary and thoughtless restrictions of liberty and leave, ships blindly following the rules of the senior officer present that liberty will not start until X-o'clock in the afternoon, despite the fact that they had just come back from a very long deployment and hadn't seen their families for six months. But the captain or the exec was not man enough to take exception to some of these things, and if he didn't have the guts to ignore them, to just go and get official permission to hold an early liberty which his men deserved. There were many little things. Some officers didn't ensure that the quality of the food was good. Neither the exec nor the captain sampled the ration every day and took quick action if the meals fell below standard. There are so many things that a ship's administration can do for habitability and comfort and just human dignity that the average people might think of.

Q: Was saluting included in any of those things?

Captain Noel: No, I don't think saluting was ever an onerous thing. It was never particularly liked by the free, the young American, unless he understood that it was a mutual mark of respect. Very often young sailors and young officers are shy about saluting seniors; they don't want to intrude and they look upon it sometimes mistakenly as something subservient.

Q: That, I think, is the crux.

Captain Noel: Right. But if it's explained and taught as a traditional and happy custom of the service.

Q: And we're all together in this and we're sort of saying hello to each other.

Captain Noel: You salute and say good morning to your division officer the first time you see him as a matter of respect, and he salutes you and says good morning, and you've started the day off with a feeling of some mutual responsibility perhaps.

Q: I was amused. I went to an officers' club and, of course, as a commander female in civilian clothes, I'm sure that the young man at the gate, although I gave him my ID card, had no thought of saluting. I like it and I used to like to do it.

Captain Noel: Well, it certainly is an important part of the military atmosphere that even in the Navy we maintain to a minimum. Certainly the sanctity of the quarterdeck is an important mark of a good and smart ship. A ship that allows people to wander around the quarterdeck in dungarees, smoking cigarettes and skylarking, is a ship that doesn't have an officer of the deck that knows what he's supposed to do. Of course, the quarterdeck is supposed to be reserved for ceremony and greeting people coming aboard. There's supposed to be a certain air of dignity about it. Otherwise, the serious work of the ship, the maintenance of a proper watch in port, even a proper lookout from the quarterdeck, could be impaired if the men are allowed to hoot and holler and race around.

Q: We haven't mentioned up 'til now women in the Navy, particularly in BuPers, the Bureau of Naval Personnel. Did you have any relationship, any problems, or any matters that were interesting in which you were involved?

Captain Noel: No, I don't recall any. I was always impressed by the quality of the WAVES that I encountered in the Office of the Secretary of the Navy and the Chief of Naval Operations, mostly in the Secretary of the Navy's office. It was obvious from the few that I met--I didn't meet any at sea--the few that I met ashore, it was obvious that they were first-rate people. I did not foresee the problems that would evolve when we sent them to sea in tenders and they had to have at least special bathrooms.

But recently, in the last few years, in revising The Division Officer's Guide, I've had to take out all the supposedly sexist language, and I had an interesting time with the last edition in which I resolved, of course, to make it very, very non-sexist. My publisher, Tom Epley at the Institute, recommended a WAVE in Pennsylvania to whom I sent the manuscript of the new edition with a request that she make it more neutral.* Well, she, of course, substituted "he or she" every other line, or "his or hers" the whole thing. It was abominable.

Q: I think it would sound ridiculous.

Captain Noel: So I compromised. I started off with a paragraph in the introduction that said that any place where the reader sees "he," substitute "he" or "she." Where the reader sees "his," substitute "his or hers." And at the same time, we tried not to use "your men" as a generic term for sailors; we used sailors, crew, your people, and this worked out. I haven't heard of any complaints.

Q: I was wondering if you were involved with any jobs that they could or couldn't do, because I know that in the bureau--and I'm not sure what year--there was a great hassle between the bureau and OpNav and SecDef as to jobs women would or would not be

---

*Thomas F. Epley, director of the Naval Institute Press. WAVE is a term formerly applied to women in the U.S. Navy. It stems from the World War II acronym WAVES, for Women Accepted for Volunteer Emergency Service.

permitted to do.* I wondered if you were involved in any of that.

Captain Noel: No. Very happily, I wasn't. I think it was inevitable. There are always a lot of old fuds who see problems in everything new, and there are always a few people that are a little strong on innovation, but I think they shook down without much of a problem. The Army has more of a problem, the infantry has, because there's a question of physical strength sometimes in people.

I think it's only fair to say that since my active duty and in revising The Division Officer's Guide and talking to people at the Surface Warfare Officers School, where they train division officers, I've gotten the distinct impression that the women division officers are superior across the board because of their greater motivation. Probably the best thing they do for the Navy is, they keep the male junior officers up to snuff, because if they don't stay up to snuff, they'll look very sad indeed as division officers alongside the women.

Q: That's interesting. So we're finished with your duty in BuPers.

---

*OpNav--staff of the Chief of Naval Operations; SecDef--Secretary of Defense.

Noel #2 - 137

Captain Noel: Yes. This is 1958, and it was time to go to sea again. I was able to pick my deep-draft command, the AKS Altair. AKS stands for supply ship, auxiliary ship, for the Sixth Fleet. This was homeported in Barcelona, Spain. The Altair was an old bucket with the Navy's first computer for the 30,000 items that she carried to supply the Sixth Fleet under way. We had a new helicopter platform aft and were able to pioneer underway replenishment by helicopter. We were really a floating supply depot, and I had a talented group of Supply Corps officers to initiate a new era in fleet support.

Q: A new era, you say. So this was a new concept that you instituted?

Captain Noel: The concept wasn't mine, but I had the pleasure of commanding the ship that instituted this more advanced form of underway replenishment. It took such a long time for the carriers particularly to be replenished. They had to pick up fuel and ammunition and stores and fresh food. Anything that could speed it up and thereby decrease the vulnerability, particularly of the carriers, who were forced during replenishment to steam at the replenishment speed, which was 12 to 15 knots, that anything that could reduce this vulnerability was very much welcomed. One of the things, even before we got our own big helicopter that could carry a load, the carriers would lend us their rescue helicopters, which could only carry 200 or 300 pounds, but still they could snap this off the deck, drop it on their carrier, come back and snap up another one. It did speed up replenishment considerably.

Q: So that's how it worked. Explain an incident so I can picture what actually happened.

Captain Noel: The replenishment force was made up of ships such as ammunition ships, oilers, ships like mine, the supply ships, reefers that had fresh food, and these ships belonged to the service squadron. The commodore was homeported generally in Naples. Periodically, every three or four weeks perhaps, he would gather his replenishment ships together in formation and go to a certain rendezvous, hopefully in the lee of some island where the seas were not rough, and the carriers would appear over the horizon at dawn and come charging up, and we would replenish them. This was the operation of the theory that some fleets do not need a home base. Now there were certain ships homeported abroad. This meant that they came into this home port instead of going back to Norfolk, and they had their families there. Some of the replenishment ships were homeported and the flagship was homeported. The carriers, however, deployed with their destroyers and cruisers, deployed every six months or so from Norfolk.

Q: When they would all get together, you had your helicopter and transferred it that way. Did all the other other ships also?

Captain Noel: The helicopter was just an additional tool. We didn't change going alongside. Every supply ship generally had two ships alongside to get their food or their supplies, a destroyer on each side, a carrier on one side, maybe, and a destroyer on the other. But while this was going on, the helicopters would be making pickups from our helicopter platform and dropping material on the appropriate ship. So the helicopters were just a device to speed up the whole process which generally took three or four hours. Sometimes it took a long time to fuel some of those ships.

Q: How did it get from one ship from another? I'm sounding naive because I want you to give me a picture of it. In a net?

Captain Noel: By helicopter where there would be small nets. From ship to ship, the ships would maintain station alongside of each other and lines would be put over, and the material would be transferred in nets that would travel on a wire from one ship to the other and then be hauled back.

Q: That must have been a spectacle to see that operation.

Captain Noel: It was, particularly in bad weather with seas breaking over the bow and sometimes ships having trouble keeping station. But it was sort of exciting. Some of us who were most directly concerned finally persuaded the staff to be more perceptive in looking for a lee somewhere. If the wind was blowing hard from the northwest, there was no use replenishing on the northwest side of Corsica. It made a lot more sense to go through the Straits of Bonifacio and find a lee on the east side of Corsica. This became standard procedure.

Q: It seems to me that one hears of the military aspect of it, whereas this is really the background, the basis for the whole thing. It's not heard about a lot.

Captain Noel: No, perhaps not. It's rather routine. This ship-to-ship replenishment has been going on, of course, for a long time, since World War II, even before. Destroyers normally went alongside a bigger ship and got their fuel oil.

Q: With that I'm familiar, but with this other . . .

Captain Noel: Replenishing a whole fleet was a new concept and rather peculiar to the Sixth Fleet.

Our job in the <u>Altair</u> was to replenish the Sixth Fleet under way with everything needed except food, oil, and ammunition.

There were separate ships, of course, for these three commodities. The Sixth Fleet had no logistic support ashore, although a few ships such as the flagship, some oilers, and the Altair were homeported in the Mediterranean. This meant that the families for these ships were sent over and the ships periodically returned to their home port, in our case, Barcelona.

It was a great experience for the Noels to have a home abroad. They travelled widely in Europe, learned some Spanish. I'm speaking now of Mary and the children particularly. They studied Spanish and the European culture and made many good foreign friends.

We entertained for visiting Sixth Fleet ships and arranged their visits. Barcelona, as you can guess, was very popular. Unfortunately, the consul general there was an ineffective alcoholic, and as senior captain of the three ships homeported there, it fell upon us to sort of do the honors for Barcelona, and this was a pleasure. Spain in 1958, Barcelona in particular, was for Americans primitive, cheap, and charming.

Q: You told me that you selected the Altair. Was it because of its home port?

Captain Noel: Yes. Mary had never been able to follow me anywhere in the Pacific. I'd spent my whole life in the Pacific. There's a lot of water and very little else. I was determined not only to see something of the Atlantic and of Europe, but to give my family a chance to see that. It was tremendously stimulating and interesting for Mary to live abroad. It was the sort of a job where I really needed a charming and intelligent wife, because there were a lot of people for us to entertain that Mary was the major part of the receiving committee.

While we lived in Barcelona, our daughter Carol, at 18, went to the local university. Jackson, at 15, went to St. Peter's in York, a British public school. Joy went to a private church school in Barcelona.

The <u>Altair</u> was a challenge, a very old hull and engineering plant containing an expensive computer to handle the 30,000 items we dispensed. It was essentially a floating supply depot staffed by outstanding Supply Corps people. The rest of the crew was a mixed bag who needed lots of attention.

Q: How large was your crew?

Captain Noel: I'd say 300-400. We used the computer to record their birthdays, which was about as far as we could go with enlightened personnel administration. But the computer showed every day if anybody was having a birthday, and if they did, they came up to my cabin and had a cup of coffee and a piece of cake.

Q: That was nice. I was going to ask you, at the risk of

interrupting, whether you were able--I know you did--to put into effect your personnel management ideas on this large and important ship.

Captain Noel: Oh, yes. We were big in enlightened management. I'm sure we did a lot for the habitability of the ship. We paid a great deal of attention to the men's welfare. We had an interesting problem in that the men were so taken by Barcelona and so many of the men had a relationship with very fine Spanish girls, but these were girls they'd just picked up in a bar. Because Spain in those days, in 1958, was so dreadfully poor, there were many girls of respectable families who just had to take to the streets to stay alive. They were sort of B girls. They hung out in bars. They were picked up by the sailors, but they were really attractive, for the most part far superior to any girls of this type that would be found in Norfolk, and they made a great impression, particularly on the members of the crew. Some of the young lads had come from very poor families and from ghetto neighborhoods where they had never really had anybody to love them. These girls that they picked up and lived with and supported took wonderful care of them and gave them a great deal of tender loving care, and were there to greet them when the ship came back to its home port. As a result, of course, we had many requests for permission to get married. We didn't discourage too heavily this idea, but we did try to put the matter in perspective to the man. But if he persisted in wanting to marry the girl, and the police report on her was negative, she had no criminal background or connections, we gave permission. I remember one case in which I was persuaded to let one of my storekeepers marry a woman who had an illegitimate child and was raising this child. This was really stretching things to a point, but I had a lot of faith in this man whom I had persuaded to stop going ashore and raising hell so he could hang on to his promotion. He eventually became a chief petty officer. I saw him when he was retired in Rota, and the marriage was a huge success. They had children of their own, the children went to college, and this really was almost a typical example of the kind of women that our men in Barcelona were associated with.

I'm going to pick up a description of the ship and what we did here. The engines of the <u>Altair</u> were old and cranky and often broke down while we were en route to our station. Our general routine was that we'd be in our home port for a week or ten days, and then we would go and meet the other replenishment ships at the rendezvous and replenish the Sixth Fleet. Then if we didn't go off and visit some other port, we'd come back to our own port. We had to come back to our own port to meet the ship that came over from Norfolk that kept us supplied with supplies. Sometimes when we had engine trouble and were on our way to our duties, we would break down and have to cut off all power. We'd lie to with an oil lantern in the rigging if it was at night. And it might be several hours. Of course, a strict interpretation of regulations required us to notify Commander Sixth Fleet immediately if we had any casualties, but we never did. We were able to persuade the staff to give us a speed of advance of 13 knots and we could make 17 if we had to, so with that four-knot differential, if we were hung up for a few hours repairing ourselves, we didn't have to tell anybody as long as we could make the rendezvous. I saw no reason to worry Commander Sixth Fleet or anybody and blacken our reputation.

As an aside, my legalistic and foolish successor, when he took over the Altair, filled the air with distress messages every time the old engines needed repairs, and when he was called on the carpet to explain why the Altair was now in such bad shape from the material point of view, he blamed me very severely. I gather that this rather amused the staff.

The shiphandling of this old, small, and underpowered ship with a single screw was something new, although as the author of several books on seamanship, I was sort of a self-appointed expert. The only hairy part was joining up at night with the other logistic ships prior to a scheduled fleet replenishment at dawn. The service squadron staff at first often put out confused signals and directed somewhat dangerous procedures until it learned its job, and this led to a few danger signals and emergency backing bells.

Replenishment courses were sometimes far from ideal in rough weather and the gang on deck and the winchmen earned their pay as we put the stores over the side to ships alongside, to which we had rigged wire highlines. The winchmen were the very important men who ran the winches that were used to pull the cargo out of the holds and started off on its way across to the other ship.

This is from some notes I kept at the time. I took command of the <u>Altair</u> in the shipyard at Norfolk, not the best time to take over a ship unless the old skipper is exceptionally responsible to ensure that all shipyard work has been checked.

Leaving Norfolk was most hectic; wrestling with the shipyard to test and finish their jobs, preparing for and enduring an administrative inspection, testing our new helicopter replenishment at sea and holding an open house aboard ship were some of the major items. There were dozens of minor crises such as finding two homosexuals in the act in the library, a chief petty officer who had just learned that his wife was being unfaithful. On a small ship, the captain handles these things.

On departure, coming down the Elizabeth River in a narrow and crowded channel, the rudder jammed full left, and we had to back emergency and drop both anchors. We did not go aground and were able to make repairs and proceed. No harm was done, but it was an indication of what was to follow until much of the machinery was worked over and the crew retrained.

We sailed for refresher training at Guantanamo Bay, Cuba, a

routine procedure after a long overhaul. The training command put us through the wringer with repeated supervised drills and exercises and a final examination. We survived and the Altair emerged fit and competent, although we had to replace the executive officer who could not handle the job. He had not had enough recent shipboard experience.

We returned to Norfolk from Cuba briefly to load stores for our departure. At the open house, we received the various Navy Wives Clubs who had collected nearly 100 boxes of used but clean children's clothing for the children of Barcelona. This is our Children-to-Children program, later expanded to include toys and protein powder for the very poor orphan children of Spain. I believe we were the first to do this. At any rate, all ships leaving the U.S. are now doing it. It was heartwarming to see the effect of this project on the children. Protein added to their diet made an instant and noticeable effect on their appearance and activity levels.

Q: Were you in charge of that program?

Captain Noel: As I remember it, we either initiated it or we were one of the first ships to do it. I think it became quite common and I think it was taken up on a larger scale. But the poverty of Spain was so obvious that it just seemed the sensible thing to do, to pick up old toys and old clothes in Norfolk, and later on, some of this food for millions that was high in protein. It was really astonishing to see the effect of this small amount of protein physically on the orphan children who, as you can imagine, were living on a very austere diet, mostly starch.

Q: To whom did you turn it over? Who handled it ashore?

Captain Noel: We had made arrangements through the consulate in Barcelona to meet with some of the Catholic charitable organizations in Barcelona, and they told us about the poor orphanages not supported by any organization, that were really hard up. There was one in particular that took the little girls 10 and 12 off the streets who were child prostitutes, and rehabilitated them. Occasionally we would have a shipment of chocolate candy kept on board ship too long and starting to get a little discolored. It was perfectly healthy, but we couldn't pass it along and sell it, as it were, to our clients, so we'd load up a truck with this candy and take it up to the orphanage. That was a great scene.

Q: You actually saw the children yourself?

Captain Noel: Yes. We had a good friend in Cadiz who was a doctor, who, as charitable work, was taking care of an orphanage.

He told us that he could tell a block and a half away, as he walked toward the orphanage, he could tell by the sound of those children playing whether there had been a recent shipment of protein from any naval source. That's a touching thing, isn't it?

Q: It surely is, for those of us who have so much.

Captain Noel: The voyage across was uneventful, marked by good weather and the visits of some migrating birds. There were gales to the north, but all we felt were moderate quartering swells which had Altair rolling. The loud clatter of loose gear below decks forced us to get squared away quickly. As we left Norfolk, we found a rain squall and washed away the dust of the shipyard.

Approaching Gibraltar, we passed the Spanish town of Tarifa, from which our word "tariff" is derived. We put into Gib for a few hours for fuel. The current was so strong off the Rock that I could not maintain steerageway at 5 knots. I went ashore to have a swim, phone Mary in Barcelona, and buy some Dak flannels. Found the Daks at half the U.S. price. Phoned Mary from the Rock Hotel and had to wait an hour, but five minutes only cost 60 cents. Dick Leighton, my senior supply officer, and I had a swim in a small cove where Nelson's body was landed in a cask of Navy rum after the Battle of Trafalgar.

On 20 September we arrived in Barcelona. What a joy it was to see Mary, Carol, and Joy! Jackson had fortunately been accepted by a very old and good English public school near York, St. Peters. The list of headmasters went back almost 1,400 years. Many of the men and officers had not seen their families for six months. It was a joyous and moving homecoming. Many of the single men do indeed feel that Barcelona is home. The people here have been looking after sailors for at least 2,500 years, and they do it superbly. Barcelona is a large modern city with all the amenities of an old and advanced culture. The people are very poor, however.

I saw these two good-looking blondes on the dock and I recognized my 17-year-old daughter and I wondered who the other one was at first, and it was Mary. She looked like a million dollars. The new life was agreeing with her.

The crew loved Barcelona, and every man who wanted one could find a faithful and attractive friend who was ready to set up housekeeping ashore. Mary and the children were settled in an attractive apartment with a large terrace overlooking the harbor. We were only in port six days, so we did little sightseeing. I played golf with Mary, rode with Carol--my aching back--and took Joy up to the amusement park on Tibadabo to visit a very scary enchanted castle. Went out on the town once or twice, which in Spain is almost an all-night project. Dinner starts at 10:00, and the nightclubs do not get warmed up until just before breakfast.

After a short and glorious six days, we went to sea to join the fleet for the first time. The Altair reflected her hard training period and did very well. We left our first replenishment of the fleet on 6 October and returned to Barcelona eight days later. What an experience! The first ship to come alongside was a cruiser with ComSixthFlt himself aboard. It was blowing hard, and the sea was making up. The crew behaved like veterans and did a grand job despite the heaving decks and slippery footing. We had helicopter operations all day working from the new helicopter platform aft, and, at the same time, ships were coming alongside port and starboard. We replenished a carrier and a destroyer both by helicopter alone--a Navy first. This was reported back to Washington by ComSixthFleet, much to our satisfaction.

For three days we maneuvered and came alongside ships, received ships, and operated helicopters provided by the Forrestal. It was a great experience, and we all learned a great deal. It takes time and a few tense moments to learn to handle these slow, heavy ships nimbly, particularly at night in formation. We had a few misunderstandings about signals before we were shaken down. I had a very green gang on the bridge, but they were all eager to learn, and my executive officer was a tower of strength when the going got rough.

We were in Barcelona, this time for two weeks. Mary and I

joined a tennis club, played golf, did some sightseeing, and met many charming Spaniards. Barcelona is a very old and very civilized city that had a great deal to offer every taste and inclination.

One of our memorable shore trips during this cruise when I had command of Altair was possible when Altair was sent to Villefranche for ten days on a routine port visit. Mary drove over from Barcelona, and together, when I took leave, we drove to Italy to see my cousin Katerina. When my grandmother, about 1875, divorced my grandfather, Dr. John V. Noel from Canada, she took her sister and her son, my father, and went to Italy. There in Sienna they both met and married officers in the Bersegliere, a famous regiment known to tourists by the long plumes in their hats. After her Colonel Ferrari died, my grandmother returned to the USA with my father, of course, then a teenager, but her sister remained. The daughter of this sister married the Count di Segardi, and it was in her house in Livorno that I saw many family pictures and other mementos and we met many Italian cousins. This dear Katerina is still alive. She is a very poor contessa. She's so poor and is such a modest person that she doesn't use her title. She had two daughters. One lives outside of London, married to an Englishman, and the other married a very poor Italian peasant in Sienna and, of course, had a dozen children or so, and they've all had quite a struggle.

Our next port visit after a stretch at sea replenishing the

Sixth Fleet was Palma in Majorca. Many of the wives, friends, and children came over to Palma for the visit and we took them back to Barcelona in the <u>Altair</u>.

Q: Wives and families?

Captain Noel: Of course, you could only do it if there wasn't any nighttime involved. This day-long trip was a great experience for the families and was marked by very heavy weather as we entered our home port.

Q: Your description of life in Barcelona makes it very attractive, and you enjoyed your command. But it didn't last very long.

Captain Noel: No. Commands are necessarily short, a year to a year and a half. A lot of people have to have their turn. Life in Barcelona was marvelous, it was inexpensive, it was exceedingly luxurious in terms of living, restaurants, servants. The tennis club was magnificent, the golf club was magnificent, the friends we made were magnificent, the Spanish were friendly. Barcelona was a fairly cosmopolitan city. There were a good many foreigners there.

Q: Is Las Ramblas the main street running down to--Barcelona is important, I think, because Columbus came back there, and wasn't he met by Queen Isabella?

Captain Noel: He was, on the steps of the cathedral, which are visible today, and his ships were overhauled in the old shipyard there, which is now back from the waterfront about 500 or 1,000 yards, and is a maritime museum.

Q: I remember seeing those steps, and my mind just expanded 'til I could hardly stand it to realize on those steps was Queen Isabella and Ferdinand and Columbus coming up there. It was wonderful.

Captain Noel: It was quite exciting. They've done excavation since we were there around the cathedral and have found magnificent Roman ruins.

Q: Down underneath?

Captain Noel: Yes. It was probably a barbaric temple of some kind, and then it was probably a Roman temple, and then it was a cathedral.

Q: Around in back, isn't it?

Captain Noel: Exactly.

Q: Isn't there a replica of his ship that's tied up at the waterfront?

Captain Noel: There's a statue of Columbus on a big tower on the waterfront.

Q: I thought it was a fabulous city. Again, Las Ramblas, to which I made allusion, and then going up in the mountains, the black madonna.

Captain Noel: The black madonna was a sight that everybody wanted to see, because the culture of Barcelona is very interesting, in addition to being very old. At one time the Catalans, homeported in Barcelona, were a significant sea power and dominated that part of the Mediterranean.

Q: Wasn't it through there that Hannibal went over the Alps to France?

Captain Noel: As I understand it, he landed further south, near Cartagena. For some reason that I've never been able to explain, they have found remnants of the stone buildings that the Carthaginians always sent ahead of their army to store the food in, and they found remnants of these buildings when they built the American airfield at Rota in Spain, near Seville. So I think there were more movements of the Carthaginian troops under Hannibal or someone else in Spain than most of us are aware of.

Q: It's fascinating to be there, and you're a student of history, I know. You like to write and read about it, so it was especially rewarding.

Captain Noel: It was. Spain is where we lived at Sotogrande on the coast east of Gibraltar. There was a larger population in Roman times than there is now.

Q: Really?

Captain Noel: You go back in the hills, in country that is quite desolate now, eroded, lost, lost their topsoil, and you run across the ruins of a Roman amphitheater, which tells you that to support an amphitheater, there had to be a lot of people, and to support a lot of people, there had to be a lot of arable land. But like most of the Mediterranean coast, and particularly the Middle East, the same story--cut down the trees, lose the topsoil, and then they're forced to turn to goats and raising grapes and olive trees because they don't have any soil for anything else. It's really a tragic land if you look at the

Noel #2 - 157

damage that has been done to their ecology, which most of them are probably not even aware of today.

Q: But isn't that a lesson for us in the U.S?

Captain Noel: It certainly is. It's a great lesson. We have one of the few unravaged--yet--countries in the world, and yet we're losing topsoil.

Q: Acid rain.

Captain Noel: And we're losing trees to acid rain, and we're losing topsoil to wind and erosion on a very large scale.

Q: Now we're going back to Washington, D.C.

Captain Noel: In 1959 we returned to Washington, where I was detailed as senior aide to the Assistant Secretary of the Navy for Personnel. Richard Jackson was an intelligent, likeable, and scholarly lawyer who knew little about the Navy and less about personnel. Unfortunately, he could not get along with Vice Admiral Page Smith, one of my squadron commanders during World War II and now the Chief of Naval Personnel. I was caught in the middle of this bitter feud to the detriment, eventually, of my future in the Navy. Admiral Smith was opposing a strong civilian-backed move by the Navy's lawyers to form a Judge Advocate General Corps, which meant more flag officer billets for them. Jackson, a lawyer, was in favor of the proposed corps. For some reason Smith assumed that I was helping Jackson, when in fact I was working to defeat the idea. It was an emotional issue and I was not politic enough to see Smith and get my position clear. Smith thought quite sincerely that I was being loyal to the civilian secretariat instead of to him. On this basis he persuaded the Chief of Naval Operations to instruct my selection board not to consider me for promotion to flag rank.

Q: I was in the Navy and I was in Washington at this time. As a lawyer, I was somewhat aware of this, but not to the extent you were, and I'm supposing that you perhaps know more about it than anyone. I wonder if you would care to expand on this conflict about the JAG Corps.

Captain Noel: As I've said, it was an emotional issue because the straight line officers resented the Uniform Code of Military Justice. At least some of them did and to some extent. There were many good reasons to have a new Uniform Code of Military Justice. On the other hand, its implementation and its concern for the rights of the individual put a great strain on the line officers who had to administer men and to run a ship. The lawyers believed--and I'm sure sincerely--that it was very important to go through the legal rigamarole before you punish somebody who was obviously a bum.

Q: Hang you right after you've had your trial.

Captain Noel: The line officers were rather impatient with this, and I think the whole struggle was hopeless from the beginning. The lawyers had their way, as they have had in our society, which is becoming largely a society devoted to litigation. Now it sort of horrifies officers of the old school to see that the legal officer is called a judge, and we have elaborate courtrooms set up ashore, and large staffs of bureaucrats to process these fellows who jumped ship or deserted or got drunk and disorderly. I'm not so sure there were a great many injustices done under the old system, but perhaps this is just an indication of the change that we have to have.

Q: You said Admiral Smith was your squadron commander. Didn't you at one time save his ship from being attacked?

Captain Noel: Well, Admiral Smith and I have had a curious relationship, and I haven't seen him since I retired. The first time I had met him was when he reported from Admiral King's staff as one of those fellows who were really just getting their ticket punched at the end of the war.* He had to have a good sea command under his belt. He was made a squadron commander and, frankly, most of these fresh-caught squadron commanders were a blasted nuisance to us who had been at sea during the whole war, and they would let their little staffs exercise the screen and changing station all during the night, not realizing that the commanding officers needed a few hours of sleep. Thus, I think he was aware of his equivocal position as a fresh-caught squadron commander vis-a-vis some of us who had been out there the whole time. He gave me a marvelous fitness report as a commanding officer, but I think he felt rather uncomfortable about this. Perhaps not.

Q: How was it you saved his ship?

Captain Noel: One of the incidents was that when we left the anchorage at Iwo Jima, where he was the senior officer and had quite a few ships in there, we encountered a couple of Bettys, which we reported.** They were flying on the deck, but we were lucky enough to pick them up on our surface search radar, and we reported them in time for Admiral Smith to get his harbor darkened and in time for him to shoot them down. I didn't save

---
*Admiral Ernest J. King, USN, Commander in Chief U.S. Fleet. Captain Harold Page Smith, USN, was Commander Destroyer Squadron Four.
**"Betty" was the Allied nickname assigned to a Japanese land-based torpedo bomber.

his life personally; I shouldn't have used that expression. But we did have a very good rapport when we were at sea.

When he reported as Chief of Naval Personnel, he relieved Admiral Holloway, and this happened not long before I left, but in time to be present when I presented the moral leadership program to the Secretary of the Navy and assembled dignitaries. He would have had to take the bludgeon as my superior if the program wasn't any good. Fortunately, he could take a bow because the program was accepted with some satisfaction. At that time I felt that I had a very good rapport with Admiral Smith, although when he greeted me in BuPers, at first I noted a certain coolness.

Anyway, going back to Dick Jackson, I really can't blame Admiral Smith. I should have kept him better informed. I should have made it clear that I was working in his behalf. He was so mad about the whole thing, he wouldn't come over and even discuss these things with Dick Jackson unless he got a direct order to come over. I would sit in these meetings and uphold the position of the line against the lawyers. Of course, since lawyers were in Congress and in the Department of Defense and everywhere else, the passage of this law to form a JAG Corps was foreordained. I'm not so sure it was the worst thing that could have happened.

Q: I know all of the other services have a JAG Corps because of supporting the UCMJ.

Captain Noel: Yes. It's a little different on a big Army base. With some peace of mind you can turn over your problem children to another agency, but it's very ticklish on a ship where you don't have too many men, where your men are almost always in some key position. You have to be sure that they're being treated fairly and that they're being punished adequately and that they're being gotten rid of when they have to be gotten rid of. However, the system is working fine, and I have no particular quarrel with that.

Q: I did know the admiral who was the head of the selection board, and I know how those things work also. I bitterly resent that you didn't go over and make it clear to Admiral Smith. Would he have listened to you?

Captain Noel: He persuaded Admiral McDonald, I think, the Chief of Naval Operations, to put this in.* The only reclama I could have at that time would have been to go and see Mendel Rivers, chairman of the Armed Service Committee in the House and a very powerful man. I was on a first-name basis with him, and he remembered me at college. I knew his staff very well. I could have pointed out to Mendel what had happened. The only thing he could have done if he so chose was to refuse to approve the

---
*Admiral David L. McDonald, USN, Chief of Naval Operations from 1963 to 1967.

selection board, that as a matter of routine came over to his office before it went to the President to be signed. It had to be approved by Congress first. If he had been keen enough about my cause, he could have, the next time the list came, said, "There's a name missing there, and you better find out who it is." Secretary Gates ensured the promotion of a very good friend of mine this way, and it was damn good for the Navy, because this chap turned out to be a very splendid, very senior officer, but on his own merits he would have never made it if Tom Gates hadn't kept sending the selection board findings back to the board until it finally dawned on them whose name it was that Tom Gates wanted on that piece of paper.

Q: The story of Admiral Rickover is a classic example of having names put on the list.

Captain Noel: That sort of works in the reverse there, doesn't it, for Rickover?

Q: They wouldn't pass it until his name was put on.

Captain Noel: Congress wouldn't approve it, that's true.

Q: In any case, I am interviewing you and not setting up your case.

Noel #2 - 164

Captain Noel: We can talk more about that when we come to the incident itself.

Q: I think there must have been some more special incidents when you were with Jackson. You spoke of travelling with him and so on.

Captain Noel: He was a lot of fun to travel with and very amenable to suggestion. As a matter of fact, most of the time when we travelled on the West Coast, he was entertained by my friends, who were very happy to entertain us in Los Angeles and Seattle. They were my friends that entertained him, and sometimes in Europe. We had a marvelous tour in Europe in which we took Luis de Florez along, and he left us for a few days when we stopped in Rota. He went to Cadiz to see some of his relatives because he was not far removed from the life in Spain.

Q: Did you feel you accomplished anything during that tour?

Captain Noel: Yes, I think so. I think it was possible, because he had a tremendous amount of power and authority in the Navy and no background in personnel, and he didn't know much about the Navy. I think I was a good influence on him. I think I could point out some things on which we could possibly do some good. One of them was alcoholism, in which we did not succeed in accomplishing anything, but alcoholism was a severe problem in the Navy, particularly among the senior officers. There were too many relics of World War II. People had been promoted, and deservedly so, who had had a good war, a good reputation, but had taken to drink. These flag officers stumbling around from one naval air station to another were really a scandal. Yet there was no quick fix here because the Navy, as the rest of the military, still looked upon alcoholism as a disciplinary offense instead of as a form of illness. Since it was a disciplinary offense to be caught drunk, none of these poor chaps were ever made a matter of disciplinary action because it would have meant a court-martial; they could have lost their retired pay. Nobody wanted to do this to good old Joe.

Q: It probably would have been tragic had that happened.

Captain Noel: It would have been tragic, but it was high time that the Navy and the military looked upon alcohol as industry did.

Q: Definitely.

Captain Noel: As a physical problem. We eventually did, of course, and we do now. It's a very simple matter to report a senior officer who is perpetually drunk--to turn in any officer who uses a lot of alcohol--to turn him into a medical facility and give him his choice of either resigning or staying away from alcohol.

Q: You had just had an experience like that in Barcelona, hadn't you, when you went in?

Captain Noel: The consul general there was a drunk, yes. He made trouble for me by reporting that I never consulted him. He reported this to Commander Sixth Fleet, and Commander Sixth Fleet sent a captain over to investigate the situation. I persuaded this captain that the only reason I didn't consult him was I wasn't sure I'd find him sober. ComSixthFlt, Admiral Ekstrom, apparently believed this at the time, but he certainly did a month later when he took the consul general out on his ship for a few days.* When they went ashore in Majorca, the consul general got falling down drunk.

Mr. Jackson and I saw that we just couldn't revolutionize the Navy's thinking about alcoholism at the time. Much later, however, a remarkable Navy doctor named Captain Joe Zuska at Long Beach, on his own authority set up a rehabilitation center for alcoholics and started a program that has done an immense amount of good for the Navy, because the Navy had more than its share of

---
*Vice Admiral Clarence E. Ekstrom, USN, Commander Sixth Fleet, 1958-1959.

alcoholics and was not trying to rehabilitate them as big corporations did. But since then, the Navy has--and I think the other armed forces do, too--have very specific programs and a considerable success in rehabilitating a certain number of their alcoholics.

Q: That's not only for officers.

Captain Noel: It goes to dependents and wives.

Q: Enlisted people?

Captain Noel: Yes, mostly enlisted people. All can receive treatment there, just like dependents can receive medical treatment in a hospital.

Q: How long has that been in existence?

Captain Noel: I ran into it in '65, so I would say 20 years, anyway.

Q: But it was not too long after you'd been in the Secretary's office that some action was taken. You were in the Secretary's office in 1960.

Captain Noel: It wasn't too long that somebody took some action.

Q: You went to sea then.

Captain Noel: Since I'd been shipmates with Captain Dog Smith, who was a detail officer, I was able to get orders to sea to command the guided missile cruiser Springfield, flagship of the Sixth Fleet in the Mediterranean.* Vice Admiral George Anderson was Commander Sixth Fleet. Anderson had the reputation of being a fast charger, a very demanding but efficient officer, a tough boss who did not suffer fools gladly. There did not seem to be too much competition for this particular job. The ship was homeported in Villefranche-sur-mer, which is near Nice, and Mary and the children would be sent out there. Most of the Sixth Fleet ships were deployed to the Med for six months without families, so we were fortunate in again having a ship in the Sixth Fleet that was homeported there. George Anderson and I became very good friends, and it was a joy to be part of an able and smart team. The flagship showed the flag everywhere. We entertained heads of state and were entertained in turn. It was a great life with Mary and often Carol following the fleet.

I had orders to report to Springfield in Beirut the end of March. Mary and the children came out a bit later after school

_____
*Captain Daniel F. Smith, Jr., USN.

was over. I assumed that the Air Force transport planes were still leaving from Anacostia, but upon arrival there that day I found that they now left from Andrews Air Force Base, some 40 minutes away. I arrived at Andrews too late to board the plane; someone else had been given my seat and their baggage was beyond retrieval, so I could only go home and lie doggo until the next plane departed, sending a message in the meantime that I had been delayed unavoidably by important business. Of course, I could send this message from the Secretary of the Navy's office so nobody questioned it.

Q: I'm glad of that.

Captain Noel: I arrived in Beirut too late to take command there but before the ship departed.

I'm going to quote from a few letters that I wrote to Mary that supplement the first two installments of a sort of journal that I kept of the cruise. I plan to append this journal to this paper. One begins:

"Dearest, It's 1:00 o'clock in the morning but all these strange shipboard noises are keeping me awake. Do you remember that when I came ashore from the Lamson I had trouble sleeping in a quiet room without the roar of ship's blowers and the half-hourly ship's bells?

"The flight to Paris was normal and I was met by Chris Cagle.

We went to SHAPE, where I paid my respects to Admiral Bucky Lee, whom I had known at BuPers.* His brother is the supply officer on the Sixth Fleet staff. I had a quiet dinner with the Cagles, who took me to Orly early." This is Vice Admiral Malcolm Cagle, retired. "The Cagles send their love and want to meet you when you come through. The flight on the new Pan American 707 was great. Saw the Alps before we refueled in Rome and then passed over Capri and the Corinth Canal. From 27,000 feet we could see walls and roads going down to the water's edge and far beyond, this along the coast near Rome.

"At Beirut I was met by the commanding officer Francis Boyle, met the admiral briefly as well as the chief of staff, Hank Monroe.** Turned down a reception and took time to unpack. Got our schedule from Hank. We arrive at our home port a week before my birthday. We may visit Venice and Palma afterwards. Give my mother and the children a special hug for me. I take over at sea on Tuesday. The royal family of Greece will be aboard Wednesday. I will be very busy from now on. I miss you." Etc., etc.

Sunday morning, March 26. "Dearest, Yesterday we had personnel inspection and I looked over the ship and talked to the

---
*SHAPE--Supreme Headquarters Allied Powers Europe, the headquarters for the military setup of the North Atlantic Treaty Organization. Rear Admiral James R. Lee, USN.
**The Springfield had originally been commissioned in World War II as a gun-armed light cruiser. Captain Francis D. Boyle, USN, was her commanding officer when she was recommissioned 2 July 1960 as a guided missile light cruiser. Captain Henry S. Monroe, USN, was chief of staff to Commander Sixth Fleet.

heads of departments. We have lots of talent, in severe contrast to all my other commands, and a most willing crew. The morale seems high and I know there is a big opportunity here to achieve something.

"At 6:30 went in uniform to a reception given at the Indian Embassy for a Mr. Nehru, cousin of the prime minister. I tried to get along in French with the Russian ambassador. Met some interesting people. Went on from there to a cocktail party given by one of the U.S. Embassy people and met Ambassador McClintock, a friend of Chad's, who asked me to go swimming tomorrow. Few people here swim this early.

"The general visiting has started and some local people are peering into my portholes from the main deck. I am going ashore to stretch my legs. Little prospect of tennis. Only a commander on the staff seems interested."

Monday, early. "Dearest, Soon we get under way for Athens. En route tomorrow afternoon I take command and we arrive Athens Wednesday morning. <u>Altair</u> will be there, too. Yesterday I went swimming with Ambassador McClintock. Two years ago when he and Admiral Holloway led a parade of U.S. Marines that had been sent to pacify the place, he took his dogs along in an open car, to a general outcry in the Moslem press. Water very cold, like California, but refreshing. We were alone except for young Mellon. Paul Mellon is en route to that temple behind the Aswan Dam. We think he will be asked to finance its removal and preservation.

"Had lunch with the McClintocks. Very friendly and interesting. He's a Navy buff and dives for artifacts in restricted waters where he alone can go. Had a Phoenician ship's anchor near the front door. It was curious. It really was nothing but a big round stone with a hole in it.

"Returned to ship for long talk with the chief engineer. He was pathetically grateful for my interest. We will get along fine. We have some problems with this old plant which could have had more attention when they made the missile conversion.

"Went on to a formal dinner given by Commander Sixth Fleet. Both Andersons most cordial. Everyone asks when you are coming. Staff officers most cordial. Boyle is a respected officer, but apparently not one of the gang, speaking of the staff. Boyle will let me take her out of the inner harbor this morning--big thrill.

"This will be my last for a few days. I've not yet started to dictate the journals, so please keep these letters. All my love." Etc.

Thursday, 30 March. "Yesterday we arrived here in Athens. I relieved Boyle the day before and I've barely had time to go to the potty since. As soon as we anchored, I rushed into sword and buckler and fell in as part of the entourage to receive all sorts of VIPS. The royal family came to lunch. Queen Frederika asked surprisingly perceptive questions about the guided missiles, and the Prince offered to lend us a dragon to race with them. Since he won the Olympic gold medal at Naples racing these small sailboats, everyone who is is anyone in Greece races dragons. Finally the gun salutes, band music, manning the rail, and VIP tours were over. All went well, and Admiral Anderson sent the ship a signal 'well done.'

"That evening went to a dinner at the naval attache, Al and Patty Berg, our golfing friends in Washington.* Home late and up early for more ceremonies and then a luncheon given by the amiable Greek Navy. After lunch, signed a few papers and took a lieutenant ashore to play tennis. Not very good tennis, but better than no exercise. In an hour I leave for a theater party given by the charge. Helen Hayes will be there, and then supper afterwards. Everyone is most cordial and all goes well. Ship is in good shape, but I can make lots of improvements, mostly by being accessible and understanding.

"Joy wrote me a sweet letter but nothing from you yet. I miss you." Etc.

Saturday. "Dearest, Your wonderful letter of March 27 came last night. You are a wonderful person and a superb mother. I am so proud of you and so glad you are handling things so well. Between Nona [my mother], Carol and Jackson, you have a house full of characters. Of course, my not being there simplifies

---
*Commander Alvin C. Berg, USN.

things in that way. I'll start house-hunting about 20 April and should be able to make a decision then. I could try to nail down an apartment for 15 June and would have to sign a year's lease. House-hunting is getting tougher as summer approaches. I'll have more news after we get to Villefranche and case the joint and talk to some of the wives.

"I have mentioned the luncheon with the Greek Navy and the bad play 'The Glass Menagerie.' Helen Hayes, however, was magnificent."

I didn't say in this letter that I used to know Helen Hayes because I courted her daughter and we used to swim in her swimming pool out in Nyack. As a matter of fact, I had the distinction of borrowing Charlie MacArthur's swimming trunks once, which is my only claim to dramatic fame.*

"In an hour we will have inspection. Tonight I have the duty ashore in civilian clothes, to check on the shore patrol. Anderson runs a very taut fleet, has his own sources of intelligence and expects superb behavior from the men ashore and gets it.

"We go to sunrise Easter service ashore near the Acropolis where Paul preached. It's a hectic life but interesting. Can't wait for you to get here." Etc.

From here on a rather thin narrative starts in the first

---

*Charles MacArthur was the husband of Helen Hayes; they lived in Nyack, New York.

installment of the cruise journal. Taking Springfield alongside the tanker at sea for the first time was a thrill, then putting her alongside the dock in Split in Yugoslavia was another first. Our charts said that there was not enough water, but since the pilot assured us otherwise, we went on in.

Q: On the Adriatic?

Captain Noel: Yes. I kept the conn and asked the pilot the local conditions. There was no wind or current and few ships under way, so it was not really difficult. We came in fairly fast, backed the outboard screws and threw the lines over. I got a hearty "well done" from the flag. I found out later that my predecessor was a very timid shiphandler, which exasperated Admiral Anderson.

The 48-hour bug that I had was really a blessing, because it gave me an excuse not to attend an outing and slivovitz bash given ashore by the Yugoslavian Navy.

Q: A what?

Captain Noel: A slivovitz bash. The Yugoslavs are great for drinking slivovitz, which is to me a rather distasteful clear alcohol made from plums. The Yugoslav Navy is famous, as the Russians are, for hard drinking, and I was very happy in my weakened state not to have to go ashore and hold up my end on slivovitz.

"The toughest part of this flag captain's job is not the command work nor the staff work, but doing both head-to-toes is rugged. After being up all night in rather heavy ship traffic, I must appear instantly on the quarterdeck to greet callers with the admiral and then as part of his entourage, join them in a furious round of official and often dull calls, receptions, dinners, etc. But it is a fascinating experience and I'm a lucky man.

"This is my first command fully manned with competent officers and crew. I have a chance to improve performance and morale. My innovation of a suggestion box with all serious comments answered in the plan of the day has caused quite a stir, especially in the staff, but provides anyone in the crew a chance to communicate and gets an honest answer as well. Every morning when the chief master-at-arms brings me the scraps of paper, he and I can feel the pulse of the crew. Of course, some pieces of paper are anonymous and merely damn the master-at-arms or blow off steam in some other way, but this does no harm. As a matter of fact, it does some good."

I now append 16 installments of a rather simple ship's journal that I kept during my cruise in the Springfield. This, I think, gives a rather accurate picture of what life was like in our time in a flagship of a U.S. Navy fleet. It shows the sort of operations we conducted, the sort of operations the flagship conducted. Of course, we were the showpiece, and we had the admiral aboard, and we did the entertaining and we were entertained. The fighting part of the fleet was the carriers, and there was an admiral in command of the carriers. He didn't do quite as much socializing as we did.

Q: I thought you made a statement when you were off tape that I liked. You said, "I think it's important to put in this material because 50 years from now when someone is looking at history, this will be as different today, in this period of time, as we are now from sailing ships."

Captain Noel: Exactly. It'll be just about as remote.

I left the Springfield in April of 1962 and it was with very mixed feelings that I left that bright morning off Athens after a simple change of command ceremony. As I went over the side for the last time, the band played "The Whiffenpoof Song" instead of "Anchors Aweigh." This was arranged by the young Yale NROTC officers in the wardroom who were all good friends of ours.

My driver, Alcott, a freckled, sweet kid who was a pet of Mary's, if not the world's best driver, took me to the airport and I was met in Nice by Mary. We then had ten glorious days of leave. We went over to our tennis club, the country club of Monte Carlo, where we found that their big annual Easter tournament was about to begin. Jacques Medecin, the grand old man of French athletics, got me entered, and Gardiner Malloy asked me to play with him in the veterans doubles for the cup of the four musketeers.* It was a kind and patriotic gesture on the part of a man who had won Wimbeldon. He said there should be an American team entered. Despite my rusty tennis--I had not played much over a year--we reached the finals where a tired Malloy--he had played two final matches that day already--could carry me no longer.

On 28 April I flew to Washington for briefings before going to Paris later as the naval attache.

Q: Before you do that, I think you told me you had met some interesting and exciting people in Villefranche.

Captain Noel: We had. Our best friend in town was the commodore of the yacht club, whose name was Robert Capelier. We used to sail his boat. As a matter of fact, the children acquired a small boat. These were Comets. Jackson's best friends were the teenage sons of David Niven, who had a place on Cap Ferat. We got to know the Nivens; he had a charming second wife. His first wife died. His boys were great companions for Jack, and we had

---
*Jacques Medecin was the manager of the venerable Monte Carlo Country Club.

them out to Springfield for lunch and saw them occasionally.

Q: I don't know if you've identified for sure that Jack is Noel number two.

Captain Noel: Yes. Jack, or Jackson, is the son who was then about 17. He volunteered to show David Niven how to sail his new catamaran, and they got caught in a line squall and turned over and had sort of an amusing game of coming up on opposite sides of the boat looking for each other and then diving to the opposite side to again look for each other. Neither was hurt, but David lost his enthusiasm for catamarans and said, "Jack, you and your father can use this boat for the rest of the summer," which we did, although I never had the good fortune to find that much wind and I was only able to take her out once.

We made friends, of course, with some charming French people, the Antonettis, who lived in Villefranche. The consul general there was also a good friend of ours, with whom we stayed later on when we were assigned to duty in Paris. All in all, it was a delightful and charming place to live.

Q: You started to say you went back to Washington for a briefing before you went to Paris.

Captain Noel: Yes. My friend Admiral Smedberg, the Chief of

Naval Personnel, agreed to let me take French lessons at home in Villefranche during the summer instead of going to language school in Washington.* Thus we had a pleasant two months at home in Villefranche, swimming with the children at la Plage de Sable, playing tennis and golf at Monte Carlo, and making a serious effort with all this playing together to learn French. Believe me, it was a serious chore, because we both realized that to make a success of the new job in Paris we had to know a little more than just saying "hello" and "good morning." Neither of us are naturally good linguists, and it really was some time into our tour in Paris before we felt perfectly comfortable, without a couple of stiff drinks, to be at a dinner party that went on for three hours, all of it in French.

Q: Were you prepared for any sort of intelligence duty that might have been part of your job as naval attache?

Captain Noel: Somewhat. In Washington, before I returned to Villefranche to study French, I did go to the intelligence school at Anacostia. And I did get some idea of the kind of responsibilities that I was to have. I also, of course, asked all the so-called experts in the Office of Naval Intelligence

---
*Vice Admiral William R. Smedberg III, USN, Chief of the Bureau of Naval Personnel from 1960 to 1964.

Noel #2 - 181

what we would need to discharge our obligations and duties in Paris, and we got a lot of very poor information about taking a service for 12, silver for 20, and this and that. Most of it we didn't do, and it was fortunate, because it was much simpler and less expensive to find whatever we really would need in Paris, particularly in London.

Q: I would have expected it to be all furnished.

Captain Noel: These were personal possessions. Yes, you would think they would be furnished, but each naval attache had to outfit himself and his family with all the things necessary to entertain rather well.

Q: That makes it an expensive billet, doesn't it?

Captain Noel: Yes. There were some extra expenses, but then there were some extra good times that we had.

After our holiday in Villefranche, we moved to Paris to enter a new world as a U.S. naval attache at the American Embassy. General Gavin was our ambassador, a splendid retired Army officer. Cecil Lyons, a career Foreign Service officer, was the DCM, Deputy Chief of Mission. The embassy staff was large and competent. My office was blessed with three very able officer assistants and two superb secretaries, all of whom spoke and wrote excellent French. This office had a serious purpose, to gather intelligence for the U.S., particularly on the French Navy. Despite General de Gaulle's anti-Anglo-Saxon bias and his orders to his military to be secretive, we had for years cultivated the top French officers and had their trust and good will. We also collected whatever intelligence came our way, through personal contacts, on Russia, China, and other countries, exchanging information with some of our especially competent friends such as the Israelis. This intelligence-gathering was not all that casual; it was carefully planned and was our major task.

In addition, we led an intense social life, entertaining and being entertained. This was no little strain on our health. The quality of the food and wine can be imagined. The naval attache is a part of the ambassador's immediate staff and assisted at all embassy functions together with their wives. The wives, in addition, were expected to assist Mrs. Ambassador in the various official and charitable activities.

Mary had some amusing incidents in her efforts to keep up with Mrs. Bohlen's standards. This was after the Gavins had left and the new ambassador was Chip Bohlen, a marvelous professional who spoke fluent Russian and a man who had friends and relatives in Europe and was a thoroughly able and competent fellow.[*] But

---

[*]Charles Bohlen, a career Foreign Service officer.

Mary got her signals crossed once and wore a short dress to an embassy dinner when long dresses had been the prescribed uniform. She barely could conceal her embarrassment at first but was delighted to find that the guest of honor, a French woman, also had on a short dress, thereby Mary saved everyone's peace of mind.

Going back a minute to collection of intelligence . . .

Q: I wanted to ask you if it was appropriate to tell me and put on the tape how you did that.

Captain Noel: Mostly by having assistants on the staff. These officers would visit the French installations and see what the French had, and ask their friends what was new, and then would write up a report. I didn't do that much direct detailed technical intelligence collection, but my officers knew what was going on in the field of weapons and electronics, and they knew where the things were that were supposed to interest Washington.

My only real experience with intelligence was rather amusing. I was invited one summer with my daughter to the wedding given for his daughter by a prominent French industrialist who had been a hero of the Resistance and was thoroughly trusted, of course, by everybody. This chap told me the following story. When aircraft from the western world were not going into Moscow as frequently as they do now, he was invited by the Russians to bring his own plane into Moscow. He went to the American Embassy, got in touch with our CIA and offered to let them put cameras on his own plane as it went into Moscow. The Americans were very glad to put cameras on the plane, and this chap's pilot pretended to be lost and flew all around Moscow taking pictures of their antiaircraft installations while, of course, the Russian air controller was howling at them to come down and land. They thought they would see fighter planes launched very soon. But they did manage to stumble their way around convincingly, getting some fine pictures of Moscow and its installations.

The Americans told the French to be very careful not to try to develop those pictures, that it was a new film that required new processing and they would, of course, give the French a copy of everything they took. The French, unfortunately, didn't trust the Americans, tried to develop the film and ruined the whole batch. The whole expedition came to nothing.

Well, with this preamble, my friend said, "Jack, I've been invited to take my plane into Peking." I think most of us remember that at the time when de Gaulle was one of the first Western leaders to call on the Red Chinese and was attempting, as he always did, to be one up on the Anglo-Saxons and be a good friend of somebody. The Chinese were keen to get some modern electronic equipment and had invited my French friend to fly his own plane into Peking. My French friend said, "You are perfectly free to put any electronic equipment you want to on my plane to get electronic intelligence from the Chinese."

I went and told our CIA representative at the embassy about this. I told him I could vouch for the Frenchman, but he, of course, would check on him. I thought no more of this until a few months later I ran into my CIA friend and said, "Oh, by the way, whatever happened about that caper that I told you about, going into Peking?"

"Oh," he said, "Jack, we checked out that Frenchman and we just don't think he was very solid, so we didn't do anything about it."

I started to sputter, because I knew that this Frenchman was probably closer to de Gaulle and more anti-Russian than anybody I could think of. I started to sputter, and then it dawned on me that this was exactly the right answer. I had no need to know a damn thing, and he was telling me very politely that he couldn't talk about it. But it was sort of negative reassurance. I assume that they did it and they got something.

Q: Do you think that's the same thing that happened over Moscow, or do you think that really did mess them all up?

Captain Noel: No, I think they really got the intelligence, because it would be very difficult to mess up the electronic tapes that you got, getting the signatures and getting the frequencies and everything. I think it worked.

Q: You think over Moscow as well?

Captain Noel: No, at Moscow the whole mission was futile because all the film was ruined by the French trying to develop it.

Q: But I was wondering, did they tell you that and was it really ruined, like this second instance?

Captain Noel: I think it's possible. Anything is possible, but I doubt it. Maybe de Gaulle found out about it and told them to develop it. He used to make a profession out of distrusting the Anglo-Saxons.

Q: Oh, he definitely did. How many CIA people were on the embassy, or did you even know at that time?

Captain Noel: I had no idea. I knew that a couple of them worked more for the agency than they worked for anybody else, but I didn't have too much to do with them. They may have collected intelligence in their own way, but all the intelligence collecting was coordinated back in Washington anyway.

In addition to collecting intelligence, a major job that we had was taking care of the many senior naval officers and naval civilian dignitaries who found it imperative to visit Paris and see the rest of France and who required extensive logistic support. They had to be met, hotel reservations made, tours arranged, sometimes entertained--in general, made happy. Wives had to be treated, of course, with great care. Grown children of friends and acquaintances often showed up, sometimes without warning and sometimes without funds, to be provided with care and hospitality. Needless to say, Mary was a tower of strength in all these matters and played a major role.

We lived in a large apartment on the rue Fontaine near the Bois de Bologne, 16th arondissment. The government paid most of the rent, of course, and provided a car and a driver. Through friends we were able to join the tennis club of Paris and the Golf de St. Cloud, both rather difficult to get into unless one had some leverage and a diplomatic passport. I also joined the Travelers, a men's club at the Ronde Point near the embassy.

In connection with the official visits of U.S. naval ships and commands to French ports, Mary and I saw a great deal of France. These visits involved my office with preparations such as berthing and a schedule of official calls and entertainment. Mary was needed, since official wives were always present and part of the drill. The American admirals often brought their wives, and French admirals had their wives on deck, and the entertainment was always coeducational. So Mary was important. There were no funds to pay for her transportation by any standard means, so I would draw an automobile from the embassy pool and we would drive. We saw no need to break any speed records. We'd always take an extra day and drive into Brest or Cherbourg or Toulon. Along the way we would look for the quaint country inns, look up the best restaurants we could find in the Guide Michelin, talk with the natives, and really get some of the real flavor of France.

We found outside of Paris (and possibly around Nice and Cote d'Azur) that the people of France are relaxed and amiable and friendly toward Americans. If sometimes they appear to be bad-tempered or mean, it is perhaps explicable. Paris is a very crowded town. We found out that they're not mean and rude occasionally because we're Americans; they treat their fellow Frenchmen the same way.

The French, particularly in Normandy, still remember with great warmth the soldiers who drove out the Germans, and the soldiers and G.I.'s who, when they were children, gave them some candy. There was nothing de Gaulle could do, despite his obvious Anglophobia, to persuade the French people that the Americans hadn't come over and saved them.

Tennis was a major part of my life, for fun and for keeping fit and for meeting people. Through Barotra and Brugnon, two of the famous four musketeers of tennis who still played, I was asked to join the International Lawn Tennis Club of France and played for France against England and Belgium.* These matches

---

*Jean Barotra; Toto Brugnon.

were, of course, mostly social events for old tennis players to renew their friendship. At Le Touquet every year, a resort on the channel, the two teams, French and English, with wives and grown children, would take over a hotel and play golf in the morning and serious tennis in the afternoon, for a silver bowl given by the Maharajah of Kutch. Mary wound up playing golf for France when they found out that she was a better golfer than most of the tennis players.

In 1964 the Under Secretary of the Navy, Red Fay, and Anita came to Europe on a farewell trip and asked us to join them.* We went to Nice and to Rome and always played family tennis and had a great time. We were traveling in Red's own plane, of course, and it was a great deal of fun to make no pretense of doing anything serious except just travelling around and playing tennis and seeing people whom we enjoyed.

Q: You might identify who Red Fay is.

Captain Noel: Under President Jack Kennedy he was the Under Secretary of the Navy. He had been with Jack Kennedy in PT boats. He and Anita were great friends of the Kennedys and spent a lot of time at the White House. He was in a way a court jester, in that if the President was ever feeling the strain, he

---

*Paul B. Fay, Jr., Under Secretary of the Navy from 1961 to 1965.

enjoyed Red Fay making jokes or introducing him to amusing people and so on.

Q: I'm going to indicate that at the end of your cruise on the Springfield you wrote an article called "The Navy and the Department of Defense," which appeared in the November 1961 Proceedings.

Captain Noel: It was actually after leaving the Altair, when I was working for Mr. Jackson, that I wrote this article based on my experiences as Assistant Chief of Naval Personnel for Special Projects and my experience in working in the Department of Defense. It took some time to write it and some time for it to be published. It actually appeared at about the time that Admiral McDonald relieved Admiral Anderson as Commander Sixth Fleet.*

One of the major reasons the newspapers picked this up, particularly Mark Watson of The Baltimore Sun, who first picked it up, was that it was seen as an expression of dissatisfaction with the Department of Defense by Admiral Anderson, since Admiral Anderson had just taken over as Chief of Naval Operations and was listed, as all Chiefs of Naval Operations are, as the president of the U.S. Naval Institute, the professional organization of the

---

   *Vice Admiral David L. McDonald, USN, relieved Vice Admiral George W. Anderson, Jr., USN, so the latter could become Chief of Naval Operations in August 1961.

Navy. So poor Admiral George Anderson, who had never seen the article, was thought to have sponsored it, and this was supposedly his expression of dissatisfaction with the way the Department of Defense worked.

When Admiral McDonald came aboard, I thought I should tell him about it, since I just learned that there had been a bit of a flap, and I was amused to find that he wasn't sure what the Naval Institute was. But he learned quickly. Of course, when he became Chief of Naval Operations due to the intervention of John Connally, his great and good friend, he became the honorary president of the Naval Institute.*

Be that as it may, this article, which is actually a rather moderate analysis of some of the shortcomings of the people in the Department of Defense, caused some uproar but not a great deal and not a serious amount, and all that resulted was to my credit. Admiral Anderson told me that Mr. McNamara called him one morning and said, "Have you seen this article in the last Proceedings by some Captain Noel?"**

George Anderson said, "Yes, I have, Mr. Secretary. Have you read it?"

The Secretary had to admit he hadn't read it; he'd just been told about it.

---
*Admiral McDonald served as Chief of Naval Operations from August 1963 to August 1967. John B. Connally had been Secretary of the Navy from January 1961 to December 1961.
**Robert S. McNamara, Secretary of Defense from 1961 to 1968.

Noel #2 - 192

George Anderson said words to the effect of, "Mr. Secretary, I suggest you read it. I think it is fair and accurate. Captain Noel was my flag captain and is a reputable officer, and I think this is a worthwhile article."

No more was heard from Mr. McNamara. His Assistant Secretary for Public Affairs, Mr. Sylvester, whom I got to know later very well and personally in Paris, was slightly put out because technically it hadn't been sent to his office for clearance.* Given the kind of mice that worked for him, if it had gone to his office, it would have been killed.

Q: Mice? Like plural of "mouse"?

Captain Noel: Yes. This was the bad part about this censorship that the Department of Defense tried to exercise. Little people working for Mr. Sylvester could never lose their jobs by refusing something for publication and always took a certain amount of risk in passing something. As a result, they passed almost nothing, nothing that they could possibly help. So I'm glad I didn't send it in.

Q: Did you do that deliberately?

---
*Arthur Sylvester, Assistant Secretary of Defense (Public Affairs).

Captain Noel: It never occurred to me to send it in. I figured if there was any clearance required, the Naval Institute would do it. They took refuge in saying that they thought that I had done it. So we made up this little passing the buck. Nobody was really mad at anybody, and I got really dozens and dozens of letters from old friends and new friends saying, "Great stuff, Jack. You're telling it how it was."

It was an article that didn't cause any great impact on the body politic, but I think it probably provided a little cheer for those hands who were struggling with the Department of Defense. Nobody had very bad motivations, except there was a very distinct anti-military group of civilians in the Department of Defense who had come from the services. They had not done well in the Navy or the Air Force, and they saw a chance for better promotion, so they went over to this new office of the Department of Defense, which was growing fast and had lots of promotions and lots of GS-15s.* These characters didn't like the military. In such matters as air-conditioning for housing and things like that, they really made it tough on the military.

Q: Put that on the record, because I thought that was interesting about the air-conditioning.

---

*GS grades are used to indicate the relative levels of Civil Service employees; GS-15 is near the top of the scale.

Noel #2 - 194

Captain Noel: It will be in the article, I'm sure.

Q: It is.

Captain Noel: One of the things we had to struggle with was to get permission to install air-conditioning in our military housing for the enlisted people and junior officers in Texas, at Corpus Christi. The FHA, the Federal Housing Administration, wouldn't guarantee a loan unless there <u>was</u> air-conditioning in these houses, which is an illustration of how small some of these people working for the Secretary of Defense were. On the other hand--and I think I made it plain in the article--if you wore a uniform, you had to have a certain amount of understanding for the other fellow's point of view, an understanding that there was tremendous pressure from Congress and the administration to save money. And there was no reason why, just because we'd fought a good war, we could be given carte blanche for anything. All of us, if we were honest and knew anything about what went on in the Army and the Navy and the Air Force, had to admit that there was a lot of waste and boondoggling and the kind of stuff that is appearing today, spare parts being horribly overpriced. Of course, they always were. Even in those days, it was apparent to most people that the way armaments were procured was to give a contract to somebody like Grumman, one of the Navy's favorites and a damn good company. But contracts were not really competitive; they were issued to some company at a cost for a new weapon that was obviously less than it was going to cost. Then the overruns were paid. There wasn't any real competition in the deal.

I think that that's about all that I need to say about this article. It was received with some enthusiasm, I think, by most people in uniform, and gave the newspapers a chance to speculate on Admiral Anderson's antagonism for Mr. McNamara.

I might say here that I had mixed feelings about McNamara. When he tried to assure that the black shoes that the Navy wore were bought by the same manufacturer at the same reduced price as the black shoes that the Army wore, this was in general a good thing. There could be big cost savings in getting a common usage factor introduced in military procurement. However, he lacked a certain sophistication in these things as he tried to force the Air Force's fighter plane on the Navy.* It just wasn't a plane that was made for carrier operations. He did not have much tact.

I might mention an incident about the Cuban Missile Crisis, which I'm sure Admiral Anderson has put in his oral history. Mr. McNamara went down to the war room plot where Admiral Anderson was in charge and where all the ships of our blockade of Cuba were shown on the plot, and the blockade was in progress. Mr.

---

*The plane in question was the F-111. The Navy successfully fought off having to accept a carrier version and instead developed the F-14 Tomcat to serve the role of carrier fighter.

McNamara entered with two people that George Anderson had never seen before, and asked Admiral Anderson what that destroyer was doing way up there 200 miles from the formation. To answer that question honestly, Admiral Anderson would have had to reveal matters about special intelligence that he wasn't sure these two unknown people were cleared for, so he very properly gave a sort of evasive answer, for which Mr. McNamara rebuked him and told him to get things in order down here and get all these ships together, which really made Mr. McNamara look like a complete ass, which he could be if he tried hard.

Later on, George Anderson took him aside and explained why he had had to give him an evasive answer, and essentially rebuked him for bringing those odd types in who weren't obviously cleared for special intelligence. I'm sure that this and other stories of troubles Admiral Anderson had with McNamara are a matter of record. My sympathies, of course, were thoroughly with George Anderson. When he wasn't reappointed, McNamara didn't have the guts to tell him. He sent Mr. Gilpatric to see him before breakfast one morning to tell him he was fired.* Jack Kennedy felt so sorry for George Anderson that he appointed him as ambassador to Portugal. Later on we had the pleasure of visiting the Andersons in Portugal.

---

*Roswell Gilpatric, Deputy Secretary of Defense.

Q: Did you ever have any personal dealings with McNamara?

Captain Noel: No, I never did.

Q: There's a lot on the record about him and how he ran a war 6,000 miles away.

Captain Noel: He didn't lack self-confidence. I think he probably had a greater bad influence than he had a good influence, although I really shouldn't judge. Stemming from his days we have a situation now that is very similar. If there's ever an emergency in any part of the world, to get permission to take any definitive action, communications have to go back from the commander on the scene through the Pentagon and to the White House. By the time anything is decided on--as turned out in the Pueblo incident, by the time anybody's made up their mind, it's too late. We didn't have to lose the Pueblo to the North Koreans. We had carrier aircraft that could have reached that scene and sunk the Pueblo in deep water, but by the time the carrier admiral had been able to correspond with the White House or with the Pentagon, first with the Commander in Chief Pacific, all the way back to the White House, then all the way back to him, by that time the Pueblo had been taken into North Korean waters and couldn't be sunk.

Noel #2 - 198

Q: I interviewed Admiral Sharp on that.*

Captain Noel: He must have been unhappy.

Q: He was unhappy.

Did you ever have any personal experiences with Admiral Zumwalt?**

Captain Noel: Oh, yes, I knew Bud very well. He was a major supporter of ours in our moral leadership program. I relieved him, took his place as aide to Mr. Jackson. He picked me to be Jackson's aide. I had a great admiration for Zumwalt; I still have. I'm not so sure I like his politics, as expressed. They're not as bad as some of the retired military who are a little bit to the right of Ghengis Khan but, nevertheless, he was a superb Chief of Naval Operations.

Q: I, of course, heard from the captain who was in charge of women in the Navy and who had a conflict with Admiral Zumwalt.

Captain Noel: Over what?

---

*Admiral U.S. Grant Sharp, USN, Commander in Chief Pacific from 1964 to 1968. His oral history is in the Naval Institute collection.
**Admiral Elmo R. Zumwalt, Jr., USN, Chief of Naval Operations from 1970 to 1974.

Q: Over women in the Navy and jobs they could do.

Captain Noel: Was he conservative about that?

Q: Very.

Now we're coming up to the year 1965. Is that correct?

Captain Noel: Right. When I decided that I would retire rather than stay in the Navy longer. It was apparent that I was not going to be promoted, although there was another selection board due to be held, and my name could have come up again. But there was a certain temptation, despite the blow to my ego, in thinking about civilian life and making a little money. The Navy, during my active service, was very badly underpaid as all military were. I earned $12,000 a year when I retired, and I was supposed to educate children on that. I probably should have left the Navy some years before. I had been offered a job as the VP for personnel of McKenzie, the management firm. Chester Nimitz, Jr., my classmate, had given my name, and the man came down to Washington to talk to me. It was a great temptation to go, as Chester Nimitz had, into business and make a more comfortable living for my family. But I was too fond of the Navy and enjoying it.

Q: When did you know that you were not selected for admiral?

Captain Noel: 1964.

Q: The year before, at the end of the selection board?

Captain Noel: Yes.

Q: Did someone tell you? How did you hear about it?

Captain Noel: Admiral Griffin told me.

Q: He told you that your name wasn't . . .

Captain Noel: My name didn't appear. People were surprised and a lot of good friends commiserated with me. Then Don Griffin, who was on duty in London as Commander Naval Forces Europe, a friend of mine, came through Paris and said, "Jack, I don't know what you've done to get yourself in bad odor, but we were instructed not to consider your name on the board."* So that was that.

Q: He was the . . .

Captain Noel: He was the president of the selection board.

_____
*Admiral Charles Donald Griffin, USN, whose oral history is in the Naval Institute collection.

George Anderson later wrote me and said that I had queered myself somewhere with somebody in BuPers, which was all he could find out. You see, the procedures of the board are very secret. People take an oath and don't talk about it. They burn the minutes of the meetings and everything.

Q: I've been on a board. I'm sure you have, too.

Captain Noel: Never.

Q: You haven't missed much. I know the procedures that they follow. There weren't many senior women officers to act on selection boards for junior officers.

When did you find out about Page Smith and that?

Captain Noel: I knew right then, of course, because the directive has to come from Admiral McDonald, who was Chief of Naval Operations. The only person in the world who would have persuaded him that I was more loyal to the civilian secretariat was Page Smith. I've never confirmed it, but it couldn't have been anybody else, because that was the issue in our disagreement. He thought I was loyal to Jackson, but we never discussed it. I was too foolish to go over and see him and talk about these things. I knew that he was unhappy with Jackson. I never suspected he was unhappy with me.

Q: It's awfully difficult for me--and I've said it before--and I'm not the protagonist, naturally, for you, except I had thought maybe when you had this publication that wasn't cleared that maybe someone got a real angle on that.

Captain Noel: I think that's very unlikely. I never heard anybody seriously criticize that article, certainly not in the Navy.

Q: In the Navy they'd like it.

Captain Noel: Yes, they did. Admiral Anderson told his staff meetings that it was required reading for all of his people. He spoke about me with--I think it's in my file there of commendations--glowing terms.

Q: Again, I know I'm off base, but I've interviewed many admirals, and I can almost tell when you see what they've done on big ships and shore duty, they've gone to other big ships, they've gone to other commands, they've gone to a different type of ship, and you see them constantly going up the ladder, and they have a charming wife, which is important, that there's no place to go except to be admiral.

Captain Noel: Even among those, even if you took the select

group, as I was, that had had the right jobs and the right fitness reports, even among those, it can't be all of them because there aren't that many spots. The people who do the best, of course, are those people who are non-controversial, who haven't made any enemies. I was reasonably controversial. I guess I was pretty bullheaded and confident, but I never did make any enemies as far as my record. My fitness reports don't reflect that. The only thing that isn't absolutely perfect in my last ten years of fitness reports is that Admiral McDonald, who gave me my last fitness reports at sea, didn't mark me in one particular little column. In the fitness reports of those days had "Is this a poor officer, a good officer, an excellent officer, an outstanding officer, or one of the most outstanding officers you've ever seen?" And he didn't check me off on that right-hand one, but checked me off in the next one. You really can't consider that a down-check.

Q: The point is, your record didn't even go to the board. Had it gone to the board and they looked at all these people and said, "Well, everyone is here except this," but it never went to the board.

Captain Noel: No, that's true. George Anderson, if he had been CNO, would never have. If he'd been reappointed, I would have had no problems. But Admiral McDonald was not as great a friend of mine as George Anderson was. Admiral McDonald was a hillybilly from Georgia who was a very fast learner. He came aboard full of the normal prejudices of a redneck from Georgia about Jews and things like that. He would make a few jokes at the staff meetings and he wouldn't get a smile. George Anderson had picked himself a very fine staff, as everything George did, he had good people working for him. His people weren't about to say, "Ha, ha, ha" when the new admiral made some stupid joke about Rickover being a Jew. But he learned fast; he stopped it. He didn't do it anymore. He used to make fun of us on the ship going off and diving with the scuba team. We found a Roman village under water. He used to make fun of our interest in archeology and things like that. A month later we heard him bragging to his visitors about how his flag captain and flag captain's wife were out diving and looking for Roman villages. He learned fast. He learned that it was not politic to take certain hillybilly attitudes that he'd taken all his life.

Q: How did he get to be an admiral?

Captain Noel: Mostly, I think, John Connally. He served with John Connally in a jeep carrier during the war. McDonald was the epitome of a Georgia politician. He and Carl Vinson could have exchanged positions. If he'd been a congressman, he would have been like Vinson, spitting into a big brass spittoon and coming down with all the political bromides. He was a good politician and he was a good detail man. He did things carefully, and he wasn't a bad guy to work for on the ship. I think I antagonized him in some way, or perhaps he never gave non-aviators the best marks. He was, as ComSixthFlt, far inferior to George Anderson. I was told never to upstage George Anderson.

Q: George Anderson?

Captain Noel: Yes, I'm going back to George Anderson. I was told never to upstage George Anderson. I was advised not to, because he was very proud of his French and he was very proud of all the things he did. And I didn't upstage him.

But I think I upstaged McDonald once, because we were going through the straits off Sicily in a northwest gale and the ship was rolling very heavily but perfectly safely. But he'd never been on anything except a carrier, and he was uneasy about the ship's motion. His foolish flag lieutenant was telling him that things were coming adrift here and the barge was coming adrift there. Well, a few things came adrift, and we secured them. He wanted me to change course and lie to, you know. Maybe I should have, but it was a bright, sunny day, it was one of these fair weather northwesters blowing in the Atlantic and Mediterranean that blows hard, the seas are big, but to lie to, I'd have been the laughingstock of the world. We were perfectly seaworthy, safe. I'm not so sure he was ever happy with me after that, because if I'd been a proper and subservient flag captain, I would have said, "Yes, sir, this is dangerous," and I'd have come around and we would have lay to for a while. But he wasn't a good seaman. Other than that, he was very pleasant. When I was in Paris, they came several times and I saw them. I had no great admiration for him, but he didn't treat me badly.

Q: That you know of.

Captain Noel: I know. I'm sure it was at the instigation of Page Smith, who told him about how I had supported Jackson.

Q: That insight relating to all that is so scary because you didn't know whether someone was going to take that against you.

Captain Noel: In every profession and business, everywhere in life, you take those chances. I think I've been as lucky as anybody.

Mary was not at all unhappy with my leaving the Navy. She had great reservations about being an admiral's wife in a place like Guantanamo, for example. There were an awful lot of dull jobs in the Navy. I'd had better jobs as a captain than I would probably have had as an admiral for years, although with Bud Zumwalt as Chief of Naval Operations, I think I would have had some pretty good jobs. Still, Mary was not at all unhappy about the prospect of leaving the Navy.

Q: But you had said, I believe, that you had no rancor.

Captain Noel: I had no rancor against Page Smith or the Navy or anybody else. That would have been foolish.

Q: When did you then finally decide you would retire? I don't have your retirement date.

Captain Noel: June of '65.

Q: That was in Paris?

Captain Noel: In Paris. I retired there. But six months before, I had met a man at dinner at the Ritz Hotel. It was a big golf tournament that somebody put on at Saint Nom de Breteche, and for some reason a lot of important people came over. They had a dinner at the Ritz, and I met this man. It turned out that I knew his wife's brother, with whom I had served in the Korean War. He had just bought a mud company, Milchem, in Texas.

Q: Mud?

Captain Noel: Mud. These are the chemicals they use in digging oil wells and drilling oil, barite, bentonite, those kind of things. He was looking for somebody to take over their operations in the Western Hemisphere, in Europe, Africa, the Middle East. He offered me the job.

I went back to Washington. They said, "Yes, you can retire early."

I went to Texas, talked to the people. I was offered a very good salary. Then I started a very interesting experience. I don't think if I'd known what I know now I'd have ever taken the job. The people working for me were all castoffs and rejects and maladjusted characters from the United States who had been sent to staff the overseas office. They were all guys who couldn't get in their expense accounts because they could hardly read and write. They were drunk--some of them.

Q: Was this in Paris?

Captain Noel: All over, Rome, Paris, Africa, the Middle East. I had the whole works, so I had people everywhere. None of them had ever been an officer; they were all ex-enlisted men. None of them really were educated. They didn't keep any central office files. Everybody did their business by personal correspondence, which they put in their pocket. They took great umbrage at the fact that I insisted that these affairs were company affairs and not their affairs.

Q: Did you give me the name of this company?

Captain Noel: Milchem. So it was a very educational, financially rewarding experience for a couple of years. They finally closed most of their operations abroad, and I was out of a job. I was not unhappy with that.

We had moved from this rather glamorous, expensive apartment that the government paid most of the rent of, to a very attractive and much more comfortable, much less expensive apartment in the neighborhood. We'd settled down to a different life in Paris. I did a good deal of travelling in business. Mary went with me on some of the trips. I had to go to Rome a good deal, to London. We were setting up an office in London. I had to go out to the Middle East. We had a man in Bahrain, a man in Kuwait. I never did get down to Nigeria.

This went on until Milchem folded up their operations in Europe. I kept telling them that they didn't have a chance of being successful. I sent my own geologist that I hired to go around looking for barite, because we needed a source. In the United States they had their own mines and they could compete with Magabar and the other companies. In Europe they had to buy their barite and bentonite from a rival mud company and then try to resell it. The kind of people that I had inherited over there were the old-time mud salesmen who figured if you got the man on the rig that was drilling drunk enough, he would buy anything you had available. Now this was the old days of drilling, perhaps, but what they didn't realize was that all these drilling companies had some smart young accountants who were computing the cost per foot of drilling every well at every time and under every condition. You couldn't get away with unloading a lot of stuff on them because he became a friend of yours. You had to use some skill and you had to use some expertise in purchasing.

Anyhow, after this great experience was over, I went to work as a consultant for the Garrett Corporation and Grumman. Grumman had built with Garrett, using a Garrett jet engine, had built a hydrofoil. This was going to be the boat that inaugurated fast passenger service, over 45 knots, in so many parts of the world where it was needed. But at the same time Boeing built a hydrofoil. They were technically different. The Boeing hydrofoil today is successful; it's been bought by the Navy as their hydrofoil gunboats. The Grumman hydrofoil is dead as a mackerel and it should have been dead before it became alive, because it was an impossible boat to sell. I went everywhere in Europe and North Africa, finding people very much interested in fast water transportation, across the channel, along the French coast, the Mediterranean coast. The highways had been expanded and overloaded, the railroads were overloaded. In the summer the only way to go from the airport at Nice, say to Monte Carlo, is on a road that will take you the rest of your life to do it. A 45-knot seaworthy boat would be a godsend. But the boat didn't work. They sold the first model being made by Blohm & Voss in Germany, and they sold the first model to some Spaniards who were running it in the Canary Islands. This was a great mistake because they were running it in the open sea. This boat was only good for 6-foot seas.

I had the head of Vickers come down with me to the Canary Islands to demonstrate the boat, and we got out half an hour and bang! The gear broke down and we had to come back on our diesel. This particular boat transferred the power of propulsion from those big jet engines to a supercavitating propeller driven through a very elaborate gearbox. The gearbox was very expensive and took a long time to design and to build, and yet it hadn't been designed to resist the lateral thrusts of a big sea. It was just poorly designed and it failed. I had a very interesting time working for a couple of years, but at the same time I was only a consultant on this job trying to sell this hydrofoil on a half-time basis.

The rest of the time I was looking for companies in Europe to sell for American companies. I had come into this game really after it was over, although I did succeed in finding a good French radio company that we sold to ITT, and I made a good commission on that.* But by and large, the time had passed when

---
*ITT--International Telephone and Telegraph

people like ITT were buying every good European company they could. It was a great way to transfer your taxes offshore and then not pay them. It was a marvelous tax advantage and they were doing it on a large scale, and people like me, brokers, who were finding companies and showing them to ITT, were making a bundle. I got in on the tail end of it, but it was quite an adventure.

I did a few other things. I started a small company to build outboard propellers. I had a French friend with an unusual invention, a weed-free propeller. We started to build them in Italy. We ran into a strike of the Italian customs people, so we couldn't get anything out of Italy for about four months. We were selling some outboard motors from Canada that looked promising, and then they went bankrupt. So our little venture in boating gave us mostly just good experience.

Then I had a Yugoslav friend who had great connections in Yugoslavia. He had gotten a lot of business for MK, Majenska Kumminica, something like that, but it was called MK, a very sophisticated printing house in Yugoslavia. It's in northern Yugoslavia. For a while we had great prospects because this publishing company had bookstores all over Yugoslavia that they were going to turn into drugstores in the French style. You've heard of the drugstore in France, the first drugstore. The Yugoslavs were dying for Western luxury goods, sophisticated dark glasses, cigarette lighters, jeans. The only stuff they had in

Yugoslavia came from East Germany, which was mostly junk. They were just watering at the mouth to get their hands on some of these marvelous Western goods, and they were going to make all these bookstores into drugstores selling these things. We had the inside track, and we were buying all kinds of things--Danish furniture, German silver, French baccarat. We started off great guns, and then Tito took one of his changes of course.* The way he kept the balance between East and West, one of the ways he did it in Yugoslavia was, he would open towards the West and encourage his people to have dealings and business dealings and social dealings with the West, and then he'd get nervous and cut that off and go back towards the East a little bit and kowtow in a very small way to the East. By shifting back and forth, he never let anybody get in a position of political opposition. We got caught in one of the shifts from West to East, and the ball game was over. We hadn't invested any great amount of money because I figured out a way to buy these things with back-to-back letters of credit. It was a little amusing that the orthodox socialists in Yugoslavia could not stand to be charged for a commission or a profit. If we had bought this stuff and added 10% and sent them the bill, they were horrified; they wouldn't pay anything like that. So we had to buy the stuff in our own name and then sell it to them so that no profit appeared. Of

---
*Josip Broz, generally known as Tito, was President of Yugoslavia.

course, we took a very nice profit.

Q: Did they think you were doing it for the exercise?

Captain Noel: No, they didn't, but this was just part of their hang-up. So with back-to-back letters of credit, which I thought was pretty clever, we'd get a guaranteed letter of credit from them and then the Bank of America, which was the only outfit in Paris that understood what I was trying to do, would issue a guaranteed letter of credit backed by that letter of credit to our supplier in Holland, at a smaller amount, of course. The difference would be our profit. Well, Mary and I had some great times travelling in Yugoslavia. We made enough sales, I suppose, to pay for the trip. But then all of a sudden this whole thing came to an end because our friends in MK were on the outside and pro-Russian executives had the inside track and we were out in the cold.

Q: So then what did you do?

Captain Noel: At about that time I think we left Paris and went down to live in Spain. While we were in Paris we had taken our holidays at this golf resort in Sotogrande and found it a charming place to go. We met some attractive people who were building houses, and we saw building costs going up 15% every year. We thought, "Well, why not look toward the future? We may want to retire down there some day. In the meantime, it would be nice to have a house in Sotogrande."

We were selling our house in Minorca. We sold our house in Minorca, which had been built as a summer house. When you are in Paris in the summer, you've got to get out, and we had three kids and they all had three friends each. By the time you've rented a large establishment on the beach somewhere, you've paid $5,000 or $6,000 as a very minimum, usually $10,000. So it made a lot more sense to build a house, which only cost us about $20,000. We built a small house on a wonderful place to swim with four little bedrooms and eight beds. We went down there. Mary and the children and the dog would go down there in the summer, and I'd come down for two weeks in July and two weeks in August. But we sold that house in order to build the house in Sotogrande. At Sotogrande we built a pretty big house which we still have, and which I'm sweating blood to sell right now.

Q: Where is this?

Captain Noel: Near Gibraltar. Sotogrande is within sight of Gibraltar.

Q: You said east of Gibraltar, didn't you?

Captain Noel: Yes, just east of Gibraltar. It's got two Robert Trent Jones golf courses, two polo fields, a beach club, a tennis club. They have a lot of rich people there. Now it's rather changed. Now they're getting a lot of moderately well-off English people who build little houses. For a while there, Nick Biddle built a great big house, and the King of Belgium came down to build a big house, and there was a lot of big money there. Now there's still some very well-healed Spaniards who live there. The community is about half Spanish and half foreign.

Q: You're trying to sell that house now? Is it rented?

Captain Noel: Yes, it's rented this month. We kept a house all the time when we were in Paris and then when we were in Iran.

Q: When did you go to Iran?

Captain Noel: In '73.

Q: Travelling or business?

Captain Noel: On business, as the country director for the

International Executive Service Corps. We left Paris about '70 and gave up the flat, and had to get all the papers necessary to get out of Paris! I not only had to get a certificate saying that I'd paid all my taxes and that I was a man of good character, but then I had to go to some other functionary and get him to certify that that man had signed my piece of paper. We got out of Paris with all our stuff and took up permanent residence at Sotogrande. It was a big and very comfortable house. At the time we enjoyed the place very much. We had come down there on holidays. It still had an aroma of holidays. Just about that time, a year after we had moved down there, or a year and a half, we were roaming around New England in the summer. We never stayed at Sotogrande in the summers. It was too hot and too crowded, full of crazy Frenchmen and Spaniards jamming up everything. It was a great month to get away and we'd rent our house for a lot of money.

We were staying with Frank Pace, the head of this International Executive Service Corps, and he said, "Why don't you be our man in Morocco? We need a country director." The way this International Executive Service Corps works--it's a non-profit organization started by David Rockefeller with the blessing of Lyndon Johnson to help the Third World with technical assistance in the form of retired executives.*

---
*David Rockefeller, chairman of the board of Chase Manhattan Bank.

Q: I've read of that, I think.

Captain Noel: And their wives, who give their services, but they get their expenses, and go abroad for three or four months. Every country where they operate needs a country director who goes out and finds the projects and describes them, then convinces New York it's worthwhile, then greets the volunteer and his wife. Mary played a big part in this picture because half the time the wife is reeling from cultural shock and somebody has to hold her hand for a little while, particularly when you go to a place like Iran. We had to put them in a local but adequate hotel because nobody could afford to put them up at the Hilton.

So it's a fascinating job for a couple. I enjoyed it thoroughly. We thought Morocco was marvelous. Of course, it was just across the straits from where we lived, so it was very easy. I drove my own car down there and had a marvelous time, which I've just relived in a way, because I've been in touch with a man that's going down there to reopen the IESC operation. When I left, they closed it. I was handling Tunisia, Algeria, and Morocco. I'd gone down there, driven my own car, done my own paperwork, hadn't hired anybody. I had a cheesy little apartment. I'd taken them seriously. I was a real idealist. I was going to get started on the cheap and so on. Well, I soon learned that nobody in IESC that had any sense did things on the cheap. All the staff in New York flew around the world first class with their wives and stayed at the local Hilton. I felt like a chump. But anyhow, they all came and saw that I was sincere and economical and that my French was good and that I had made friends. I had just made friends with the chief of the king's cabinet through some adopted children of ours in Paris I haven't mentioned. Bensouda, the number two man in the government, when I called on him, said, "Where's Mrs. Noel?"

I said, "She's out in the car."

After he read the letter I gave him, he said, "Bring her up here." That day we went to this chap's house for lunch. Boy, when you do that in a Moslem or an Arab household, you are a member of the family. We were. I was so happy with this connection because now I could get big support.

But they suddenly said, "Close up everything. Do you want to go to Iran?"

I said, "Sure." We were always ready to travel. So we went to Iran. It was a damn shame, because we were doing something in Morocco. Algeria was tough, but I was making the connections to get in there. Those Algerians are as tough as nails. You couldn't even get a hotel room at the St. George without having a personal representative there who would go over and get you a room, because they wouldn't pay any attention to a telex. A confirmed reservation by telex was about as good as a pack of cigarettes. So Algeria was tough. It was tough just to get into the place, but I had some friends there. A woman lawyer, incidentally, a brilliant woman, and that's unusual in a Moslem country, but she had worked for my associates in Paris. But they folded us up in North Africa, and we went to Iran.

I've sort of overrun a few things here. In Paris I became associated in the last two years--and I had forgotten this, that the real reason I left Paris was the collapse of my best French friend, Richard Klehe, a marvelous and important French banker who represented Charles Allen and Company over there. He was taken with a stroke and is today just a vegetable. As soon as that poor chap essentially died, I had nowhere to go. We had all kinds of fascinating things going. We had a timber project in Africa; we had a magnesium project in Bahrain; we had a lot of things going, and he was the money man and the important man. My function was to find the team, to find the collaborators, to find people with the separate expertise, and to put this group together and exploit something like the timber in Africa or the cheap electricity in Bahrain.

Q: Called an entrepreneur.

Captain Noel: Then when all this was put together, I'd have a couple of percent which would make me very comfortable for the rest of my life. I knew the former ambassador in Bahrain. He had left there with the right to build a magnesium factory, using surplus standby power that they already had in Bahrain to make aluminum. The soil of that whole damn island is dolomite, which is the raw material for magnesium. We really had a good thing going. All it needed was a few more people in the act and a revival of the light metal market. But here poor Richard Klehe disappears from the scene.

Q: Still alive but only in words.

Captain Noel: Just a vegetable. God, I'd hate to go that way.

Anyhow, it was this that convinced me that we might as well give up the Parisian scene. We could afford to live on what I'd saved and my retired pay.

Q: How many years early did you retire?

Captain Noel: As far as pay was concerned, none, because I got credit for my enlisted service.

Q: But you could have stayed on until when?

Captain Noel: I could have stayed on for another year. My 30 years would have been up in '66.

Q: Then from Iran . . .

Captain Noel: We left Morocco and we went to Iran for almost three years.

Q: Doing the same thing that you'd been doing?

Captain Noel: Country director for IESC, yes. That was a very tough place to live and to work, but a fascinating place.

Q: Tehran?

Captain Noel: Yes. The Iranians are very abrasive people, very un-Western, un-European. I didn't find the Moroccans at all unsympathetic or not understandable, although they had some weird customs. You never knew whether a fellow was coming for luncheon or dinner or cocktails when he said he was. He might never appear or he might come with ten of his relatives. That was the custom of the country. So you just were braced for it. But the Iranians were really tough people. The man in the street was a suspicious fellow. There wasn't anything you could do for him that would convince him that you were his benefactor, no matter how much you gave him. We used to have caddies. Everywhere in the world Mary and I have taken caddies under our wing.

Q: Golf caddies?

Captain Noel: Yes. But no matter what you gave a caddy at the Imperial Country Club as a tip, he'd spit in your eye. He'd rant and rave and say it wasn't enough.

Q: He'd take it, though?

Captain Noel: Yes. He'd take it, but he'd expect to get more.

Q: How did you get along with language?

Captain Noel: We didn't learn Farsi; we learned a few polite phrases. We didn't learn the language. All the educated classes spoke English or French, so with English or French I could do everything. Sometimes it was all French. The upper classes are all educated. There might have been one German I couldn't communicate with, but I don't really remember, because the upper class always sent their children to France or England or Germany. The Germans always learned either English or French, so there was no trouble with the language. There was a lot of trouble with the people, the man on the street. It was dangerous to drive. It is a disheartening place for a couple of kindly people to live, where everything you try to do for your associates, for your servants, for the people you associate with on a certain level, is rebuffed. My secretary, who was educated in England, was a marvelous woman that I correspond with to this day. My

Iranian assistant was another marvelous chap. We still have marvelous Iranian friends. But the man in the street was damn near impossible. The businessmen, many of the bureaucrats that I did business with, were very unreliable. The Arabs were much better people to do business with.

Q: Did they care about this program at all?

Captain Noel: Yes, theoretically they did. The Shah was for it, the prime minister, Hoveda, who was shot out of hand or hanged or something as soon as Khomeini took over, Hoveda was a friend of mine and he cared about it. Some of the more enlightened bankers, the heads of some of the banks, thought it was marvelous. But the average Iranian fellow who had a factory somewhere, even though he could see in theory that it would help them, was difficult to deal with. His subordinates were immediately suspicious that your volunteer was planning to take over his job. Dealing with the bureaucracy was fantastic.

I tried to help them form a university and provide people to train the faculty and help them build some of their buildings, and I got the damnedest runaround from some of these petits functionaires who either wouldn't pay their bills or who would not honor a written agreement to have a man come over. They were just slippery, unreliable people, in part. In some other way, they were marvelous.

Noel #2 - 225

Q: When was the Shah deposed? What year?

Captain Noel: I think about '79, probably. I was there from '74 to '77.

Q: Did you see it coming?

Captain Noel: No, I didn't see it coming and there was no reason for it to come. The Shah was just a chicken-livered, sick man, and our intelligence was very damn bad. Because I have an Iranian friend who saw it coming and got out with millions. But our intelligence was bad, although, my gosh, Dick Helms, ex-CIA, was our ambassador. He should have known. Actually, there was no way to predict it because it shouldn't have happened. When these religious fanatics got too big for their britches, the Shah should have had his army chase them out of town again. But he was a sick man. He was much sicker than any of us realized. He lost all his guts. We put him back on his throne once before when he fled to Italy, when Mosadegh tried to get in. We propped him up. But he was a sick man and an ineffective man in many ways. Power had corrupted him to the point where he was an authority on everything.

Q: Did you know him? Did you meet him? Did you ever have anything to do with him?

Captain Noel: No. He talked to God and Allah perhaps, but that's about all. I couldn't even get an audience with him for Frank Pace. But he would issue dicta arbitrarily, quickly, without warning, such as 40% of all the stock of a company has got to be sold to the workers. Nobody told anybody how it was going to be paid for. Or all workers in these categories must have an immediate raise of 10%. This would screw up all sensible business planning.

Q: Did anyone do it?

Captain Noel: They had to do it. Everybody adjusted and compromised. In the meantime, the oil was flowing like crazy and he had lots of money. But his abdication was a great tragedy for that country, and it never should have happened. It didn't have to happen. His army was loyal, a bit corrupt.

Q: So what's new?

Captain Noel: But well-armed. But they were the most difficult people to help. To give you an example, the military assistance group later told me that the F-14s that we sold them, they didn't want to admit that they couldn't maintain them, our people, all with good intent, tried to persuade them that they had to do certain things in order to maintain the planes. So one pilot thought he would show them. He left his plane that he was flying that they took care of, an American pilot. He went on a holiday. Before he left, he disengaged two wires behind the dash. When he came back, he asked for his plane and they walked it around. Finally they had to admit that they didn't have it ready, that they couldn't find out what was wrong with it. Well, he said, "I just want to show you that you people need this kind of training." He went back and showed them the two wires. They flew him out of town in 48 hours.

Q: He was an American?

Captain Noel: An American pilot. He was an ex-Navy pilot. He was hired by some company or by the Iranian Government to fly those planes and help them learn about them.

Q: That was usually part of our deal, wasn't it, to send someone to train them?

Captain Noel: There was a very important man that apparently nobody recognized who used to play golf by himself.

Q: How do you do that?

Captain Noel: Play golf by himself? Sure. He'd never join a

foursome or a twosome. He'd just start off and play golf. He had several times asked to go through this foursome of women. This is bad golf etiquette, because a single man has no standing. But it didn't really cost anybody anything. Well, he did it again a third time and these people were just about ready to tee off. He asked permission to go up ahead of them, and this woman turned around and said, "No, why should we? You're by yourself. You have no stature here. There's no reason why we should wait for you." That woman and her husband were out of town in 30 hours.

Q: Who was this man?

Captain Noel: Somebody close to the Shah. I don't even know his name. He was a minister or a cabinet member.

Q: And who was the woman, an Iranian?

Captain Noel: No, she was an American. She was the wife of one of the local businessmen. They were both out of town, bang!

Q: Being there those three years must have been miserable for you then.

Captain Noel: No, it was marvelous. We travelled. We had to

get out of town every three months. In the first place, the organization would send us home every year and since we were about halfway from home, which was Seattle, technically, we'd go around the world every summer because we'd go home one way and come back the other.

Q: Your home was Bremerton, because of Mary's family.

Captain Noel: Yes, and because our children were there and that's where we headed for. So we'd go around the world, we'd stop and have an adventure somewhere. So we had marvelous travels. Then every three months, because we didn't want to get anything except temporary, short-term visas, for many reasons, including taxes. We were there very illegally. The Shah knew all about us and approved of us, but there is no provision in Iranian law for a non-profit organization, so we were a non-organization since we couldn't register ourselves. So we were highly illegal, technically.

Q: Did you get scared ever?

Captain Noel: No, I knew the prime minister. They knew we were there to help them. But we had short-term visas, so every three months we'd have to get out and get a new visa. So that meant we could go to Turkey and have a week there. We could go to Kuwait if it wasn't too hot. So we saw a great deal of the world, we saw a great deal of Iran. We went to Afghanistan. We knew some of the royal family in Afghanistan. We went over the Khyber Pass, flew a plane over the Hindukush. We had a lot of great adventures.

Q: When did you get back to Santa Fe?

Captain Noel: We went back from Iran. I left Iran after three years. We'd had enough. We went on a safari in Kenya, saw the Pyramids, went back to Sotogrande where we lived for three years and I wrote these two dictionaries.* Then we decided to pack it in. In the meantime, Mary had come through Santa Fe and bought this house.

Q: How did she happen to come through Santa Fe? Did you have a son here?

Captain Noel: Yes. Jack had called us from here once before we were ready to come back for the summer, and I had something else to do or somewhere to go, but Mary said she'd come through Santa Fe. He wanted a little help in buying a farm out in the country.

---
*The VNR Dictionary of Ships and the Sea and The Boating Dictionary - Sail and Power, both published by Van Nostrand Reinhold.

Some of the counterculture who had come back out of the cold, more or less, from Berkeley, had come into this country over here by Ojo Caliente, something like that, and they were doing a little homesteading, buying a little land from the Indians. He wanted to do that, so he knew we were always ready to help him with something substantial like buying a farm. He urged Mary to come through. She came through on the Fourth of July. The land he wanted, thank God, had been taken off the market. In self-defense she figured she'd better buy something. She thought it was a great town, she loved it, and so she saw this house and bought it over a weekend. The smartest thing you can imagine. So anyway, Mary bought this house in '78, and two years later we decided just to pack everything.

Q: Where did you come from?

Captain Noel: We were living in Sotogrande.

Q: You were still in Spain.

Captain Noel: Right. We came here and Joy was having a terrible struggle with a bum of a husband.

Q: Joy is the third daughter?

Captain Noel: Third child. So Mary went up to help Joy through this divorce. It was messy because she had to get a sheriff to throw Mike out of the house. It was the house that we'd bought for Joy.

Q: I think that it's sweet that her name is Joyeux Noel, meaning "Merry Christmas."

Captain Noel: Right. So Mary went up to hold Joy's hand and help her out for the summer. I came here. One of Jack's friends is a very skilled carpenter, he's really a contractor but doesn't do it much, and he came down here from Ojo Caliente in northern New Mexico. He brought some labor with him and together we remodeled the house. I mostly swept out the place on weekends, bought fried chicken at night for dinner--they all camped out here except for weekends--and wrote checks. That was my major contribution.

Q: It's an absolutely charming house.

Captain Noel: Mary designed the remodeling. There was much work to do.

Q: Just for the record, it's done in the lovely style of Santa Fe with everything white on the walls, and the ceilings are traditional latilla vegas. Those are the beams.

Captain Noel: I took the bark off those, most of them. There were some things I did. I painted the whole place with one assistant. I found a fellow to dig a trench we needed for a new sewer line, and it turned out he said he was a good painter. I said, "Great, let's paint the place." And we did.

Q: I think it's interesting that you insulated it on the outside, so it actually never has heat. Any heat is basically solar.

Captain Noel: It's mostly solar.

Q: And you have two fireplaces. How many rooms do you consider this has?

Captain Noel: It's hard to say. It has a sunroom, a dining room and study, master bedroom, guest bedroom, kitchen. That's all.

Q: That's almost ten rooms, isn't it?

Captain Noel: About 2,000 square feet.

Noel #2 - 234

Q: It's absolutely charming.

Captain Noel: It was what we decided before we left Spain, what we decided we wanted--small, comfortable, attractive, simple house. We can live here until we're dead.

Q: I wanted to ask you some questions basically relating to your own character and traits. You said in 1966 you made a French TV documentary called "War in the Pacific."

Captain Noel: Yes. I had forgotten about that. I helped them with the script. They did the research. It was a wonderful team from French Television. It was a great example of how you can do things modestly. They had a director, a producer some of the time, but always a director, a cameraman, a man to carry the camera, and one other hand. They had a party of five. If the Americans had done it, they would have had 25 people and three Rolls-Royces.

Q: Did you go to Pearl Harbor?

Captain Noel: Yes. After we put the script together and they'd done the research and did all the clips, we went out to Pearl, where I was in the film myself. The pattern of these great documentaries which include "The Battle for Stalingrad," "The

Battle for the Atlantic," "The Battle for Paris," they would take all the best clips they could from everywhere, and in between the pictures they would splice a narration by somebody who had been there. So having been at Pearl Harbor, I was able to make a little talk there to the camera with the ships as the background. I made another talk on Admiral Nimitz for that series. We did this film right after the Navy had supported a private film made called "Tora, Tora, Tora," which you may not remember.

Q: That means "Attack, Attack," doesn't it?

Captain Noel: Yes. They hired the Navy pilots on their off hours to fly World War II planes over the hills and simulate the Japanese. It was a good film, and the Navy supported it so enthusiastically with so much PR money, that the General Accounting Office got on them and issued a report. There was a small scandal and the Navy got its knuckles rapped for being too keen to toot its horn. The result was, us poor Frenchmen coming over to make a film, we didn't get anything. We had to hire a boat to go out to the Arizona. I was hoping to put all my friends up at the BOQ.* I stayed with old friends, the McCains.** We really had to do it on the cheap because the Navy

---

*BOQ—Bachelor officers' quarters.
**Admiral John S. McCain, USN, was then Commander in Chief Pacific.

was so gunshy.

We had a grand opening of this film in Paris. There we had the then-Ensign Gay, the only survivor of Torpedo Eight, who was a TWA captain.* And I met a kamikaze pilot who had survived. This was on the film.

Q: What do you consider your best traits?

Captain Noel: If you asked Mary, she'll tell you I don't have any good ones.

Q: Oh, come now. Tell me. What do you think your best characteristics are?

Captain Noel: I think I'm competent, reasonably intelligent, and have no great aversion to hard work when necessary. And perhaps in my profession it's been worthwhile to be interested in a great many aspects of life and the world. Perhaps I'd have done better if I'd have concentrated on something and discovered a new kind of spider.

Q: I think it's been fascinating. Your family relations, your

---

*Ensign George S. Gay, USNR, was a member of Torpedo Squadron Eight during the Battle of Midway in June 1942. The planes in the squadron were all shot down; of the group only Gay was rescued. He was subsequently a pilot for Trans World Airlines.

religious beliefs, any of those things, have they ever affected you? I have not heard you talk about any religious beliefs other than that you are liberal.

Captain Noel: I was raised an Episcopalian of sorts and I'm sort of a backslid Protestant. We go to the Unitarian Church because we believe in what they believe in, and we enjoy the company of people we consider more enlightened than the average religious person.

Q: That's good. I go to the Unitarian Church.

Captain Noel: Good for you. You can see that my religion is A-1.

Q: And all the moves you've made, have they had an effect on your family?

Captain Noel: This is hard to speculate on. Sometimes we think yes. I'm sure they've had an effect. I'm sure our children are better educated, have broader vision, are more cosmopolitan, perhaps have better manners than they would have had had they been brought up in one place. On the other hand, there is a certain amount of stress in frequent moves for children. Sometimes they miss old friends.

Index

to

Reminiscences of

Captain John Vavasour Noel, Jr.

U.S. Navy (Retired)

Abandon Ship
   Noel and other crew members from Lamson (DD-367) jump from the destroyer after fierce Leyte Gulf action in December 1944, pp. 57-60

Ainsworth, Rear Admiral Walden L., USN   (USNA, 1910)
   As Commander Destroyers Pacific in early 1945, threw beer party for ships that straggled into Pearl Harbor after tackling kamikazes and a typhoon, p. 66

Air Conditioning
   Navy fight to get air-conditioning for quarters in Corpus Christi from tight Defense Department fists in the early 1960s, pp. 193-194

Alcoholism
   U.S. consul general in Barcelona in the late 1950s was rendered ineffective by alcoholism, pp. 141, 166; serious problem among senior officers in late 1950s, pp. 164-167

Aleutians
   Patrol wing commander broadcasts successes in Aleutians in 1942, p. 32; Mine Division One lays minefield in late 1942, pp. 33-34; cold weather patrols, pp. 34-38

Algeria
   Difficulty for foreigners in Algeria in the mid-1970s, pp. 219-220

Altair, USS (AKS-32)
   Implements underway helicopter replenishment for Sixth Fleet in late 1950s, pp. 137-140; duties with Sixth Fleet, pp. 140-141, 151-153; crew birthdays observed, p. 142; many requests from crew to marry Spanish girls, pp. 143-144; duty routine, p. 144; frequent trouble with engines handled quietly, pp. 144-145; preparation for deployment to Spain, pp. 146-149; charity programs for Spanish children, pp. 147-149

American Medical Association (AMA)
   While on duty in the Bureau of Personnel in the mid-1950s, Noel borrowed by Defense Department to address the AMA on dependent care, pp. 115-118

Amphibious Group One
   Noel's duties as planning officer in the late 1940s, pp. 87-88; training of Army personnel in Japan in 1950, p. 89

Anderson, Admiral George W., Jr., USN   (USNA, 1927)
   Reputation as Sixth Fleet commander in the early 1960s, pp. 168, 172; congratulates Noel on shiphandling in Yugoslavian harbor, p. 175; put in awkward position by Noel article in Proceedings while Chief of Naval Operations and president of U.S. Naval Institute in early 1960s, though he agreed with it,

pp. 190-193, 195, 202; dealings with Secretary of Defense McNamara regarding Cuban Missile Crisis, pp. 195-196; advises Noel of his trouble with flag selection board, p. 201; compared to David McDonald, pp. 203-205

Anderson, Rear Admiral Walter S., USN (USNA, 1903)
As Commander Cruiser Division Four in 1937, hosts Astoria (CA-34) officers at West Coast tennis club, p. 8; discussion of pace of operations in U.S. Pacific Fleet in 1941, p. 25

Antiaircraft Gunnery
Firing by U.S. warships under attack at Pearl Harbor on 7 December 1941, pp. 19-20; destroyer Lamson (DD-367) fires at Japanese planes off the Philippines in late 1944, pp. 56-57

Apple, Lieutenant (j.g.) Robert E., USN (USNA, 1944)
Lamson (DD-367) navigator loses his composure when the destroyer almost grounds off Bremerton in January 1945, pp. 71-72

Army Air Forces, U.S.
Pilots in Aleutians unfamiliar with radio device, p. 32; pilots not qualified for night landings in 1944, p. 50; at Leyte in late 1944, pp. 54, 56-57; See also: B-17, B-29

Army, U.S.
Noel feels given undue credit at Battle of Midway, p. 29; soldiers in Japan in 1950, p. 90; See also: U.S. Army Air Forces

Astoria, USS (CA-34)
Ensign Noel's duties in mid-1930s include tennis, pp. 6-7; one of first large ships sent to Pacific in 1937, pp. 7-8; takes former Japanese ambassador's ashes to Tokyo in 1939, p. 10; overhaul at Bremerton in 1937-1938, pp. 11, 13; See also: Captain Charles Gill, USN; Captain Richmond Turner, USN

Attache Duty
Intelligence gathering, pp. 180-186; social life, pp. 182-183, 187; handling of VIP guests, pp. 186-187

B-17 Bombers
Japanese unnecessarily intimidated by B-17s at Pearl Harbor, p. 21; inflated claims of success in 1942 Battle of Midway, p. 29

B-29 Bombers
Lamson (DD-367) monitors and assists B-29s, guiding fighters from the Marianas to attack mainland Japan in 1945, pp. 79-80

Bahrain
Noel's business dealings here in the 1970s, pp. 220-221

Bar Harbor, Maine
Site of USN-Royal Navy tennis tournaments in 1930s, p. 6

Barbers Point, Hawaii
  Rumor of Japanese landing here during Pearl Harbor attack generated by some Japanese, pp. 21-22

Barcelona, Spain
  Appeal to American Navy personnel and dependents, pp. 141-142, 150, 153; Altair (AKS-32) participates in charities for children, pp. 147-149; social life, pp. 150-152; historical significance, pp. 154-157; U.S. consul general in the late 1950s an alcoholic, pp. 141, 166

Bluejackets' Manual
  Noel writes current version in early 1950s, p. 92

Bohlen, Charles
  Assessed as U.S. ambassador to France in the early 1960s, p. 182

Bremerton, Washington
  Lamson (DD-367) repaired here after December 1944 kamikaze attack, pp. 71-75, 79

Bureau of Naval Personnel
  See: Naval Personnel, Bureau of

Burgess, Carter L.
  Assessed as hardworking Assistant Secretary of Defense for Personnel in the mid-1950s, p. 128

Cagle, Captain Malcolm C., USN (USNA, 1941)
  Entertained Noel in Paris on his way to take command of Springfield (CGL-7) in March 1961, pp. 169-170

The Caine Mutiny
  Realistic portrayal of destroyer duty in South Pacific, pp. 42-43

Case, Chief Gunner's Mate
  Sicard (DM-21) chief makes valiant attempt to down Japanese planes at Pearl Harbor with antiquated gun, p. 19

Central Intelligence Agency (CIA)
  Gathered information through U.S. Embassy in Paris in the early 1960s, pp. 184-186

Chaplains
  Navy chaplain influential in Navy's adopting moral leadership program in the mid-1950s, pp. 119-120; Bureau of Naval Personnel arranges conference of NATO chaplains in the U.S. in the mid-1950s, pp. 124-126

Charleston, South Carolina
  Exposure to naval officers while attending college in Charleston spurs Noel to apply for U.S. Naval Academy in 1932, pp. 3-4

China
   U.S. handling of attempt to collect intelligence on China through French civilian in the early 1960s, pp. 184-186

Coding Machine
   Sicard officers get reports of Midway battle from shipboard ECM, p. 31

Cold Weather Operations
   Danger and discomfort for units of Mine Division One operating in Aleutians in late 1942, pp. 33-36

Cuban Missile Crisis
   Secretary of Defense McNamara put Chief of Naval Operations Anderson in awkward position regarding classified details of this October 1962 incident, pp. 195-196

Daniels, Josephus
   Noel approves of former Secretary of the Navy's decision to make U.S. Navy dry, pp. 11-12

De Florez, Rear Admiral Luis, USNR
   Convinces Secretary of the Navy Gates to implement an enlisted education program in the mid-1950s, p. 111; travels to Europe with Noel and an Assistant Secretary of the Navy in late 1950s, p. 164

De Gaulle, General Charles A.
   French President in the early 1960s, notorious for distrust of Anglo-Saxons, pp. 182, 184-185, 188

Defense Department
   Noel writes article critical of department in the early 1960s, pp. 190-195; tight-fisted about installing air-conditioning in Corpus Christi quarters in early 1960s, pp. 193-194

Discipline
   Examples of leadership in Rochester (CA-124) in the mid-1950s, pp. 101-102, 104-105

Division Officer's Guide
   Noel translates need in Navy into Naval Institute publication in the early 1950s, pp. 92-94; neutered to apply to all readers, pp. 134-135

Dyer, Fred
   Civilian worked with Noel on implementing a moral leadership program for the Navy in the mid-1950s, pp. 119-120

Ekstrom, Vice Admiral Clarence E., USN (USNA, 1924)
   As Sixth Fleet commander in the late 1950s, dealings with U.S. consul general in Barcelona, who was an alcoholic, p. 166

Embassy Duty
   Intelligence gathering, pp. 182-186; social life, pp. 182-183, 187; handling of VIP guests, pp. 186-187

Empress Augusta Bay
   Mine Division One lays mines before action here in November 1943, p. 41

Enterprise, USS (CV-6)
   Enterprise planes coming to Pearl Harbor the night after the Japanese attack are shot at by Americans, p. 23

F-111
   See: TFX

Fay, Paul B., Jr.
   The Noels join Under Secretary of the Navy and Mrs. Fay on trip through Europe in 1964, pp. 189-190

Fighter Director Ship
   Lamson (DD-367) served as director for Army Air Force and Marine pilots around Leyte in 1944, pp. 50, 56-57

Flagships
   Pros and cons for vessels with an admiral and his staff embarked, pp. 99-100, 131

Flaherty, Captain Michael F., USN (USNA, 1928)
   Seamanship and navigation department head in the early 1950s encourages instructor Noel's professional writing, pp. 91, 93

Flusser, USS (DD-368)
   Rescues crew members from Lamson (DD-367) who abandoned ship after fierce Leyte action in December 1944, pp. 59-60

Forrestal, USS (CVA-59)
   Provides helicopters for replenishment duty to Altair (AKS-32) in the late 1950s, p. 151

France
   Visited by touring Noels in 1962, pp. 177-180; U.S. Embassy personnel in Paris in 1962, pp. 181-182; embassy social life, pp. 182-183, 187; French distrust of Americans results in lost opportunity for intelligence on Soviets in early 1960s, pp. 183-184; Noels travel through France, pp. 187-189; Noel scripts documentary for French television in 1966, pp. 234-236

French Frigate Shoal
   Sicard (DM-21) lays a minefield here after Pearl Harbor attack to impede Jap flying boat refueling here, p. 26

Gates, Thomas S.
   Secretary of the Navy a proponent of naval enlisted scientific

education program in mid-1950s, p. 111; persuaded to implement a moral leadership program in the Navy in the mid-1950s, pp. 118-119, 129; ensured promotion to flag rank of a favored officer, p. 163

Gehres, Captain Leslie E., USN
Patrol wing commanding officer in Kodiak, Alaska, in 1942, ties up communications line broadcasting his group's success, p. 32

Gill, Captain Charles C., USN (USNA, 1907)
Astoria (CA-34) skipper in the mid-1930s an enthusiastic tennis player, p. 7

Goldberg, Captain Joshua L., CHC, USNR (Retired)
Jewish chaplain suggests conference of NATO chaplains that is held in the mid-1950s, pp. 124-125; suggests U.S. naval attaches in Paris in the early 1960s increase rapport with Israeli attaches as a good source of information about the Russians, p. 127

Greece
Royal family visits Springfield (CLG-7) in spring of 1961, pp. 170, 172-173

Griffin, Admiral Charles D., USN (USNA, 1927)
Head of flag selection board in 1964 and Noel's friend, advises him that board was instructed not to consider him, p. 200

Grumman Corporation
Grumman hydrofoil could not compete with Boeing's in the 1960s, pp. 210-211

Halsey, Vice Admiral William F., Jr., USN (USNA, 1904)
Noel considers it fortuitous that Halsey was hospitalized in May 1942 and replaced by Rear Admiral Spruance before Midway, pp. 29-30; congratulates Sicard (DM-21) after patrol while disabled, p. 40; criticized for leadership during December 1944 typhoon, p. 53; attends party at destroyer officers' club at Pearl Harbor in January 1945, p. 67

Handy Billies
Used in repairs on Lamson (DD-367) at Bremerton in early 1945, pp. 78-79

Haraden, USS (DD-585)
Proves to be poor guide to Lamson (DD-367) on way to Bremerton in January 1945, pp. 69-71

Hawaiian Islands
Pleasant living arrangements in late 1930s, pp. 12-13; Japanese allowed into Hawaii under diplomatic immunity cause problems during Pearl Harbor attack, p. 21; See also: Pearl Harbor; Barbers Point

Hayes, Helen
  Noel recalls acquaintance with actress Hayes through her daughter, p. 174

Henderson Field, Guadalcanal
  Noel put up in VIP quarters while awaiting flight home in early 1944, pp. 43-44

Hill, Captain Andrew J., Jr., USN (USNA, 1931)
  Seventh Fleet staff officer in mid-1950s specific about what space in Rochester (CA-124) would be allocated for staff, p. 100

Holloway, Vice Admiral James L, Jr., USN (USNA, 1919)
  Met Noels at Annapolis party in 1950, p. 110; as Chief of the Bureau of Personnel in mid-1950s, hesitates before implementing moral leadership program, pp. 119-120

Homeporting
  Greater replenishment capabilities in the late 1950s enabled fewer ships to have overseas home ports, p. 138

Hoover Commission
  Noel considered many recommendations of this committee on cost-saving and personnel reduction to be ill-advised, p. 128

Horn, Commander Roy de S., USN (Retired) (USNA, 1915)
  U.S. Naval Institute managing editor in the mid-1950s felt naval officers should not be paid for professional writing, p. 96

Hydrofoil
  Grumman's model could not compete with the highly successful Boeing hydrofoil in 1960s, p. 210

Indian Island
  Lamson (DD-367) unloads depth charges here in January 1945, pp. 69-70

Indianapolis, USS (CA-35)
  Flagship of Commanding Scouting Force Pacific in late 1930s, pp. 10-11; Panama Canal transit in late 1930s, p. 11; East Coast cruise in late 1930s modified due to worsening relations with Japan, p. 11

Industrial College of the Armed Forces
  Noel not inspired by his one-year program here in the mid-1950s, pp. 108-110

Intelligence
  Noel interprets pre-war intelligence as showing that the Japanese could not attack the fleet, p. 17; quality of Japanese intelligence at Pearl Harbor, p. 18; importance prior to

Midway, pp. 26-27; Noel attends intelligence course in Washington before serving as naval attache in Paris in 1962, p. 180; intelligence-gathering through U.S. Embassy in Paris, pp. 182-183; French distrust of U.S. causes lost opportunity to gather covert intelligence on Soviet Union in early 1960s, pp. 183-184, 186; U.S. handling of covert intelligence on China, pp. 184-186

International Executive Service Corps
   Explanation of this enterprise that the Noels joined in the mid-1970s, pp. 217-220, 222

Iowa, USS (BB-61)
   Difficulty refueling Lamson (DD-367) after she is damaged in December 1944 attack, pp. 63, 65

Iran
   Noel's experiences here in the mid-1970s, pp. 222-224, 227-230; assessment of the Shah, pp. 224-226; ill-trained military, pp. 226-227

Iwo Jima
   Importance for air operations in 1945, pp. 79-80; Lamson (DD-367) sights Japanese plane in time to warn Iwo Jima to darken the harbor, p. 160

Jackson, Richard
   Assessed as Assistant Secretary of the Navy for Personnel in the late 1950s, pp. 157, 164; feud with Chief of Bureau of Personnel, Vice Admiral Page Smith, over formation of Judge Advocate General's Corps, pp. 157, 161, 201; looks at problem of alcohol abuse in the Navy, pp. 164-166

Japan
   Worsening relations with Japan in late 1930s cause change in Indianapolis's East Coast cruise, p. 11; Japanese allowed into Hawaii under diplomatic immunity compound difficulties during Pearl Harbor attack, pp. 21-22; at Empress Augusta Bay in November 1943, pp. 40-41; at Leyte in late 1944, pp. 56-57, 64; See also: Pearl Harbor; French Frigate Shoal; Kamikazes

Japanese Americans
   Loyalty during World War II, p. 22

Judge Advocate General's Corps (JAGC)
   Controversy in the late 1950s over possible formation of this body of officers, pp. 157-159, 161

Kamikazes
   Around Leyte in mid-late 1944, pp. 50-51, 54; caused great concern by early 1945, p. 67

Kaskaskia, USS (AO-27)
    Directs escort ship Sicard (DM-21) to proceed at a hazardous speed in the Aleutians in 1942, p. 35

Kauffman, Rear Admiral James L., USN (USNA, 1908)
    Fumes when Lamson (DD-367) is not able to go right out to forward area because of crew shortcomings in mid-1944, p. 49

Kennedy, John F.
    Relationship with Paul Fay, pp. 189-190; appointed George Anderson as ambassador to Portugal in 1963 to assuage his firing as Chief of Naval Operations, p. 196

Kimmel, Admiral Husband E., USN (USNA, 1904)
    Preparations for war as Commander in Chief Pacific Fleet in 1941 defended by Noel, pp. 24-25

King, Commander Ed R., Jr., USN (USNA, 1936)
    Noel's classmate co-wrote shiphandling book published in 1954, p. 95

Kinkaid, Admiral Thomas C., USN (USNA, 1908)
    Favorable appraisal as Commander Seventh Fleet in 1944, pp. 54-55

Knight's Modern Seamanship
    Noel gets involved in revisions on this classic in the early 1950s, pp. 94-95

Korean War
    Amphibious Group One sent to Japan in spring of 1950 to train troops, p. 89

Lamson, USS (DD-367)
    Prospective commanding officer Noel sent to sonar school before assuming command in March 1944, pp. 45-46; inexperienced officers complicate shipyard overhaul in mid-1944, pp. 46-47, 49; Noel's difficulties with navigator, pp. 47-48; held up at Pearl Harbor for training, p. 49; supports Army and Marine pilots at Leyte in 1944, pp. 50, 54; disabled after 7 December 1944 kamikaze attack, Lamson passes within 90 miles of typhoon, pp. 51, 64; operations around Leyte in 1944, pp. 56-57; Noel abandons ship by jumping overboard, pp. 57-59; on the verge of being sunk by U.S. ships after damage in Leyte Gulf action in December 1944, able to be towed instead, p. 60; damage sustained in attack, pp. 60-64; temporary repairs in Indonesia, p. 64; refuels with difficulty from Iowa (BB-61), pp. 63, 65; to Pearl Harbor for repairs, pp. 65-68; trip to Bremerton in January 1945 includes a near grounding, pp. 68-73; repairs at Bremerton, pp. 78-79; returns to duties near the Marianas and Iwo Jima in early 1945, pp. 79-82; used in Bikini tests, p. 85

Leadership
  Noel perceives shortcomings of leadership training for midshipmen in the early 1950s, pp. 93-94; innovations successfully used in Rochester (CA-124) in mid-1950s, pp. 101-102; Noel implements moral leadership program for Secretary of the Navy Gates in mid-1950s that evolved into LMET program, pp. 118-121, 129-134

Leadership and Management, Education and Training (LMET)
  Moral leadership program Noel implements for Secretary of the Navy Gates in the mid-1950s evolved into the Navy's LMET program, pp. 118-121

Legal Officers
  See: Judge Advocate General's Corps

Leyte Gulf
  Lamson (DD-367) supports landing and expansion of the beach in mid-1944, pp. 50, 54, 56-57; Army supports landings, pp. 50, 54, 56; Lamson hit by kamikaze in December 1944 during landing, p. 51

Liquor
  Noels host mint julep party for Sicard (DM-21) wardroom in San Diego in 1943, pp. 36-37; Sicard skipper breaks out medicinal whiskey for officers after collision in the Aleutians, p. 38; Tulagi officers' club established in 1943, p. 41; inequity between availability of liquor to officers and enlisted men, p. 42; Noel trades liquor for produce on Guadalcanal, p. 44; Lamson (DD-367) crew share stiff drink after harrowing Leyte Gulf action in December 1944, p. 61; as commanding officer of Springfield (CLG-7) in early 1960s, Noel invited by Yugoslavian Navy to party where Slivovitz, a potent native alcohol, is guzzled, but illness prevents his attendance, pp. 175-176

Little Creek, Virginia
  Little Creek officers' club cited in 1950s as example of well-planned and successful operation, p. 122

London, General
  British flag officer tries to entertain Noel aboard Flusser (DD-368) during fierce action in Leyte Gulf in December 1944, p. 60

MacArthur, General Douglas, USA (USMA, 1903)
  Expresses concern over ships in Leyte area through Commander Seventh Fleet, Admiral Kinkaid, in 1944, p. 54; Noel disagreed with MacArthur's plan to attack the Philippines, p. 55

Mann, Ensign Hoyt D., USN (USNA, 1936)
  Loans Noel money for a car in 1938, p. 14

Mare Island Navy Yard
    Questionable character of some workers during World War II, p. 38; repaired Sicard (DM-21) after May 1943 collision, pp. 38-39; Lamson (DD-367) overhaul in mid-1944 complicated by inexperienced officers, pp. 46-47

Marine Corps, U.S.
    Marine sentries at Pearl Harbor on 7 December 1941 man antiaircraft guns, p. 19; Marine fighter pilots used for night flights at Leyte in 1944, because Army Air pilots not qualified, p. 50

Matsonia
    Noel comes home for leave on this luxury liner-turned troop carrier in early 1944, p. 45

McClintock, Robert
    Noel's relationship with U.S. ambassador to Lebanon in the early 1960s, pp. 171-172

McDonald, Admiral David L., USN (USNA, 1928)
    Negatively influenced about Noel by Admiral Page Smith, pp. 162, 201, 206; in 1961 as Commander Sixth Fleet, knew little about U.S. Naval Institute; two years later he was president, p. 191; fitness reports on Noel in early 1960s, p. 203; assessed by Noel, pp. 203-206; compared to George Anderson, p. 205

McNamara, Robert S.
    Reaction to Noel's Proceedings article on the Defense Department in the early 1960s, pp. 191-192, 195; assessed as Secretary of Defense in 1960s, pp. 195, 197; dealings with Chief of Naval Operation Anderson regarding Cuban Missile Crisis, pp. 195-196

Medical Care
    Noel addresses American Medical Association in mid-1950s to iron out terms for dependent medical care, pp. 115-118

Mellon, Paul
    Financier swims with Noel and Ambassador McClintock off Beirut in 1961, pp. 171-172

Midway, Battle of (June 1942)
    Impotence of B-17s, pp. 21, 29; importance of intelligence before battle and necessity to keep knowledge secret, pp. 26-27, 29; Noel feels importance of battle never fully realized, p. 29; Sicard (DM-21) gets news of battle from coding machine, p. 31; See also: Halsey, William F.; Spruance, Raymond A.; Yorktown

Milchem
    Noel's difficult post-retirement position with Milchem in the mid-1960s, pp. 207-210

Mine Division One
   Homeported in Hawaii for many years in the late 1930s, ships were undermanned when war approached, p. 16; commander gives liberty to men with families ashore the afternoon of 7 December 1941, p. 22; deploys to Port Townsend in June 1942, p. 32; laid mines off Alaska, pp. 33-34

Mine Warfare
   Mine Division One uses World War I mines to lay a field off Kodiak, Alaska, in mid-1942, p. 33; earlier use of mines in South Pacific might have prevented losses in the Battle of Savo Island in August 1942, pp. 39, 41; mines laid before Empress Augusta Bay action in November 1943, p. 41

Minorities
   Shown to advantage by Rochester (CA-124) in mid-1950s, p. 103

Monte Carlo
   Noel plays with tennis greats at Monte Carlo Country Club in April 1962, pp. 177-178, 180

Morale
   Noel feels morale was good in South Pacific destroyers in 1943, p. 42; in Rochester (CA-124) in mid-1950s, pp. 100-102

Morocco
   Noels lived here as part of International Executive Service Corps in mid-1970s, pp. 218-219

Mount McKinley, USS (LCC-7)
   Flagship of Commander Seventh Fleet in 1944, call sign "Warhorse," p. 54

Naval Academy, U.S.
   Admittance of Naval Reserve candidates in early 1930s, p. 3; Noel's recollections from 1932-1936, pp. 4-5, 86-87; Noel unchallenged by instructor duty in early 1950s, pp. 90, 94; Noel perceives shortcomings in leadership training for midshipmen in the early 1950s, p. 93; seamanship and navigation department instructors tackle revision of Knight's Modern Seamanship in the early 1950s, p. 94; Noel serves as secretary to the board of visitors in the early 1950s, p. 97; Noel established course in international law patterned on War College course, pp. 97-98

Naval District 13
   As Lamson (DD-367) commanding officer, Noel calls on Commander Naval District 13 upon arrival at Bremerton in January 1945, pp. 73-74

Naval Enlisted Scientific Education Program (NESEP)
   Noel instrumental in origination of this program in the mid-1950s while working in the Bureau of Personnel, pp. 111-112

Naval Personnel, Bureau of
  Established education program for enlisted personnel in mid-1950s, pp. 113-115; studies medical care for dependents, pp. 115-118; establishes moral leadership program, pp. 118-122, 129; studies officers' clubs, pp. 122-123; arranges conference of NATO chaplains, pp. 124-126

Naval Reserve, U.S.
  As avenue to U.S. Naval Academy in early 1930s, p. 3; Noel credits role of reservists in World War II, pp. 48-49; growth of Reserve programs after World War II spurs enlarged professional book publishing effort at U.S. Naval Institute, pp. 91-93

Naval Shiphandling
  Published by U.S. Naval Institute in 1955 to compete with a similar book co-authored the previous year by Noel, pp. 95-96

Naval Terms Dictionary
  Proposal to original publisher resulted in Noel's handling of this book for U.S. Naval Institute, p. 95

Naval War College
  Noel observed international law course here in order to implement a simplified version at U.S. Naval Academy in the early 1950s, pp. 97-98

The Netherlands
  Protestant chaplain from The Netherlands relies on U.S. to pay way for NATO chaplains' conference in the mid-1950s, p. 125; U.S. conference was the first time Protestant and Catholic chaplains from The Netherlands met socially, p. 126

New Orleans, USS (CA-32)
  Officers play tennis at Bar Harbor, Maine, in mid-1930s, p. 6

Night Operations
  Difficulty for Sixth Fleet service squadron in late 1950s, p. 145

Nimitz, Admiral Chester W., USN (USNA, 1905)
  As Assistant Chief of the Bureau of Navigation in mid-1930s, maneuvers tennis players for U.S.-Royal Navy tournament, pp. 5-6; appoints Admiral Spruance to replace Rear Admiral Halsey before Midway, p. 30; tells patrol wing commander to send only important messages on secret communications line, p. 32; met with all ship skippers as they passed through Hawaii, p. 40; sympathy for subordinates, p. 55; Noel preferred his suggestion for by-passing the Philippines to MacArthur's, p. 55; Noel calls on Nimitz when Lamson (DD-367) limps to Pearl Harbor after December 1944 kamikaze attack, pp. 66-67

Nimitz, Rear Admiral Chester W., Jr., USN (Retired) (USNA, 1936)
  Noel's classmate a success in business, pp. 5-6; recommends Noel for civilian job in early 1960s, p. 199

Niven, David
  The actor and his family become friends of the Noels at Villefranche in the early 1960s, pp. 178-179

Noel, Captain John V., Jr., USN (Retired) (USNA, 1936)
  Explanation of name and ancestors, pp. 1-2; 152; birth and youth, pp. 203; wife and children, pp. 11-15, 17, 22-23, 25-28, 33, 36, 45, 77-78, 82-85, 88, 90, 110, 124, 141-142, 149-152, 168-174, 177-183, 187-189, 206-207, 215, 222, 229-233, 236-237; hobbies, pp. 88-90; health, p. 90; as an author, pp. 90-97, 190-195, 202, 230; self-assessment, pp. 236-237; midshipman at U.S. Naval Academy (1932-1936), pp. 3-5; duty in Astoria (CA-34) (1936-1938), pp. 5-11; communications watch officer, staff Commander Scouting Force (1938-1940), pp. 10-15; duty in Sicard (DM-21) (1940-1944), pp. 15-43, 75; command of Lamson (DD-367) (1944-1945), pp. 43, 45-82; medals and commendations, pp. 75-77; duty in OpNav concerning surplus ship disposal (1945-1947), pp. 85-86; master's degree at Stanford (1947-1948), pp. 86-87, 94; planning officer, staff, Commander Amphibious Group One (1948-1950), pp. 87-90; instructor in navigation and seamanship at U.S. Naval Academy (1950-1953), pp. 90-98; executive officer, USS Rochester (CA-124) (1953-1954), pp. 48, 98-108; student, Industrial College of the Armed Forces (1954-1955), pp. 108-110; head of Personnel Plans Branch, Bureau of Naval Personnel (1955-1958), pp. 110-135; commanding officer, USS Altair (AKS-32) (1958-1959), pp. 137-153; senior aide to Assistant Secretary of the Navy for Personnel (1959-1961), pp. 157-167, 190; commanding officer, USS Springfield (CLG-7) (1961-1962), pp. 77, 168-177; naval attache, Paris (1962-1965), pp. 14, 180-189; retired in June 1965, pp. 199, 207, 221; post-retirement positions, pp. 210-230; work with French TV in documentary in 1966, pp. 234-236

Noel, Mary Hess
  Visits in-laws in Mexico in 1939, p. 11; meets husband in Bremerton in 1938, pp. 13-14; tribute by husband, pp. 14-15; in Hawaii during early part of World War II, pp. 17, 22-23, 25-26; flew to San Diego on Pan Am Clipper, pp. 27-28; ill-fated trip from California to Washington, D.C., in 1945, pp. 83-84; joins husband in Spain in 1958, pp. 150-152; letters from husband as new commanding officer of Springfield (CLG-7) in early 1961, pp. 169-176; in Paris as naval attache's wife in early 1960s, pp. 180-183, 187-189; joins husband in International Executive Service Corps in Morocco, pp. 218-219; buys home in Santa Fe, pp. 231-232

North Atlantic Treaty Organization (NATO)
  While working for the Bureau of Naval Personnel in the mid-1950s, Noel arranges a conference in the U.S. for NATO-member chaplains, pp. 124-126

O'Connor, Lieutenant John J., CHC, USN
  Influential in Navy's devising a moral leadership program in the mid-1950s, pp. 119-120

Officers' Clubs
  Bureau of Naval Personnel studies clubs with financial difficulties in the mid-1950s and finds "people problems," pp. 122-123

Ormoc Bay
  Lamson (DD-367) damaged during action here in December 1944, pp. 56-59, 65

Pan American Clipper
  Mary Noel flew from Hawaii to San Diego in 1942, pp. 26-28

Pay
  Poor quality of military pay tempted Noel to retire early, but he chose to stay in, p. 199

Pearl Harbor, Hawaii
  Reinforced with more ships in the late 1930s in response to Japanese threat, p. 12; Noel rules out Japanese attack in party conversation on 6 December 1941, pp. 16-17; Noel's recollections of 7 December 1941, pp. 17-20; shortcomings of Japanese attack, pp. 20-21; confusion generated by Japanese allowed into Hawaii under diplomatic immunity, pp. 21-22; positive aspects of attack, p. 24; four destroyers collide during exercise as part of pre-war training, pp. 24-25; Lamson (DD-367) crew given beer party when their ship limps to Pearl Harbor after December 1944 attack in the Philippines, p. 66; Noel goes to Hawaii in 1966 to film documentary for French TV, p. 234; See also: USS Pennsylvania (BB-38)

Pennsylvania, USS (BB-38)
  Quality of Japanese intelligence dooms this battleship at Pearl Harbor, pp. 18-20

Pershing Missiles
  Flaws in production reduced by zero defects program, based on a Navy moral leadership effort, pp. 121-122

Personnel
  See: Naval Personnel, Bureau of

Philippines
  Noel disagreed with strategy of invading the Philippines rather than go straight for Japan, p. 55; Lamson (DD-367) damaged in battle for Philippines off Ormoc in December 1944, pp. 56-59, 65; See also: Leyte Gulf

Portland, Oregon
  Extends great hospitality to Astoria (CA-34) in 1937, p. 8

Pride, Vice Admiral Alfred M., USN
   Popular as Commander Seventh Fleet in mid-1950s, p. 100

Proceedings, U.S. Naval Institute
   Noel serves as Professional Notes editor in early 1950s, p. 92; Noel writes about Rochester's "showing the flag" cruise in mid-1950s, p. 99; Noel writes about Defense Department in early 1960s, pp. 190-193, 195, 202

PT Boats
   Plan to tow PT boats into Attu to attack Japanese shipping dropped as unfeasible in late 1942, p. 34

Pueblo (AGER-2)
   Noel feels that if moral leadership had been implemented by the Navy in January 1968, when this ship was seized, the North Koreans would probably not have gotten all the secret material aboard, pp. 129-130, 197

Puget Sound Navy Yard
   Destroyer Lamson (DD-367) makes perilous approach and undergoes repairs in early 1945 after being damaged in battle, pp. 71-75, 79

Quarterdeck
   Noel feels a well-maintained quarterdeck is a mark of a good ship, pp. 133-134

Quinn, Captain John, USN   (USNA, 1928)
   Picks Noel as his executive officer in Rochester (CA-124) in 1953, p. 98; oversees reorganization in Rochester, p. 99; assessed by Noel, pp. 101-102, 104; buys silver service for Rochester, p. 104; handling of discipline cases, pp. 104-105; excellent pistol shot, pp. 105-106; highly regarded by Rochester crew, pp. 106-108

Reeves, Admiral John W., Jr., USN   (USNA, 1911)
   Persuades Secretary of the Navy Gates to implement a moral leadership program in mid-1950s, pp. 119-120

Refueling at Sea
   Rough sea conditions for the Sicard (DM-21) and Kaskaskia (AO-27) in the Aleutians in 1942, p. 35; tragedy refueling convoy during December 1944 typhoon, pp. 52-53; difficult refueling of Lamson (DD-367) by Iowa (BB-61) using phones after destroyer is damaged in December 1944 Leyte action, p. 63

Replenishment at Sea
   Altair (AKS-32) institutes underway helicopter replenishment in the late 1950s, pp. 137-140, 151

Rickover, Rear Admiral Hyman G., USN (USNA, 1922)
   Thwarted in effort to get engineers through enlisted education program in mid-1950s, p. 111; political intervention on his behalf concerning promotion, p. 163

Rivers, L. Mendel
   Noel considered going to Rivers when he was passed over by flag selection board in the late 1950s, pp. 162-163

Rochester, USS (CA-124)
   Noel evaluates two best officers in mid-1950s, p. 48; Noel selected to be executive officer while at U.S. Naval Academy in 1953, p. 98; ship's organization reworked in mid-1953, p. 99; show-the-flag cruise to Far East in 1953, p. 99; social activities, p. 100; good morale and quality of crew, pp. 101-102; Captain Quinn buys silver service for ship out of his own pocket, p. 104; crew given flexible paydays, pp. 106-107; high marks on important inspection, p. 107; See also: Captain John Quinn

Royal Navy
   Successful at tennis tournaments with U.S. Navy in Maine in 1930s, p. 6

Saluting
   Misunderstood by some young sailors, pp. 132-133

Santa Fe, New Mexico
   Description of work on Noels' home there, pp. 230-234

Savo Island, Battle of
   Noel feels earlier laying of minefields in the South Pacific could have prevented this costly August 1942 engagement, pp. 39, 41

Scouting Force Pacific
   Noel's duties as communications watch officer on staff in late 1930s, pp. 10-11

Selection Board
   Discussion of 1964 flag selection board that was instructed to pass over Noel, pp. 200-203

Seventh Fleet, U.S.
   Lamson (DD-367) supports landing and beach expansion in Leyte Gulf in mid-1944, pp. 50, 54, 56-57; Rochester (CA-124) serves as flagship of Commander Seventh Fleet in the mid-1950s, pp. 99-107

Shiphandling
   Book Noel co-authored in mid-1950s for another publisher results in rival book from U.S. Naval Institute, pp. 95-99

Sicard, USS (DM-21)
   As minelayer, still retained characteristics of destroyer, p. 15; during Japanese attack at Pearl Harbor, pp. 19-20; lays minefield in the Aleutians, pp. 33-34; escorts Kaskaskia (AO-27) under hazardous conditions, p. 35; trained as control vessel for amphibious landings around San Diego in 1943, p. 36; Noels host mint julep party for wardroom, pp. 36-37; collision with destroyer off Komandorski Island in May 1943, p. 37; repaired at Mare Island, pp. 38-39; main feed pump failed during patrol, p. 40

Sixth Fleet, U.S.
   Whole fleet replenishment practiced for Sixth Fleet in late 1950s, pp. 140-141, 151; Springfield (CLG-7) serves as flagship of Commander Sixth Fleet in the early 1960s, pp. 170-177

Smith, Captain Daniel F., Jr., USN (USNA, 1932)
   Noel gets command of cruiser Springfield (CLG-7) in 1961 through his detailer and former shipmate, Smith, p. 168

Smith, Vice Admiral Harold Page, USN (USNA, 1924)
   As Chief of the Bureau of Naval Personnel in the late 1950s, feud with Assistant Secretary of the Navy Jackson about formation of Judge Advocate General's Corps, pp. 157-158, 161, 201, 206; relationship with Noel, pp. 157-158, 161-162, 201; assessed as destroyer squadron commander towards the end of World War II, pp. 159-161

Soviet Union
   French mistrust of U.S. results in lost opportunity to gather intelligence on Soviets in the early 1960s, pp. 183-184

Spain
   Appeal to American Navy personnel and dependents, pp. 141-142, 150, 153; Altair (AKS-32) participates in charities for Spanish children, pp. 147-149; social life, pp. 150-152; historical significance, pp. 154-157; U.S. consul general in the late 1950s an alcoholic, pp. 141, 166; Noels build retirement home in Sotogrande, pp. 214-217, 230-231

Springfield, USS (CLG-7)
   Noel misses plane from Washington, D.C., and is late in reporting in to take command in March 1961, p. 169; Noel's letters to wife detail first days of command, including crew, port visits, and visitors, pp. 169-177; assessment of Noel's predecessor, Captain Boyle, pp. 172, 175; operations in rough water off Sicily, pp. 205-206

Spruance, Rear Admiral Raymond A., USN (USNA, 1907)
   Noel considers it good fortune that Spruance replaced Rear Admiral William Halsey before Midway action, pp. 29-30

Stanford University
   Noel excels while pursuing a master's degree here in 1947-1948, pp. 86-87

Surfing
   In Hawaii in the late 1930s, pp. 12-13; experience serves Noel well when abandoning ship during World War II, pp. 58-59

Suggestion Box
   Used in Rochester (CA-124) in the mid-1950s before it became de rigueur in Navy ships, p. 101; in Springfield (CLG-7) in the early 1960s, p. 176

Sylvester, Arthur
   Assistant Secretary of Defense for Public Affairs miffed when Noel published article about Defense Department in Proceedings without running it by him, p. 192

Tennis
   Noel plays on U.S. Naval Academy team in 1930s, p. 4; U.S. Navy-Royal Navy tournament in mid-1930s, p. 6; mid-1930s Astoria (CA-34) skipper's enthusiasm for, p. 7; Noel plays with tennis greats at Monte Carlo Country Club in spring of 1962, pp. 177-178; Noel plays in Paris while a naval attache in the early 1960s, pp. 188-189

TFX
   Secretary of Defense McNamara criticized for lack of sophistication in trying to force Navy and Air Force to share plane to suit disparate functions, p. 195

Thomas, Charles B.
   Supports suggestion to hold conference of NATO chaplains as Secretary of the Navy in the mid-1950s, p. 125

Tokyo Express
   Noel feels earlier use of minefields could have curtailed the Tokyo Express' tremendous damage at Savo Island in August 1942, p. 39

Tulagi
   Officers' club established in late 1943, p. 41

Turner, Captain Richmond Kelly, USN   (USNA, 1908)
   Leadership style as commanding officer of Astoria (CA-34) in mid-1930s, pp. 9-10

Typhoons
   Despite danger of typhoons in South Pacific during World War II, they provided a welcome relief from enemy aircraft, pp. 50-51; U.S. Navy unfamiliar with typhoons before World War II, pp. 51-52; ships lost refueling in December 1944, pp. 52-53; Lamson (DD-367) weathers double typhoon near Iwo Jima in 1945, p. 81

Underway Replenishment
  Carried out by the supply ship Altair (AKS-32) in the late 1950s, pp. 137-141, 151; See also: Refueling at Sea

Uniform Code of Military Justice
  New code caused controversy in late 1950s, pp. 158-159, 161

Villefranche, France
  The Noels enjoyed sailing and their neighbors here in the early 1960s, pp. 178-179; Noels study French here prior to duty as naval attache in Paris, pp. 179-180

Vogeley, Commander Theodore R., USN (USNA, 1933)
  Skipper of the Flusser (DD-368) loans Noel clothes after he is rescued from Leyte Gulf in December 1944, p. 60

Washington, D.C.
  After a precarious trip to Washington, Noel enjoys duty there at the end of World War II, pp. 84-86

Watch Officer's Guide
  Noel's first writing endeavor with U.S. Naval Institute from the early 1950s, pp. 91-92

WAVES
  Noel impressed by Navy women he dealt with in various government offices, pp. 134-136

Wentworth, Commodore Ralph S., USN (Retired) (USNA, 1912)
  Instigates revision of Knight's Modern Seamanship in the early 1950s, p. 94

Wouk, Herman
  Paints realistic picture of destroyer life during the war in The Caine Mutiny, pp. 42-43

Yorktown, USS (CV-5)
  Salvage tug skipper who hears news of Midway battle and damage to Yorktown during poker game at Pearl Harbor correctly anticipates orders to go to her aid, p. 31

Yugoslavian Navy
  Invites Noel to heavy drinking party with potent native liquor at Split in the early 1960s, but brief illness prevents his attendance, pp. 175-176

Zero Defects
  Program sold to Navy by civilian firm to alleviate flaws in missile, aircraft, and armament production was based in Navy's own moral leadership program from the mid-1950s, pp. 121-122

Zumwalt, Admiral Elmo R., Jr., USN (USNA, 1943)
　　Noel felt short-lived moral leadership program he helped
　　institute in the mid-1950s would have dove-tailed nicely with
　　Chief of Naval Operations Zumwalt's initiatives in the early
　　1970s, pp. 131, 198

Zuska, Captain Joseph MC, USN
　　Set up a rehabilitation center for Navy alcoholics in the mid-
　　1960s, p. 166

Appendices to

Reminiscences

of

Captain John Vavasour Noel, Jr.

U.S. Navy (Retired)

DD367/A16-3　　　　　U.S.S. LAMSON (DD367)

Serial: 04

22 December 1944

CONFIDENTIAL

From: Commanding Officer.
To :   Commander in Chief, U.S. Fleet.
Via :   (1) Commander Task Unit 78.3.10.
            (2) Commander Task Group 78.3.
            (3) Commander SEVENTH Fleet.

Subject: Action Report - BAYBAY Operation, 5 - 6 December 1944.

Reference: (a) PacFlt Conf. Ltr. 2CL-44.

Enclosure: (A) Two (2) Anti-aircraft Action Reports.

    1.   This report is written entirely from memory as all records were lost during the ORMOC operation on 7 December when the USS LAMSON was struck by an enemy plane.

    2.   On 5 December 1944 DesDiv NINE consisting of USS FLUSSER, with ComDesRon FIVE as CTU78.3.10, USS DRAYTON, USS LAMSON, and the USS SHAW was ordered to escort nine LSM's and three LCI's to BAYBAY, LEYTE for the purpose of supplying Army troops. The force was to arrive off BAYBAY at 2300 5 December and be off the beach by 0100 6 December.

    The force got underway with the USS LAMSON as Fighter Director ship. Although the operation order of CTG78.3 stated that "Air cover has been requested" it was only after the most earnest entreaties had been made via the MT MCKINLEY to the Army Control station on 2530 kcs. (interfighter director net) that a combat air patrol was sent out. The Army did not seem to know anything about the operation and it was only the initiative and cooperation of the MT MCKINLEY after the time and date group of the mailgram operation order had been forwarded that produced results. Needless to say, by the time air cover had been arranged for over a period of about four hours by voice over 2530 kcs., the enemy had a fairly good idea of what was going on. This method of arranging for air cover is not recommended. The C.A.P. of four P38's arrived on station about 1500 and departed at dusk. Four F6F's arrived at dusk and remained until after dark.

    The convoy hugged the coastline all the way, sometimes being as close as 700 yards off the beach. On the way numerous native craft contacts kept Combat busy plotting and evaluating. The arrival off BAYBAY was made without incident at 2245. Due to confusion and apparent misunderstanding, the Army was not prepared to unload and it was 0015 before the operations were progressing satisfactorily.

- 1 -

DD367/A16-3
Serial: 04

U.S.S. LAMSON (DD367)

22 December 1944

CONFIDENTIAL

Subject: Action Report - BAYBAY Operation, 5 - 6 December 1944.

During the unloading the USS LAMSON lay to about 3000 yards off the beach. The night was dark and clear with the moon about 6 days past full. A night fighter controlled by the Army Control station patrolled overhead at 10,000 feet and hence proved worthless in the snooper attacks which followed. Since we were unable to give an accurate estimate of the altitude of our bogies, the night fighters could make no interceptions. From the time of our arrival until 0230 a Black Cat (almost always picked up by Sugar George radar) caused many false alerts because its IFF was so weak it would not indicate until the plane was in as close as 8000 yards. Sometimes it even had to be identified visually. At about 0300 a low flying plane with running lights crossed our stern from port to starboard and dropped a large bomb about 500 yards off our quarter. Through the USS MT. McKINLEY in San Pedro Bay, we asked Army Control to have our night fighter turn off his running lights in order to avoid any confusion.

From the time of dropping the first bomb through the remainder of the night we were continuously harassed by snoopers and our own Black Cat. Plots were relayed to Army Control through the USS MT. McKINLEY with always the same question relayed back, "What Angels?" It is remembered we once answered Angels four to nine and once Angels two. Other than that we could only answer Angels low. This was because of our landlocked position plus the fact that most snoopers came in very low allowing only a few plots. About 0200 we picked up two bogies coming in from the West, range 17,000 yards on the SG. When in to 8000 yards the closest contact showed the familiar weak IFF of our Black Cat. At 6000 yards the bogie and friendly changed course to 010° and disappeared from the SG scope, still flying parallel courses about 4000 yards apart. This was the last we saw of our Black Cat.

At 0245 another bomb was dropped 1000 yards astern. At 0300 the convoy began to form for the return trip. At 0330 a plane made a near miss off the stern of the USS DRAYTON. Then the snooper went down the center of the convoy strafing and receiving machine fire return from the LCI's and LSM's. At about 0400 after passing QUATROS Island we saw a snooper vainly trying to sink HIMUQUITAN Island with two bombs.

Our urgent request during the night for an early dawn C.A.P. was granted in the form of four F6F's whom we contacted simultaneously with the very first hint of dawn. At about fifteen minutes before sunrise the C.A.P. accidentally intercepted a bogie at the same time first contact was picked up on the SC 15 miles to the

- 2 -

A

DD367/A16-3　　　　　　U.S.S. LAMSON (DD367)
Serial: 04
　　　　　　　　　　　　　　　　　　22 December 1944
CONFIDENTIAL

Subject:　　　Action Report - BAYBAY Operation, 5 - 6 December 1944.

Northwest over land.

　　　From then until we were halfway up the SURIGAO STRAITS we were not molested. At about 1100 with four P38's for C.A.P., Control suddenly spotted twelve to fifteen Vals almost directly overhead at an altitude of 8000 feet. The sky was partially overcast, visibility fair. The enemy must have come in low over LEYTE until in the straits then climbed through the clouds until overhead. The fact that they dove instead of coming in low is the only reason that only one LSM was sunk, one destroyer, the USS DRAYTON, and two other LSM's were damaged. One plane barely missed the USS SHAW and the P38's got three others. At least seven Vals were seen to hit the water or ships. All attacks were suicidal and no bombs were seen to drop. We immediately received twelve more fighters, but the remaining enemy planes, if any, had left.

　　　At this time we were joined by the USS MUGFORD and the USS LAVALLETTE, who were patrolling the SURIGAO STRAITS. The USS SHAW escorted the USS DRAYTON and all except three of the remaining undamaged LSM's and LCI's went on ahead with four of our P38's as cover. The remaining four destroyers circled the survivors and damaged LSM's during rescue operations. It took about two hours to pick up all survivors and transfer the injured to destroyers for treatment. This vessel sent its motor whale boat to an LSM under tow for three patients and at the same time received an LSM alongside to transfer four more patients.

　　　We were barely underway again when our SC contacted a small bogie fifteen miles to the West over DINAGAT. Of our sixteen P38's eight remained, as the original four had returned to base and the other four were covering the damaged USS DRAYTON. Four planes were vectored out at 5000 feet on the strength of the one plot. The next plot showed the bogies on a westerly course. Control spotted two Haps on that bearing at ten miles simultaneously with the SC operators report of a merged plot. However the P38's were too high to intercept. With visual information relayed to Control through the evualator the FDO did manage to intercept one of the Haps and get him splashed. The other Hap started a run on the USS MUGFORD but a P38 on its tail caused it to break off. The Hap than crossed in front of the convoy just off the water and circled TAYTAY POINT, LEYTE, where it was seen to jettison its bomb and was lost momentarily by both P38's and the ships. It than came back in low and fast hitting the USS MUGFORD at the base of her stack on the port side and causing her to lose all headway. Again we received a reinforcement of eight P38's in a hurry but again they were to late.

- 3 -

A

DD367/A16-3   U.S.S. LAMSON (DD367)
Serial: 04
                                          22 December 1944
CONFIDENTIAL

Subject: Action Report - BAYBAY Operation, 5 - 6 December 1944.

- -

Shortly afterward at about 1530 the USS FLUSSER and the USS LAMSON were relieved by the USS SMITH and the USS CONYNGHAM and proceeded to San Pedro Bay without further incident. During this operation the importance of the assistance given us by the USS MT. MCKINLEY in San Pedro Bay cannot be over emphasized. At no time were we in direct communication with the tower on the beach controlling our C.A.P. The USS MT. MCKINLEY relayed all information, gave much valuable information herself, and acted as a perfect coordinator. Except for a brief period when we were directly south of LEYTE we always heard her five by five, although from dawn until dusk of 6 December the IFD circuit was partially jammed with music and C.W.

It is evident that enemy planes are homing on our SG radar. While off the west coast of LEYTE bogies would be detected at thirty to seventy miles heading directly toward us. At about ten miles they would seem to lose the beam and would then circle at low altitude until they could sight us visually. This seems to indicate that the enemy is using a radar receiver which indicates direction by the intensity of the incoming signal. When close to our vessels the signal is to strong all around to afford any detection of bearing; in other words the enemy radar receiver is saturated. The securing of all air search radars is recommended at night on the theory that high flying planes cannot see you and low flying planes will be detected by SG radar.

The following observations on fighter direction and suicide plane attacks are the result of this and previous operations and were firmly substantiated by the ORMOC BAY operation which immediately followed. Traditional fighter direction dependent on radar detection alone is not possible in such restricted waters as those around the PHILIPPINES. A combination of visual and radar direction is called for based on numerous alert, well trained air lookouts supervised by an officer who can make quick decisions and estimates of bogie altitudes. Most suicide plane attacks are now coming in at masthead level, using land whenever possible to mask the approach. This necessitates placing part of the C.A.P. at very low altitudes, breaking up the usual four plane division into sections or even units of a single plane. It is recognized that the four plane division is the normal tactical unit of Army fighters and was so designed to afford maximum effectiveness against fighters. Since Japanese fighter oppositions seems to be seldom encountered in any strength it is suggested that four planes are too many to be in one group if the C.A.P. consists only of one or two divisions.

DD367/A16-3   U.S.S. LAMSON (DD367)
Serial: 04
                                          22 December 1944
CONFIDENTIAL

Subject: Action Report - BAYBAY Operation, 5 - 6 December 1944.

   It is not recommended that destroyers be used in an operation of this kind. PT boats would have been ample protection against possible enemy PT boats. If the landing craft had traveled only at night very close to the beach and had run ashore and camouflaged themselves with nets and palm branches during the day it is believed that no losses would have been incurred.

                                          J.V. NOEL, Jr.

Copy to:
    CominCh (AdvAirMail).
    CinCPac.
    ComDesPacFlt.

A

THE START OF THE KOREAN WAR

In May and early June, 1950, elements of Amphibious Group One (RADM James Doyle, USN) arrived in Japan to conduct amphibious training of units of the 8th Army. The naval forces involved were very small; the Mt. McKinley (AGC 7), flagship, the George Clymer, an APA and the Union, an AKA. Aboard the Mt. McKinley were Tactical Air Control Squadron One and a small ANGLICO unit. A TACRON is organized to train the air support personnel of a projected amphibious landing in the techniques of close support of assault troops and also to control, during the landing, all aircraft in the objective area, particularly close support aircraft. ANGLICO means Air, Naval Gunfire, Liaison Company. It has the triple mission of coordinating, for Commander Landing Force, the air Support, the naval gunfire and the artillary fire after responsibility for the assault has passed from Commander Attack Force to Commander Landing Force ashore. There was also, aboard the amphibious ships, a Troop Training Unit of Marine officers headed by Colonel Ed Forney, USMC. These TTU personnel were skilled and experienced in amphibious warfare. Their mission was to instruct the units of the 8th Army in amphibious organization, loading debarkation, communications and the other special techniques that an assault force must have.

Admiral Doyle and his staff were seasoned amphibians, having conducted training exercises for years off California, Alaska and the Hawaiian islands. ComPhibGru One had the largest purely operational staff in the Pacific Fleet. Captain John Mcn. Taylor, USN (now admiral) was Chief of Staff. I was the Planning Officer, acted as assistant operations and was the tactical officer and navigator underway. I should have mentioned above that an important member of the amphibious group listed above was Captain Gus Roane, now in OpNav, who was ComTransDiv 12 and a strong right hand man for Admiral Doyle.

It was fortunate that this small but skilled amphibious unit was in Japan when the Korean war started. We were engaged in the first of four training excercises off Chigasaki Beach near Tokyo (Yokosuka) on 25 June. First the Air Force planes, then the 7th Fleet destroyers and finally the Landing Force were recalled to more vital duties. On July first the Mt McKinley, Clymer, and Union were ordered to Sasebo to carry part of the 24th Inf. Div. to Korea. After a voyage marked by the sighting of a Russian submarine which was tracking us, we arrived at Sasebo just before dark on 3 July. By that time most of the 24th had been ferried across the Straits of Tsushima by Scajap LST. These were demilitarized LST turned over to the Japanese for merchant ship use. They were completely manned by Japanese.

On the morning of 4 July Admiral Doyle and seven members of his staff were ordered to Tokyo and we flew up in a PBM that had come in from a routine ASW patrol. Arriving at Cincfe headquarters at the Dai Ichi building that night we were given a large office and directed to make plans for the immediate landing of the First Cavalry Division at INCHON. Target date was 18 July. That meant that the transports would have to leave on the 15th and the much slower LST on the 14th. This involved using Shimonoseki Straits which had been open only to Japanese shipping because of the mine hazards.

Tokyo-Yokosuka was the staging area. While the Navy, including the invaluable TTU, made feverish efforts to load the untrained First Calvalry Division, the question of whether or not to land at Inchon was debated on the highest echelons. The original (4 July) decision to land there was based on the assumption that the reinforced South Koreans would be able to hold a line not too far south of Seoul. The expression used at the time was that this line was the anvil upon which the First Calvery Division would, landing at Inchon, hammer and destroy the North Koreans. These rosy dreams were quickly shattered by the rout of the South Koreans and our own forces with them. On 10 July General MacArthur decided on Pohang Dong on the east coast of the peninsula. Meanwhile, the First Calvery Division was heaved bag and baggage into the makeshift shipping which we had scraped up. First, of course, we had the G. Clymer and the Union. Then we were able to get several MSTS AKA that happened to be in the area at the end of their cargo run from the states. There AKA had no assault boats, boat crews or even skids for assault boats. The boat skids were made and installed by the shipyard at Yohosuka, the boats (LCM, LCVP) were obtained from the Army, and the boat's crews were flown out from the Amphibious Base at Coronado. LSU (World War II) (LCT) were pulled out of mothballs at Yokosaka and fitted for towing to Korea, each astern an LST. The LST were Scajap, Japanese manned, no guns, no military radio. Fortunately a former LST expert from Okinawa days, Captain Norman Sears, had arrived to relieve the Chief of Staff. He was given a handfull of junior officers and a few enlisted communication specialists and directed to take charge of his collection of landing ships, load them and get them to Pohang. This he did despite a typhoon enroute and a few parted LSU towing bridles. His Japancese crews were able and skilled in dodging bad weather. Most of the LST skippers had formerly commanded large Japanese ships. They knew all the typhoon refuges.

The air and gunfire support for the landing was furnished by the Air Force and by Admiral Strubles 7th Fleet. Both sent liaison officers to our headquarters. The 7th Fleet representative was Commander Fred H. White, USN now working for Captain Sam Morrison. /We had to assume that Pohang would be in enemy hands by 16 July and make our detailed air and gunfire support plans accordingly. On the day of the landing 7th Fleet planes were overhead. But fortunately we still owned Pohang and most of the men and supplies were landed at the docks inside the inner harbor in the town. This was fortunate because our beach intelligence turned out to be very poor, and the beaches we had planned to land on were not at all satisfactory.

Upon the completion of the landing the amphibious units returned to the Tokyo area and ComPhibGu One and his staff commenced planning for Inchon. I was relieved in August and returned to the States, my normal tour of sea duty having been completed. My bout with polio started at this time - I was hospitalized soon after arrival in Coronado.

To understand how the outbreak of the Korean War affected the Navy it is necessary to understand that Commander Naval Forces, Far East, Vice Admiral Joy, USN had a small staff and very few ships. His staff was not an operational one in the sense that it was not prepared for handling large numbers of ship movements with all the attendant communications. ComNavfe had a small staff which operated the few destroyers which patrolled Japanese waters. When the war broke ComNavfe was snowed under, messages piled up days behind and the few coding personnel soon collapsed. Our lesson there was that in critical areas our staffs must be set up to expand very rapidly. Similar communication difficulties were experienced at Radio Guam which at one time was 48 hours behind on priority traffic. A second weakness at one apparent was personnel in ships. The Amphibious ships and the 7th Fleet ships were operating so far below even peacetime allowance that ships could not man all their battle stations. If Russian Air-Sea power had been used against us it would have been very rough.

There were many small things that might be termed useful lessons of the Korean War providing that we really learned them. One was the fallacy of carrying MSTS AKA on the books as AKA. They were not assault cargo ships because they had no assault boats and assault boat crews nor even adequate hatch crews. They were pressed into service as described above but should have been listed as AK.

Perhaps I am out of my field in this but from what I observed myself at headquarters, General McArthur's forces were not prepared for combat, much less trained for amphibious warfare: They had not trained in close air support of ground troops for one thing.

I hope this somewhat rambiling account of my impressions may be of some value. In addition to the officers I have named herein I could supply the names of others who are particularly well informed on certain phases of our amphibious efforts. I am also enclosing a letter I started to write home but never mailed.

A Letter from Korea

We are lying at anchor in the small bay off Pohang-Dong. The ships are dispersed waiting for "Grace" a capricious typhoon that seems reluctant to commit herself to a definite path. The LST's are moored together behind the breakwater. Two days ago we landed the First Calvery Division, MacArthurs own. It was a curious and hectic expedition, conceived, executed and sailed in 10 days, labelled top secret but common knowledge around Tokyo. There was even an army band playing Anchors Aweigh on the dock as the flagships moved out into the stream. The score of correspondants aboard, most of them war hardened veterans like Carl Mydans of Life-Time, were amazed at the lack of security and censorship.

On the 25th of June we were peacefully engaged in Lex one, an exercise for the amphibious training of units of the 8th Army. The rehearsal landing came off quite well but two days later we had to execute the landing without destroyers or Air Force aircraft. There important components of every landing were suddenly diverted to more important tasks.

Upon our return to Yokosuka we were alerted to depart at once for Sasebo to lift the 24th of InfDiv to Korea. Upon arrival we learned that the 24th had already moved across the straits by LST and the admiral and seven members of his staff were ordered to fly to Tokyo. This we did in a PBM, passing over Hiroshima on the way. Upon arrival Tokyo in the afternoon of 4 July we were shown our office in the Dai Itchi building and given chits that entilled us to very small rooms at a comfortable hotel.

The next nine days were controlled pandemonum. We planned and loaded for an assault landing of a division, an operation which normally requires three months. On 13 July the operation order was printed and that day the LST departed. A few days later the big ships left.

Mydans was my roommate for the trip and was an interesting fellow. I had met him briefly before the war at Pearl Harbor and it turned out that he was present at Ormoc in 1944 when my ship the Lamson, was badly damaged by a Kamikazi.

He had just come out of Korea a few days before and he had no good news at all. He had seen our soldiers outnumbered and outgunned with nothing to effectively fight the big Russian tanks. He had seen our men leave their wounded buddies behind-a very bitter thing to contemplate because the enemy is taking few prisoners.

2 April 1961

INSTALLMENT I

This is the first of a series of short accounts of my cruise in the U.S.S. SPRINGFIELD. They will be written in rather general terms so that I can use them as enclosures in letters to friends and relatives.

I took command at sea between Beirut and Athens 28 March, the day before we were due to arrive in Athens. The crew, officers and men, with marine guard forward, fell in on the fantail and the brief, traditional naval ceremony was held. The Chaplain opened with an invocation. Captain Boyle introduced Admiral Anderson who spoke glowingly of the fine performance of his new flagship in shaking down; Captain Boyle read his orders and I read mine. After brief remarks by Captain Boyle the SPRINGFIELD Flag was presented to me as a symbol of my new authority. I said to Captain Boyle, with a salute, "I relieve you, Sir."

I then repaired to the bridge where I remained until we anchored in Athens the next morning. During a clear and pleasant night, I made the usual trips between my sea cabin and the bridge to assist the Officer-of-the-Deck in clearing the merchant traffic that is always fairly heavy in the approaches to a major sea port. The two deck divisions forward, the 1st and the 2nd, were up at 2 a.m. rigging the canvas awnings and side curtains that had been scrubbed and dried and furled the day before. Also a great deal of dried salt had to be removed topside and a general topside scrubbing down and washing of paint-work ensued.

Our first duty upon entering Athens harbor was the firing of a 21-gun salute, which we did approaching the saluting battery ashore at 15 knots with the crew at quarters. When 2000 yards from the beach and while still saluting, the ship turned to the right and approached its anchorage. The boat was dropped quickly and went in for the Naval Attache, who brought out the details of the final arrangements for a very busy day. The highlight of the day's ceremonies was the reception aboard ship of the Royal Family of Greece for luncheon.

Anchoring was followed by a series of arrivals and departures with Commander Sixth Fleet making his calls ashore on various dignitaries (military and civilian) and these calls being returned aboard ship. All of this, of course, was done with the normal honors, sideboys, guard of honor, etc. A few moments after the last official had left, about 1230, the word was passed "man the rail." As the royal barge approached the saluting battery was directed to commence firing. No warning was given to Mrs. Anderson and her party who were inside, directly under a saluting gun, and the first shot startled them considerably. This led to a full explanation of the origin of the expression "son-of-a-gun."

The King and Queen of Greece came aboard accompanied by the Crown Prince, two princesses, and their court. After a most pleasant lunch the royal party inspected the missile battery and other parts of the ship. They are a most attractive family - alert, simple in manner, intelligent, and active. All of them race their own small sailboats inside the harbor, Dragons, and the Crown Prince won the gold medal in this class at the Olympics at Naples last year.

The royal party departed with much pomp and ceremony and I had a chance to nap for an hour or so before going to dinner at the Naval Attache's, Captain Berg. There we met many attractive people. On my way to dinner, I stopped at the Royal Greek Yacht Club for a few moments and enjoyed the spectacular sight of a full moon rising over the SPRINGFIELD which was ablaze with her "Med Lights."

The next morning was full of ship's business and much coming and going of old friends and unit commanders present who attended the usual port briefing. I accompanied VADM Anderson and Hank Monroe, his C/S, to a luncheon laid on by the Greek Navy at their base here. It was a most pleasant affair with many warm toasts to the brotherhood of free men, Greek-American friendship, and the strong ties that bound the Sixth Fleet and her NATO Ally, Greece, together. These Greeks are very sturdy fellows and good people to have on our side. I learned at dinner how important their gallant stand against the Italians was in WW II. By diverting the Germans from their move into Southern Russia, Hitler's entire timetable for his assault on Russia was disrupted, fatally as it turned out. The Greeks are very proud, and well may they be, of the famous "OHI" (No) which they said to the Italians.

After lunch I took LTJG Carter to the Athens Tennis Club and played tennis for an hour. Then back to the ship, shuffled a few papers, and off to a theatre party given by the Bergers. He is the Charge who is the senior State Department official in Greece during the Ambassador's absence. We saw a dreadful Tennessee William's play, the "Glass Menagerie," starring Helen Hayes. It seemed somehow in very poor taste to impose such a poor example of American art on these noble Greeks. The King and Queen were also at the theatre; their box adjoined our front row seats. After the theatre we had a most pleasant supper at the Bergers and arrived back at the ship at 3 a.m.

Friday was relatively quiet. I played tennis briefly with a young officer and went to the Yacht Club for a beer. The rest of the day and evening was devoted to learning about my new command.

Saturday morning was devoted to personnel inspection. The crew looked better than it had last week. Then to the FORRESTAL after lunch to a reception for the people of Athens. From there to the ship and then later to another reception, this time at the house of one of the Naval Attache's. All of these are command performances. From the party I went to Shore Patrol Headquarters where I joined a police inspector for an inspection of the local hot spots. Every night a senior officer is charged with taking a look at the liberty situation ashore and checking on how the Shore Patrol was doing. The Athens nightclubs were not too bad; the fan dancers were young women of heroic proportions. The joints along the waterfront of Piraeus were most sordid.

Back to the ship at 1 a.m. for a few hours sleep until it was time to go to the Easter sunrise service on Mars Hill near the Acropolis, where St. Paul addressed the people, opening with "Ye Men of Athens."

Easter Sunday was uneventful, but busy. In the afternoon the Chaplain and I played tennis, had a large beer at the Yacht Club, and returned to the ship.

Tomorrow we sail for Split, fueling from the MISSISINEWA as soon as we clear the harbor.

INSTALLMENT II

Athens, Greece, to Split, Yugoslavia, to Corfu, Greece

The weather was beautiful as we weighed anchor in Phaleron Bay, near Athens, and stood out to sea. My first shiphandling at sea was fueling from the U.S.S. MISSISSINEWA that morning. It was interesting and went off well. Two days later we arrived at Split after perfect weather around the Peloponnesus and up the Adriatic. By radio we received a berth assignment inside which was a bit disquieting because our chart did not show enough water. We met the Naval Attache (who had come down from Belgrade) and the pilot offshore and both assured us that there was enough water inside the harbor for us to enter. We made our approach, fired our salutes and slipped in the harbor and alongside the quay. It was my first landing and went quite well. The Admiral sent up a "Well Done" from the Flag Bridge. A hectic morning of calls followed and then we went to a luncheon given by the Chief of Naval Operations of the Yugoslav Navy. It was a pleasant, but rather drawn-out affair, and having been up since 0300 I was glad to get a short nap before going off again. The next event was a reception at the Officer's Club where we sat on a terrace overlooking the harbor and watched the sun go down and the lights go on.

Back to the ship for an hour and then to a dinner given for VADM Anderson by Ambassador and Mrs. Rankin. The dinner was pleasant; I sat next to a female dairy engineer, manager of a large milk-processing plant. We discussed books - she knew of Pasternack's poetry, but not of "Dr. Zhivago." Before dinner we talked about the differences between Russian and Yugoslav Communism. One of the major differences is that only a few of the Yugoslav peasants belong to collective farms. Another is that in Russia all major projects are State controlled and directed; in Yugoslavia the same form of socialism exists, but as a local project, peculiar to a region or district.

The next day, victim of a 48-hour bug, I missed a great lamb eating and slivovitz toasting affair given on the nearby island of Brach by the Navy. We had a large reception on board in the late afternoon, for which I arose from by bunk, and all went well. Felt fine next day and went sightseeing around the market place at 0645. Colorful peasant types, but not very exciting. This is a really poor country. At 1230 VADM Anderson had a stag luncheon on the foc'sle for about 30 people. Gave the American Consul General a bundle of U.S. celery for his ailing wife who dotes on the stuff which is unobtainable here. Underway at 1500, backed clear into the tiny basin and stirred up a good deal of mud. Cranked on 25 knots and arrived at Corfu the next morning after a pleasant cruise down the Adriatic in a flat calm; a bright, starlit night.

Corfu is a lovely place, dominated by huge, ruined castles. This was Greek Easter weekend and we all went ashore early to see a procession. A local Saint, his features visible behind glass, was carried along the streets in a long colorful parade. At 1100 the streets were cleared and there was a great throwing down of large clay pots from upper storey windows. This is supposed to bring luck -- I was unable to learn more. In the afternoon, after the usual calls were made and returned, I had the Irving Johnsons aboard with their guests. Their new 50' ketch, the Yankee, was alongside the pier near the boat landing. Mary and I had visited them in their first Yankee, a large brigantine, in Honolulu in 1939.

A reception by the Mayor ended the day's activities and I was glad to turn in and secure. Sunday, after church aboard, we went to a Greek Navy reception at noon. It was Easter, of course, and to the Greeks this is the holiday.

After the reception, where we saw native dancing and had lamb roasted on a spit outdoors, a group of us drove to a small cove on the other side of the island. There we swam, climbed a nearby hill and ate lobster. The water was cold and very clear and the lobsters, longusta really, were delicious.

Back to the ship and our last event in Corfu, a dinner for 25 in the Admiral's Cabin. I sat next to the wife of a Greek shipowner and across from the senior Greek Naval officer here. Not very sparkling conversation.

Underway at 1100 Monday, 10 April for a week of operations involving the whole Fleet.

17 April 1961

INSTALLMENT III

First real Fleet Operations and Villefranche.

The first day underway was easy but the next morning at our dawn rendezvous with the carrier life became hectic. We could not find the carrier at first, she was about 35 miles south of the rendezvous point, and as we closed at 25 knots, head on, she asked us not to join because she was starting a run in for replenishment. We first went alongside the ALTAIR (AKS-32), my old ship - it was grand to see old friends. Mike Kenefick said that Annie was expecting Mary in Barcelona in June. From Dick Colbert, the skipper, I heard the news that he had orders to the Cruiser BOSTON.

All that day we made the rounds, picking up our ammo, fuel, food and stores. Finally learned how to make a good approach at high speed and close in as well. Tuesday night we joined the carrier and her destroyers for night steaming. It was quite an experience for the first time, boiling around at 25 knots like a destroyer. We had a few tense moments - my people are still a bit green. Once I had started a turn towards the carrier from a position on her beam when she turned towards me. Trouble on the primary tactical circuit at this time did not make things easier. Finally we settled down for the night and I had a few hours sleep. The next day included more dashing around and included a firepower show by the carrier. ADMS Brown and Clarke heloed over to spend the night and I was asked to dinner in the Flag Cabin. Fortunately I could accept; we had a few hours of quiet steaming. It was a farewell for CINCSOUTH and COMSTRIKFORSOUTH who retire soon. Captain Harry Hull was in the party and it was great seeing him again. ADM Brown occupied my inport cabin.

The night's operation did not become really trying until sometime after dark. We were passing through the Straits of Sicily, northwest of Malta, where all of the eastern Mediterranean and Middle East sea traffic funnels through. We dodged back and forth, turning together while in formation, avoiding merchant ship and fishermen. No sleep that night except for cat naps "all standing" in my chair. I tried sitting in the Chart Room abaft the bridge for 40 winks but the recording paper on the fathometer started to smolder and had filled the place full of smoke before we found the source.

The next morning, Thursday, we heloed all the VIP's back to the carrier where a COD plane would fly them back to Naples. It is no mean feat of necromancy to stay close to the carrier, which is conducting flight operations, routine at 28 knots, and at the same time get the helo ready for take off. True wind over the deck has to be very low for the helo to be able to engage its rotors safely, yet the VIP's must have a short hop to the CVA. All this done on a time schedule too. Well, such are the duties of a Flag Captain. Sometimes in port I feel like a disgusting free loader but I believe I earn my social rewards.

Installment IV

Villefranche - with a few days at sea

If there is a mariners' paradise today it is Villefranche. Only those in the South Seas described by Melville in Typee could compete with it. A small, almost landlocked bay, surrounded by steep, luxuriant hills shelter the ship from all but southerly winds. The climate is mild, the scenery superb and the girls plentiful and apparently friendly. Where they come from is somewhat mysterious but every man going ashore seems to find a friend and my liberty party of 500 men disappears without a trace into the medieval rabbit warrens of the old city. Walking through the town, as I did the second day in port, I could hear rock and roll and young voices raised in song; the town is full of little bars and bistros, all alive with bluejackets who find their joint and call it home. Many of the groups such as the signal gang and divisions identify themselves with their favorite bar, support it and even defend it against outsiders.

Now that the weather is warm the beaches are full of bluejackets as well. Some of them hire the odd little pedal catamarans and pedal out to the ship on their afternoon off. If accompanied by a girl in a bikini they attract considerable attention. The married men and officers also enjoy this beautiful and relaxed spot.

I spent 10 days working aboard ship (we were having work done by the tender anchored off nearby Beaulieu) and househunting. Found a lovely little villa and relaxed but found out later that the owner was returning so the lease I had signed was worthless. During this period the generals revolted in Algeria and civil war in France seemed imminent. Despite my messages and telephone calls to Mary to come by way of Spain instead of Paris, that wise girl kept her head, kept to her original plans and came thru Paris on schedule.

On 27 April we went to sea for a few days, participating in an amphibious landing on the southwestern coast of Sardinia. Our gunfire support was simulated and it was rather routine until we returned on 29 April to pick up our 30 Marines who had been ashore working out in field exercises. It was squally and blowing up to 40 knots when we took them aboard by helo. The Marine helo pilots did a grand job under most difficult conditions and we were all much relieved to have them back safely.

On 2 May Mary and Joy arrived and I had a family again. It was wonderful. We dashed about seeing people and people kept coming by the hotel with flowers and/or champagne and it was very pleasant. We sailed just before daylight on 4 May. I returned to the ship at midnight and was amused by the men who brought their wives and girls along in the bumboats that chugged out to the ship. Songs were sung and much gaity prevailed as the girls said goodbye and returned to the landing. These little passenger boats are a Villefranche institution and have been for many years. They are run by old men who operate the single cylinder engine while a passenger gravely handles the tiller.

An example of CO earning his pay was fueling Thursday afternoon. COMCARDIV 4 and his people had not performed their first replenishment fast enough to meet VADM Anderson's high standards so with the SPRINGFIELD in formation he made a 25 knot run in from the beam. Even at 1000 yards we were still abeam of the tanker and I had to slam the ship into position at the end of a high speed turn, going from ahead at flank speed (25 knots) to back two thirds! Calculating the ship's advance (sliding sideways through the water during a turn) was tricky. With the Lord's help we pulled it off, ending up 80 feet from the AO's quarter while still turning and slowing. COMSIXTHFLT put up a flag hoist meaning "Well Done SPRINGFIELD", and I waited quietly for my knees to stop knocking together.

Mail from home, heloed over from our CVA, was most welcome. So was some steaming by ourselves enroute a rendezvous with the SHANGRI-LA and COMCRUDIV 4, RADM Williamson, in the LITTLE ROCK. A target plane towing a sleeve from the FORRESTAL provided services for an AA shoot but a low overcast resulted in dry runs only. Thursday night I got 7 hours sleep.

Friday and Saturday night were spent rocketing around at 28 knots, darkened ship, 1000 yards astern of the LITTLE ROCK in NATO maneuvers. We were in confined waters, not at all well charted and full of merchant ships. It was interesting, to say the least, and recalled the old days in cruisers when 500 yards was standard distance and none had radar. During the day we charged around with the CVA FORRESTAL. It's a great experience to whip this big ship around at high speed - she handles like a destroyer. Sunday we fueled from alongside the tanker for the last time and headed for home, up the east side of Sardinia and Corsica. Tomorrow morning we anchor off Villefranche and the next day go in and pick up our mooring which the Gripsholm will be leaving.

Installment V

Missile Shoot - Naples - At Sea

We left Villefranche just before dawn and arrived off Ceres, the French missile range near Hyeres (just east of Toulon), about 0800 where we joined LITTLE ROCK. Observers were exchanged; we received four French Naval officers and sent some of our people ashore to the French Range Control Building. The French drone is a dandy, big and fast, and the first one launched flew normally. We fired two Terriers and the LITTLE ROCK fired a Talos. All went well and it was immensely cheering, as well as impressive. It had been eight months since we had fired and no one was sure that after all the hurly-burly of preparing for and receiving a big flag aboard we could still shoot well. It was my first missile shoot and most rewarding.

Naples was our next stop and we arrived there at noon the next day after a pleasant night passage of the Straits of Bonifacio between Corsica and Sardinia. I went ashore and called friends. Played tennis with Peggy Sinclair and went to the Hull's for a small cocktail party next door. Captain Harry Hull, an old friend, is Chief of Staff to COMSTRIKFORSOUTH, a NATO command in Naples. Met many of the NATO staff and RAdm Bush of the Royal Navy, a most attractive chap. Went out to dinner with the Hull's, and friends, among them Dick Winnispeare, their landlord, an Italian despite his name. Next day played tennis again with Harry Hull and saw some good tennis, Emerson, Fraser, Sirolla, Petriangelli, and others. Dinner that night was given for VAdm Anderson by Harry and Katrink Hull at their place, Villa Salvo, which has a fabulous view of the Bay of Naples. Way down below, decked out in her bright lights, was the SPRINGFIELD.

At sea again at midnight - shooting an anti-air practice the next day and chasing around as usual with a carrier and her screen. We replenished at night, a rather exhausting exercise that keeps us all up most of the night going alongside ships and taking on ammunition, oil, provisions, and dry stores. My first approaches at night with the SPRINGFIELD.

Gunnery shoot was terminated on first run by our shooting down the sleeve. Plane had trouble with her reel and could not stream another. Lost our surface search radar for awhile and had to join up at night with ROOSEVELT (CVA) and LITTLE ROCK and usual DD's. A mildly hairy experience, doing it from ahead by eye in the old-fashioned way. Not much sleep that night.

On Wednesday we steamed over to a small barren rock in the Aegean Sea, north of Crete, for a shore bombardment shoot. First we sent over our helo with two men and five gallons of white paint to mark a reference point. Then we took turns with the LITTLE ROCK and a DD blasting the rock, pretending that we were supporting with our gunfire an amphibious assault.

On Memorial Day, we drove to the American Military Cemetery at Draguinan where I represented Commander Sixth Fleet, made a short speech and laid a wreath. We observed the occasion with band music, color ceremonies and the usual volley and taps. We put on a good show with the band and the Marine Guard. Most picturesque of the participants were the French Ancien Combattants, grizzled old veterans of two wars, covered with decorations.

After the ceremony, we went to luncheon at St. Tropez as guests of the Edgar's. He is Consul General at Marseille. Splendid food at an attractive restaurant on the waterfront and good company. We drove home along the coast and enjoyed the scenery.

Just before we left we had Winnie Lyndon and the Douglas Flood's to dinner on the ship. The Flood's are old friends of my mother and dad before he died last fall, having a house in Cuernavaca. Mrs. Flood recognized me from my picture and introduced herself. They were both most interested in news from Mexico.

On 6 June, we put out to sea, headed for the Ile de Levant, Ceres, where we fire our missiles again.

INSTALLMENT VI   8 June 1961

Two weeks in Villefranche

We came in as usual at 0800 and made fast to our buoy in Villefranche. Mary and Joy were at the end of Cap Ferrat watching us approach and came out to the ship for lunch. After lunch, we all looked at the sunny unfurnished apartment Mary had found high on the hill back of town. It had a wonderful garden terrace with a wide view of mountains, the Cap, the harbor (including the ship) and the town. Our problem now was to find a place to stay until our furniture arrived. A hotel seemed dull so we took a small furnished apartment near the beach for two weeks. It had a terrace overlooking a garden and was within walking distance of the best beach at St. Jean, Cap Ferrat. There we swam when the sun shone; the water clear and icy cold. Pedal boats were there for hire and Joy and I pedalled out to the SPRINGFIELD. Paddle boards, called gondolys, with high curved stems, were also available for a few hundred francs an hour. Joy and I took one of these and paddled out around the Cap. The surf-washed rocks, marked by small coves and tiny beaches, were most interesting. Lovers and family groups having picnics found seclusion there and the clear cold water broke gently across the stones.

Mary and I played golf once at Mont Angel, the spectacular course above Monte Carlo. To the north the snow covered Maritime Alps shine in the sun and to seaward is the Cote d'Azur, a sheer drop of several thousand feet. The course is short but interesting and the club welcomes us as guests. We pay greens fees only on Sunday. The wild flowers were in bloom, particularly the bright yellow Scotch broom, and the lush fairways smelled of fresh cut hay. Despite a passing sprinkle or two, it was a memorable afternoon, particularly since all my woods were quite remarkably straight.

On our first Sunday in port Mary and I were invited by the Villefranche Sailing Club to take part in an American-French regatta. Three American couples sailed French boats, about the size of a Lightening. It was great fun, tacking our way out of the Darse, jockeying for a start and then making two circuits of the harbor. Mary did a noble job on the jib and as a reward for her blistered hands we took second place. Of course, we had Robert Capelier's boat, the newest and fastest in the class. At noon we had drinks and dinner on the terrace of the Sailing Club. Good company, wonderful food and altogether a grand day.

We went to a few parties and arranged details of housing, baggage, and checked over the VW which came into Marseille from New York. I went to the ship at seven every morning except for one night when the weather was uncertain when I stayed aboard. After lunch, Mary and I often played tennis at Monte Carlo. The tennis club there, known as the Country Club, is magnificent: dozens of splendid courts, terraces, and gardens and a staggering view of mountains and sea. Here too, we are guests and are received most hospitably. The club is only thirty minutes from Villefranche.

Two more days of steaming and shooting followed. We fired at drones carried and controlled by the LITTLE ROCK. These are small radio controlled airplanes that fly until their gasoline is exhausted and then pop open a parachute, which eases them into the water from which they are recovered by boat. Friday evening I had my first approach at night on a carrier. We went alongside the port quarter of the FORRESTAL to pick up mail.

Saturday we anchored off Rhodes for the weekend. We approached in formation and all ships, CVA, SPRINGFIELD and destroyers anchored precisely at 0800 on the bell. The usual calls were made and returned. That evening the FORRESTAL gave a party for VAdm Anderson at the Miramar, a resort hotel on the beach. Skits were put on lampooning both Admirals Anderson and Massey (ComCarDiv 4), as well as such assorted targets as the SPRINGFIELD and other ships. The major target was COMSIXTHFLT, who was depicted by a tall officer in a white wig. Much hilarious nonsense, all meant, of course, in an affectionate and respectful way. VAdm Anderson loved it. Sunday we had a luncheon on board and in the evening the Greeks returned the honor ashore. I got in a little tennis both days and bought Mary a birthday present. Rhodes is growing as a tourist attraction, but is still a beautiful, quiet spot. It is difficult to visualize the city as the ruling city of the Mediterranean at one time, with the island supporting a population of 300,000.

To sea again for drills and exercises. Monday we took on fuel and missiles and fired more shore bombardment at the same rock. Shooting going more smoothly now, as it should. Tuesday, more drills and AA shooting. Wednesday, air defense drills and Thursday morning we anchored at Suda Bay, island of Crete. During the night, shortly after midnight, a steam line carried away in the after fireroom. The casualty was well handled - no serious injuries to personnel and no permanent damage. We steamed for awhile on one fireroom, one engineroom, and the two outboard screws. Full steaming power was soon restored. I was particularly pleased with the skill and courage of the engineers who handled the casualty so well. They secured the fireroom thoroughly, thus avoiding serious damage.

Suda Bay was full of Greek, Turkish, and U.S. small ships. Had a short swim with Spin Epes and Don McVey (both on the staff) before a long and excellent luncheon aboard the HHMS HELLI, guests of RAdm Avgeris. Good company as usual - the Greek Navy are delightful. Received mail by air, as well as Hank Monroe, the Chief of Staff, back from the hospital and leave, and departed at sundown.

The next few days at sea were busy but routine, with much good drilling gained with aircraft testing our AAW defenses. On Sunday morning we entered Naples and anchored for two days. Two large beach parties were organized, one for each day, and athletics, beer and steak were indulged in. Coming back in the boat Sunday night with some of my men, I encountered a petty officer who had been with me in destroyers during the war. He recounted, in a most flattering way to me, some of our adventures. Sunday, some of us drove to Sorrento and Pasitano. Monday, I played tennis most of the afternoon and returned to the ship early.

Tuesday morning we fueled from the MISSISSINEWA and headed for the barn. Moored to our buoy #1 in Villefranche at 0800, Wednesday, and we were home again.

28 June 1961

Installment VII

At sea - Palma - At sea - Naples - Augusta Bay - Villefranche

Last three weeks in June 1961

After our missile shoot off Hyeres, Cote d'Azur, France we went down to the southeastern tip of Sardinia where the Italians let us practice shore bombardment against the tip of a barren peninsula. After two days of shooting our 6 inch and 5 inch, pretending that we were supporting Marines landing ashore in assault, we sailed for Palma. Mary was at the Nixe-Palace and we had a wonderful six days, swimming, playing tennis, entertaining the Spanish officials and meeting the Undersecretary of the Navy Paul Fay and his party. Mary was marvellous in greeting the Spanish, with whom we found many mutual friends in Spain. We drove out in the country one day to a place called Cala d'Or (Bay of Gold) where a friend from Barcelona had a summer place. Josefina Ferrer-Vidal, Marquesa de Comillas, lives in a spectacular house, surrounded by garden, looking down on a small inlet with pine covered shores and a perfect white sandy beach at the end. These narrow, deep coves dot this coast of Mallorca.

The Fay's and his sister, Patsie Woods, turned out to be old friends from California, Stanford and Coronado, and we had a grand time. The aides, Billy Holder and Jim Stockman, had been my close associates in Secretary Jackson's office in Washington.

From Palma we went to Naples for the 10th anniversary of the major NATO command there, Commander in Chief, Allied Forces Southern Europe. Warships of most NATO countries joined forces and we steamed in formation around the Bay of Naples. As we passed the reviewing stands the SPRINGFIELD, FORRESTAL and ROOSEVELT turned together and the carriers flew off their aircraft. It was a grand sight. We moored to the pier inside the harbor and received, that afternoon, over 6000 visitors. Across the pier was the beautiful French cruiser COLBERT and alongside was the Italian destroyer leader SAN MARCO. The inner harbor was jammed with warships and merchant ships of a dozen countries while passenger steamers came in and out and excursion ships and ferries dashed about.

In Naples I met Jackson, who had come down from school near Paris to sail with me for a few days. He and Pat Anderson and Lee Gehrmann spent Monday at Capri exploring the coast of that rocky little island in kyacks. I played tennis at the Naples Tennis Club with one of the professionals and later went to a party given by the Italian Navy. Good view from the roof at Italian Navy headquarters and interesting people of many countries.

21 July 1961

INSTALLMENT VIII

A week at sea - Two weeks in Villefranche - June 28 - July 17, '61

During the few days at sea of late June we cruised the central Mediterranean - following the FORRESTAL, shooting some AA practices and taking part in the making of a movie. The shooting went very well and our 5" director earned the coveted "E". The movie making consisted of providing background as a gunfire support ship for filming the amphibious landing at Normandy in WW II for The Longest Day. We joined the amphibious forces of the Sixth Fleet at an isolated bay on the northwest coast of Corsica and fired off blank rounds, made smoke, etc. It was interesting to see how cleverly the beach obstacles had been imitated with rubber and plywood. There were many simulated mine, bomb and shell explosions and much smoke. The Amphibs, including the Marines, of course, did a fine job and the movie makers were happy. Daryl Zanuck and some of his people came aboard for dinner. His private secretary was a Russian girl from Paris. Her name was Gagarin and she is related to the Russian astronaut. The author, who is also doing the script was along too.

We went ashore through the surf that afternoon and enjoyed a swim and some cold beer. Jackson, who was aboard ship with me for two weeks, speared some fair sized fish underwater. The water was clear, clean and sparkling and the coast uninhabited. Corsica is the place for an inexpensive summer holiday if you like to camp and rough it.

On the 3rd of July we returned to Villefranche for our long summer visit. On the Fourth we dressed ship and fired 21 guns at noon. In the afternoon Mary and Carol and I went to a big reception on the FORRESTAL anchored off Cannes. This was followed by an official dinner at the Palm Beach Casino which turned out to be an unusually gay affair. The Mayor of Cannes, assisted by one lady and two or three officials, was our host. The French had merely reserved two large ringside tables on the terrace of this very plush establishment. The music, food and champagne were all first rate and we had a ball. The star attraction of the floor show, a singer named Juliana Larson, turned out to be an old hometown acquaintance of Mary's. Official dinners of this kind are rare - we hope it's a trend.

The new Commander Sixth Fleet, VADM David McDonald, and Mrs. McDonald arrived on the 11th and we joined the principal members of the staff in meeting them at the airport. That evening the Monroe's had a small group in for cocktails and we all went out with the McDonald's for dinner.

From Naples we went to Augusta Bay, Sicily, passing through the Straits of Messina at night. Somewhat of a chore picking our way among the fishing vessels, ferries and deep water traffic. At Augusta Bay we welcomed a new carrier, the WASP, and attended her change of command ceremony. Saw old friends in the new destroyer squadron with WASP and enjoyed drinks ashore before dinner with ADM Anderson who entertained his senior officers. In the afternoon Jackson and I took the gig out to the breakwater and went swimming where the water was clean. All of gig crew enjoyed swim too. That evening a young Italian naval aviator, LT Ugo Oldano came to dinner. Ugo had visited us in Washington while training in the USA. The next morning Ugo took Jackson up Mt. Aetna in his Alfa Romeo. They were due back for lunch at 1200. At 1000 I was told by ADM Anderson to get underway as soon as practicable. We got everyone back except Jackson by 1030 and I reported ready. Fortunately the Admiral decided to wait until 1230 and Jackson was retrieved. We headed for Villefranche at 25 knots, arriving the next day. ADM Anderson had been named by the President as the new Chief of Naval Operations. To say we were pleased is putting it mildly. All of us admired and liked ADM Anderson tremendously and had been rooting for him in the CNO sweepstakes. Mrs. Anderson was sightseeing in Italy and read about it in the paper.

Our brief stop in Villefranche, until 27 June, was marked by farewells to the Anderson's and seeing them off. Carol Noel arrived from Washington by jet in time for the farewell party in the Rothschild Gardens on Cap Ferrat.

ADM Anderson's official departure from SPRINGFIELD was quite a gala. We manned the rails, fired a nineteen gun salute, and gave him three cheers. Many yachts and French fishing boats gathered and we piled the band into the motorboat and followed the barge ashore. It was really a moving ceremony as he received his last full honors, ruffles and flourishes followed by "Auld Lang Syne". He was a magnificent Fleet Commander, setting the highest standards of professional performance and conduct, yet with charm and humor. As an ambassador of good will in this part of the world he was superb. Our loss, however, will be the Navy's gain.

The evening before we sailed we had a very informal party celebrating mostly Carol's birthday. Half a dozen junior officers and their girls came - some with guitars. Carol sang Spanish songs, the boys sang all sorts of songs, to the obvious pleasure of our French neighbors.

The only unusual incident this time at sea occured in the Straits of Messina, between Sicily and the Italian mainland. We were proceeding north and approaching the electric cables which span the Straits at a supposed minimum distance above the water at the lowest point in mid-channel of 230 feet. An automatic tensioning device is supposed to ensure this but something was obviously wrong. The low point in the catenary, where we were headed, appeared to be about 100 feet above water.

SPRINGFIELD'S FIRST ANNIVERSARY CELEBRATED WITH GUSTO

☆ ☆ ☆

On the evenings of July 6th and 7th the U. S. Navy took over the Palais de la Méditerranée, Nice, to celebrate the first anniversary of the U.S.S. Springfield's arrival in Villefranche. The party was hosted by Commanding Officer J. V. Noel, Jr., and Executive Officer T. O. Tabor; and naval traditions of hospitality were honored to the full in an atmosphere both lavish and informal. It was what Captain Noel described as a "family party" organised by the officers and men for their own celebration, and not a reception for local dignitaries. There were no official guests of honor, though the presence of Captain Greenberg, Assistant Judge Advocate General in Washington, was noted by your correspondent.

A snappy French floor show was provided, but the high spots of the evening were an uninhibited charleston on the part of Captain Noel, (surely the Navy's most popular Captain) partnered by beautiful daughter Carole, followed by a spirited rendition of "Roll me Over" sung by Deana (the Springfield's Ella Fitzgerald), wife of Chief Jones, which must have caused the Palais de la Méditerranée to rock on its foundations. Happy Anniversary, we say, and many of them!

("Riviera Sun" News Service)

On the 14th, Bastile Day, we went to a reception at the Prefects and watched the fireworks at Nice from the balcony of a French friend, Jacques Medecin.

The great event of this period for the Noel family was getting into our flat and living en famille for the first time since March. It was a bit crowded but very satisfying to have a home again. The new grass was doing nicely on the terrace and the spectacular view was a constant pleasure. It was a great feeling to be able to come home, put on a pair of shorts, open a Danish beer and enjoy the sun and view on the terrace. We swam a good deal, played tennis, water-skied behind the gig, sailed in a small regatta, went to a few parties and also, of course, I did a bit of work aboard ship. A friend at the Sailing Club offered Jackson and Carol the use of a Meteor if they would help repair it. This they have started - quite a project - but they are learning something about boats and also some French since the man at the boatshed knows no English. Both of them Tom-Sawyered their friends into helping and Mary brings down lunch to the boatshed.

Carol and Jackson have started meeting people and are spending very few evenings at home. The Riviera abounds with all types - from rich titled French to grubby beatnicks, movie stars to school teachers - we are meeting a few of every category.

The day that the new ComSixthFlt relieved the interim commander, ADM Massey, was a big one for the SPRINGFIELD. The wind blew hard from the southwest and boating became precarious. The FORRESTAL, supposed to anchor in the mouth of the harbor and provide a helo platform for arriving VIP's, was forced to remain underway and could not run boats. Just as the guests started to come out a fortunate shift in the wind of about 30° put the SPRINGFIELD in a lee and everyone got aboard safely. American, French, Italian and British Admirals were on hand from all over Europe and the Mediterranean as was Princess Grace of Monaco. The ceremony went off smoothly except for an inexplicable clutch on the part of the bandleader who did not play the Merseillaise after playing the Star Spangled Banner. Upon leaving the speakers platform ADM Brown missed his footing and fell flat, injuring only his dignity, as he reported later. After the ceremony a reception was held on the forecastle and Joy met Princess Grace - an event of some significance for Joy whose eyes were as big as saucers.

Just as the first guests were due to leave the ship the wind backed to 220°, which was directly into the harbor, and increased to 30 kts. Boating was stopped while we veered more chain to the buoy and used the engines to hold the ship at one end of her yaw. This worked surprisingly well and provided a lee at the forward accommodation ladder. Guests departed, although not exactly as scheduled, and with considerable nimbleness of foot on the ladder.

Since we needed almost twice this to clear we had no choice but to hug the right side of the Strait, where deep water goes right up to the rocks of Scylla. Here the clearance was sufficient but the full strength, about 5.5 knots, of the current was flowing around Sicily, into the Straits. On the left were the whirlpools of Charybdis. It was now obvious why these twin hazards to mariners of old were so deadly and why their names are now common expressions for two dangerous dilemmas. When the current runs at full force from the northwest the whirlpool forms under the lee of the point of Sicily. As the old sailing ships saw the whirlpool or eddy they went over to the other side, where we passed, and became caught there in the strong current that sets directly onto the rocks of Scylla. Even expecting this current we were surprised by its effect and had a few uncomfortable minutes as we passed several hundred yards from the rocks. A sailing vessel, unless the wind was strong, would have been helpless.

1 August 1961

INSTALLMENT IX

At Sea - Golfe Juan - Aranci Bay - Toulon - Naples - 17 July - 7 August

It was calm and peaceful the day we left Villefranche and joined the Service Force ships just outside the harbor. We fueled, took on ammunition, food and stores - going alongside four ships in succession. It was a grand day for shiphandling. The next day, however, was unusually rough for the Med in July. Gusts to 40 kts and seas to match made the LITTLE ROCK's approach alongside for personnel transfer a real test of seamanship. We transferred about thirty-five observers for the LITTLE ROCK's Operational Readiness Inspection (Battle Problem) which took almost all day. In the afternoon the wind and seas had moderated and personnel transfer was done by helo.

After a few days of following the carrier and shooting AA practices we led the way into Aranci Bay, a very large, protected and isolated anchorage on the northeastern coast of Sardinia. Many ships of the Fleet were there and we enjoyed seeing old friends. We took the gig to a beach where we swam and ate lunch in a beautiful little cove. Our scuba divers discovered the ruins of an old town under water and were thrilled to find pieces of pottery, etc. Local fishermen, from the lone village in the Bay, knew of the underwater ruins but still our people felt like Columbus.

The next day we made a fast run, through the Straits of Bonifacio in bright moonlight, to Golfe Juan where we stayed for a day to turn in our first group of Midshipmen and pick up our second batch. These were all first class Mids, USNA and College NROTC, making their summer cruise. Mary, Carol and Joy drove down for the day and we had a fine time at Eden Roc, the very swank watering place on Cap Antibes. The manager, M. Salla, is most hospitable to the Navy, and we may use the place as guests. We swam in a wonderful little cove with Mr. Joseph Kennedy and ran into old friends from New York, Nancy and Holt Heyward. We asked them and their friends, plus children, out to the ship for tea. Peanut butter sandwiches made a tremendous hit.

After Golfe Juan we went to sea for a few days (which included a missile shoot) and then to Toulon for an official call on the French Navy. This had been postponed several times, once because of the French troubles with the Army in Algeria and again when VADM Anderson was called to Washington on short notice to be the new CNO.

We had four days of the most cordial and warm French hospitality. A spectacular luncheon in the garden of ADM Galleret, a formal dinner aboard the COLBERT and a Vin d'Honneur given by the Mayor which featured ballet dancers were the highlights of official entertainment. On Sunday we were invited to the houses of three French officers. We could accept only two of these invitations and it was an unusual and pleasant experience to be accepted into their homes and to meet their children and personal friends.

Mary and Carol and I stayed at an attractive little hotel, the Nautilus, the former home of Jules Verne. Inexpensive and unpretentious as it was we had a comfortable room with a balcony that looked over some palm trees to a small yacht harbor and the big bay of Toulon. Near the hotel was old Fort St. Louis, now a swimming club of the French Navy. From the top deck one goes down an accommodation ladder to swim off the rocks below. The water was icy during the mistral but a good antidote for the rich French food and drink.

We were at Toulon for the launching of the new French bathyscape in which the Junior Piccard took part. This was accompanied by many speeches and of course, a Vin d'Honneur which is, as one can guess, a sort of reception at which wine is consumed and toasts are made.

Captain John Lodge, USNR, former governor of Connecticut and Ambassador to Spain, came aboard for two weeks active duty and was a great asset socially since he had served with the French at Toulon during WW II.

On 2 August we put in at Naples, firing salutes on arrival and making our usual Med moor inside the crowded inner harbor.

The first morning was devoted, as usual, to official calls and I had the pleasure of greeting an old tennis playing friend from Washington, General de Martino, Commanding General of the local Italian Army area. Mary had not yet arrived so John Lodge and I played tennis. That evening we went to a reception for COMSIXTHFLT at the Allied Officers Club at NATO headquarters and on to an open air dine and dance place called the Grottoromano. There were about a dozen at the table, including the McDonald's and it was much fun. Mary and I went home to the Hull's (who were away in Germany), a magnificent old villa overlooking the Bay of Naples.

Four days of work, play, tennis and sightseeing followed. Thursday we played tennis late in the afternoon, Mary and I against John Lodge and Peggy Sinclair. That evening a charming small dinner was given for the McDonald's by RADM and Mrs. Cooper. It was a pleasant company, enlivened by a Cooper-Lodge Combo (accordian and piano) and some singing. Friday John and I played tennis with General de Martino on his private court in the garden of his official residence in the heart of Naples.

Again on Sunday, while at church aboard SPRINGFIELD, the wind came up from the southwest and we had to suspend boating and stayed aboard for lunch. Carol and Jackson were both scheduled to sail in a race that morning but the Meteors came out, had a hair-raising sail for awhile in the 30 kt wind and retired wisely to the Darse. A bold pair in a Comet stayed out and capsized. We sent a boat out and brought them in. Monday we slipped our mooring and went back to work at sea.

18 August 1961

INSTALLMENT X

SecNav Visit - Mallorca for Upkeep - Malta - Back to Homeport

Our one day in Villefranche to pick up Secretary of the Navy Connally was mildly hectic. Brownbaggers (married men) were allowed ashore until 1500 and wives and children of those having the duty came aboard to visit. At 1600 the crew fell in at quarters and SPRINGFIELD received SecNav with a 19 gun salute, full guard and band. As we slipped our mooring SecNav and VADM McDonald took a short helo hop along the coast. Upon his return we showed him the ship. He was interested in everything, particularly in speaking to the men. SecNav even went into the laundry and talked to the men there.

As we were steaming singly and in good visibility I was able to accept VADM McDonald's invitation to dinner. SecNav asked many questions and also gave us a fascinating insight into activities in Washington.

The next day SecNav hilined to the DEWEY and from there to the FORRESTAL. We headed for Pollensa Bay, Mallorca where we went alongside the repair ship SHENANDOAH. This was my first landing alongside an anchored ship but presented no problems. It was a great advantage to be alongside our tender and with few liberty demands we accomplished a great amount of repair, maintenance and general upkeep. Only officers, chief petty officers and first class petty officers could be granted liberty due to the size of Puerto Pollensa and the crowded conditions caused by many tourists and too many ships in the Bay. The weather was fair but very windy and SHENANDOAH steamed to her anchor for several days. A diver sent down to check the anchor found an old German magnetic/pressure mine four feet away. This mine, according to the Spanish authorities, was one of several dropped by the Germans during the Spanish Civil War. Although chances were remote that the mine was still lethal we shifted our anchorage and marked the mine for future disposal by the Spanish Navy after our departure.

Mary, Joy and Carol came over from Barcelona the next day and we enjoyed a quiet visit. After the first two days of calls and official luncheons all was quiet on the official social side. A most pleasant evening was spent with the Temple Fielding's. After cocktails on their terrace overlooking Formentor we dined in INCA at a typical wine cellar sort of native restaurant where everyone had to drink from the long spouted pitcher, called a perron. The object of the game was to direct the narrow stream of red wine into one's mouth while holding the perron at arms length overhead. Much fun and much red wine splattered over the landscape. After stopping at a new open air night club for dancing we finally turned in at 0400. The remainder of our social life was less hectic. The wardroom had a picnic on a beach where the surf was running big enough for some grand body-surfing. Champagne and hot dogs and much singing added to the fun. Spanish, French, English and German summer visitors with many children joined the party. Mary and I had dinner with Spanish friends and had asked them to the ship for luncheon but had to cancel out because of weather which interrupted boating.

At the Fielding's we met an Englishman who told us about a Roman village underwater. We organized a small group of our divers and Mary, Carol and Wendy Woods and I joined them for an afternoon of exploring underwater. Most of us used only face masks and flippers; the water was warm and shallow but a long swim was needed to get out to the site of the village. Silt and grass covered the old walls and buildings but we found the usual pieces of pottery. It was good exercise, we novices were all exhausted, but we were revived by a drink at Sir Phillip Dunns. This Canadian steel magnate, it turned out, had bought a large tract of land and had restored a large farm building whose stables were partly Roman. He came down to the beach and asked us up to his terrace. The area around Alcudia, south of Pollensa, was evidently the site of a large Roman settlement. There is an archaeological museum, a Roman theater and Roman tombs, as well as Roman walls. An archaeologist from New York University is working there and promised to show us the site of an ancient galley if we would dive for him. This project is planned for our next visit.

On 16 August the INDEPENDENCE arrived with her destroyers and I saw many old friends. The FORRESTAL group turned over the watch and departed for home, as did the SHENANDOAH. On 17 August we sailed for Golfo di Palmas, on the SW coast of Sardinia, where the Fleet gathered for a day or so. Here the new arrivals from the East Coast were briefed. I saw old friends and had lunch with Chick Harmer in the INDEPENDENCE. We left on the afternoon of the 18th for Malta and made a 27 knot run overnight to be off Valletta at 0800. There we picked up a pilot and the American liaison officer, LCDR Lopresti, whom I had not seen for twenty-two years. He was a quartermaster in my first ship, the cruiser ASTORIA.

Our arrival ceremonies (salutes, calls, etc.) went well and I had a short sightseeing tour after luncheon. Tennis at five and then back to dinner with Admiral Sir Holland-Martin aboard his flagship. Much good company - the British are delightful and friendly. Our assigned sister ship, the HMS GIRDLE NESS, gave a large party aboard for the wardroom. The men were hospitably received ashore. Sunday was a quiet day - paperwork and church services in the morning and a

Saturday Mary and I saw Pompeii and had luncheon in Sorrento before going back to Naples about 1600. Mary went shopping with Signora Giamberardino, wife of the Italian liaison officer to the Sixth Fleet, while Franco and I sat on his balcony and talked.

Sunday morning more tennis and then to Ischia for the afternoon on ADM Brown's yacht, the Grazia. The Chief of Staff, Hank Monroe, was host. Sightseeing and swimming in various interesting coves was followed by drinks and supper. Very plush and relaxing. Back on the SPRINGFIELD we found Jackson and his friend Barry who had come down from Rome where they had been spending a week sightseeing on their own. They were riding the ship back to Villefranche. So ended a most pleasant holiday. Monday morning we got underway and replenished again before taking a course for home, Villefranche, where we were to pick up the Secretary of the Navy and take him to sea.

18 September 1961

INSTALLMENT XI

Last of summer in Villefranche - Fleet Exercises - Athens - Istanbul-
Rhodes - Marmaris

The day after we returned to Villefranche for our last visit until October Joy came down with a severe case of scarlet fever and was not fully recovered until the day we left. Despite the miracle of penicillin, Joy had temperatures up to 105° for a week and such a spectacular skin eruption that Dr. Coates asked me to take a color picture of the poor child. Mary had a strenuous time nursing Joy and I was deprived of my favorite swimming companion.

Fortunately, Joy was well on the way to recovery when Mary and I gave our long planned "calls made and returned" party at the Sailing Club. A covey of visiting admirals from CONUS and the selection to captain rank that day of five commanders on the Staff gave the party a little more glamour. A few days later Jackson brought his friends, the David Nivens, out for lunch and a charming family they are. The two boys, David and Jaime, have been, together with Gregory Peck's boy, Jonathan, Jackson's closest friends all summer. Niven, who was a regular British Army Officer (Sandhurst) before he became an actor, is a most normal, attractive chap who shows in the flesh the same engaging humor that he does on the screen.

Just before we left VF Mary and Carol decided to follow the ship partly by Volkswagon during our eastern Med. cruise. This means driving to Brindisi, on the heel of the boot of Italy, and flying from there to Athens, then to Istanbul, Ankara, and Beirut. From there they can fly back to Brindisi.

We left Villefranche in a black squall that made lightering our vehicles aboard a little sticky. After replenishment underway we anchored the next day in Naples where we stayed only for fifteen hours.

The only unusual occurrence during replenishment was a tragic helicopter crash on the deck of a ship alongside. A man was killed on the fantail of the ANTARES and several injured, some on the stern of the SPRINGFIELD, by fragments of the shattered rotor blades. Our helo took off in record time and picked up the crewman. The pilot went down with the helo. The sound of a helo's rotors disintegrating and spinning off fragments like shrapnel is most chilling.

In Naples I went shopping at the PX in the morning and in the afternoon had a glorious hour with the pro at the Naples Tennis Club. Minus about five pounds but feeling great I returned to the ship for dinner. We sailed at 2300. The next day was our missile shoot against drones flown and controlled by the USS NEWPORT NEWS. The drones flew well, our missiles fired for hits and you can imagine how marvellous we felt. What a kick! - the reports - "Target commencing a firing run" - "Two minutes to go", (countdown), "3-2-1" - whoosh! and with a great roar and burst of smoke and flame our Terrier lifts off the launcher, picks up speed, drops its first stage and spirals into the beam, riding the beam all the way to the target. "Intercept" is sung out and everyone relaxes and grins. I had pledged a fat lamb to Poseidon if he granted us success. This seemed appropriate, considering whose waters we were in, and arose from my recent immersion in The King Must Die by Mary Renault, an excellent background book for the lands we were about to visit.

The next day the Fleet met in a large sheltered bay and we went over to the INDEPENDENCE for a briefing on Checkmate, the big NATO exercise that would engage our attention until we put into Athens on 19 September. Part of Checkmate was an amphibious landing in the far northeast corner of the Aegean, the Sea of Thrace, on the coast of Turkey opposite the Dardanelles. Here Greeks and Turks exercised as NATO allies together - an historic event, since these traditional enemies are normally about as compatible as two fighting cocks in the same chicken yard. We went ashore briefly after the Landing Force had landed and had a run on the beach and a swim.

Checkmate wound up on 18 September and we put into Athens on the 19th, firing salutes as we approached Piraeus and receiving dignitaries all day. Mary and Carol were due in at five but their plane did not arrive until ten. We managed to get two adjoining cottages at the Astir Beach Hotel, an unusual resort on the beach twenty minutes from Athens. The cottages were surrounded by lawn and flowers and the sand and warm clear water was a few yards away.

Wednesday was devoted to sightseeing and shopping. Mary and Carol bought some inexpensive furs for which Athens is renowned. We went to a wine festival at Daphne, on the outskirts of Athens, where wine flowed like water and everybody danced and had a good time. Carol danced the native dances and was a bit stiff and sore the next day. We went to official receptions, luncheons and dinners and had a most enjoyable time. Friday evening after a reception we went up to the Acropolis to see it by moonlight. It was a gorgeous and inspiring sight. Saturday morning we sailed for Istanbul where Mary and Carol would meet us.

swim in the afternoon. That evening VADM McDonald had a large formal dinner on the forecastle for our British guests.

The next morning we left Malta to join the INDEPENDENCE for a few days of work at sea before returning to Villefranche. In these brief accounts of our activities I have not described our life at sea. We usually move fairly quickly between ports, joining the carrier we operate with and then leaving. We take part in many drills and exercises, often around the clock. These include not only ship's drills but anti-air warfare and anti-submarine warfare exercises involving most of the Sixth Fleet.

Within the ship there throbs a microcosm of 1200 men and 130 officers. A small percentage have problems and in this closely integrated unit, their problems are mine. Some men cannot accept the Navy's discipline, some have women or drink troubles. Some are sick mentally or just seem to be; they lose their effectiveness. A very few turn out to be drunks, thieves, perverts.

Most of the crew and officers are fine people and work very hard indeed. With these my objective is to organize and lead a thoroughly efficient, smart, effective crew that can do all its duties very well, remain ready for instant combat and at the same time enjoy life as much as possible. This task is a complicated but fascinating one and is the active accompaniment to the large responsibility that commanding officers are fortunate to be burdened with.

October 1961

INSTALLMENT XII

Cyprus - Hard work at sea - Home to Villefranche

From Rhodes we went to Cyprus for a short visit. This curious and ancient island, 80% Greek and 20% Turkish, is run by a remarkable man, an Archbishop of the Orthodox Church, Makarios. He came aboard for luncheon and I had an opportunity to talk to him briefly about his embryonic republic which he won for his people against the British. He is an impressive man, clearly a patriot and statesman of major caliber. At Cyprus we met many attractive and interesting people, the Clerides, probably the next president (he a former RAF pilot, she half British, half Indian who met him while broadcasting in WW II for BBC), the Tranos (he the Greek Ambassador, she a well known eye surgeon), the Wilkins (he a career minister now Ambassador to Cyprus, she a Navy junior, daughter of an old shipmate in my first ship, the USS ASTORIA). In thirty-six hours we had a whirl of official parties and did little else. I got ashore for a brief swim on a gorgeous beach and an hour of tennis. Before going to dinner at the Wilkins we had an hour or so to roam about Nicosia. Not a very attractive town but I found two books by Durrell that I had been looking for: Reflections on a Marine Venus (about Rhodes) and Bitter Lemons (about Cyprus).

After leaving Cyprus we had a quiet night sailing westward but as we left the lee of Crete a strong northwest gale made life unpleasant. This was our day for replenishment and it was a tough day indeed, especially for the destroyers and the Service Force ships. We got our fuel and our ammunition, leaving food and stores for a calmer day. By the next morning the Mediterranean had regained her composure and Malta lay shining before us, surrounded by the calm blue seas we remembered.

The next three days were spent shooting near Malta - at a nearby rocky islet for shore bombardment practice, at a towed sled, and at targets towed by aircraft. One morning we accidentally passed over a fishing line that was on the surface being rebaited and we carried a greater part of it away. To compensate the fishermen, who were in two small boats, we dropped each of them five cartons of cigarettes by helocopter.

During our days of shooting we completed our replenishment, at night this time, going alongside both HYADES and ALTAIR. The seas around Malta are calm but full of ships since it lies in the middle of one of the sea's great thoroughfares. It was ticklish changing course while alongside a supply ship but the formation had to be maneuvered back and forth to avoid shipping. Most merchant ships cannot be depended upon to observe the Rules of the Road.

We fueled again on 15 October and then spent the next few days in Anti Air Warfare exercises. On 16 October we closed the INDEPENDENCE for mail and passengers. Captain Fred Bardshar, the new Staff Operations officer, Spin Epes' relief, came aboard at dusk and brought a letter from Mary. I quote part of it:

"Nev (Captain Nev Shaefer) invited us aboard for Sunday breakfast since we were leaving Rhodes that morning in the tiny Greek steamer Pandalease and we accepted with pleasure. Just as we were returning to the beach in came the Pandalease, the Courier and the SPRINGFIELD. We made a dash for the Pandalease as she has a reputation for adhering rather loosely to schedule. Captain George, her skipper, is a restless old character who shoves off when the spirit moves him. As we left Rhodes we saw a signal light flashing at us from the SPRINGFIELD. We told Captain George that it was a signal from you so he reached for the whistle cord and pulled on it for the next five minutes. Then again as we passed the Hotel Rosas he pulled the whistle; we were waving to the Ellis's.

On the way to Miknos we stopped at four islands. Captain George is known to indulge in ouzo while underway but he is magnificent in handling the ship entering and leaving port. He paces up and down on the wings of his bridge bellowing orders. The Pandalease charges up to the beach, drops the anchor and in two seconds the steamer is swarming with vendors and departing as well as arriving passengers. The tiny shore boats now load and unload cargo, from fish to furniture. While hauling aboard a large glass front wardrobe by a single tiny hook, for example, Captain George would blow the whistle as a signal of immediate departure. People would then fling themselves over the side with angry protests, replied to in kind by Captain George. Then, as the last man jumps for it the wailing of those saying farewell ceases, the air is full of cheers, flowers and smiles and with a final salute on the whistle we are off to a repeat performance at the next island.

We arrived at Miknos about eleven at night, departing the Pandalease in a small boat. As we approached the dark shore, there were not a dozen lights showing in the whole town and we wondered what we were getting into. As we stepped out of the small boat a tall blond American offered his services to Carol; at the same moment the concierge of the hotel spoke to me. A porter carried our bag the five blocks to the hotel and we had arrived.

The next morning, the American, his friend (both young engineers), Carol and I embarked in the boat for Delos where we spent the morning. About noon we decided to join the Americans, a young man taking pictures for the National Geographic and his friend, a young widow, in an excursion around the islands, departing for Athens on a later steamer. Despite the rain Carol and the Americans joined the villagers in dancing in the street. The fiesta was sparked by two miners who, overcome by ouzo, decided not to go to work that day. We finally arrived in Athens the next day after a rough passage.

We fueled Sunday morning underway and went through the Dardanelles Sunday afternoon. This was interesting from every viewpoint. At the narrows we saw the ruins of the old castles built by the Turks to isolate Constantinople before taking it. A Turkish officer aboard told us about the Battle of Gallipoli and how the Turks repelled the allies. He showed us where twenty-one mines laid early one morning in the dark after the British had swept sank four battleships when they reversed course to the right. If they had turned to the left none would have been touched. Just beyond this point was a hill behind which lay Troy. What ghosts must haunt this land! At the second narrow bend in the Hellespont we encountered a small Italian steamer which turned across my bow and came down the left side of the channel. As we entered the sea of Marmara we went alongside the MISSISSINEWA for fuel oil. That night in formation was uneventful but the fun started about seven when the Naval Attache showed up in a 75' ASR with the Time-Life men who were to do a Navy story. We had a hectic time getting the formation stopped to take them aboard and then rang up 20 kts to make our eight o'clock date for saluting the Turks. From there we had to anchor quickly in order to get the barge off to take Dr. Seaborg (new head of the AEC) to the landing to catch his plane. Dodging downstream traffic (large tankers) and a dozen rush hour ferries while anchoring in this strange port was quite a ball. At one time I had ferries coming at me from every side yet had to push in firmly to the anchorage. The current runs swiftly off Istanbul. We were all glad to get the anchor down and the barge away. We found that the ferries of Istanbul are quite considerate. Belching black smoke (they obviously all burn soft coal) they look formidable, particularly when in large numbers, but they are piloted by good seamen who know that a large ocean going ship has too many problems with the current to be able to dodge a ferry, no matter who has the right of way.

Istanbul was fascinating. We found a small pension near the landing and soon came under the benign influence of Ruby, an attractive, English speaking woman whose charm and friendliness compensated for the somewhat primitive sanitary arrangements. We had our usual round of official parties both ashore and aboard the INDEPENDENCE but we had time for a trip up the Bosphorus as far as the Black Sea. Scenery was magnificent. We went shopping in the Covered Bazaar, a well established retail outlet, founded about 1460. Copper, brass and costume jewelry were good buys, as well as a pair of Turkish handwoven woolen bedspreads. We bought several large copper pots for firewood alongside the fireplaces at Vacation Lane.

Istanbul also offered the magnificent Aya Sofia, the most impressive building we had ever seen. Larger than St. Peters in Rome, it testifies to the grandeur and wealth of Constantinople. The Blue Mosque and the mosque built by Suleiman the Magnificent were also worth seeing.

Mary and Carol stayed on for a few days in Istanbul while the SPRINGFIELD left for Rhodes. Since they were booked for Beirut and could only get to Rhodes by backtracking to Athens, Mary and Carol were planning to skip Rhodes. We arrived there on Friday and Saturday night learned that our visit to Beirut had been cancelled because of the revolution in Syria. I went to the Hotel Rosas and called Mary. Fortunately I got through and told her to come to Rhodes.

Mary's adventures in cashing in her tickets, turning the Turkish lira back into dollars and getting to Athens and then Rhodes is a story in itself. A convention of some sort was departing Istanbul and Mary and Carol almost had to hitchhike. By sitting at the airport and calling all the people they knew or had heard about in Istanbul connected with air travel they managed to do it. Carol caught a Lufthansa plane and Mary was given a ride in an old Turkish non-scheduled DC3 which hedge-hopped all the way to Athens. There they spent the night and caught a fortunate extra Olympic Airways flight to Rhodes on Monday. A synod of the Orthodox church, the first since 1873, was just finishing in Rhodes and the extra plane had been sent down to help bring out the 300 churchmen, including the twelve patriarchs of the church. I went to their final mass on Sunday and the spectacle of these twelve ancient and bearded worthies all dressed up in their splendid gold and jeweled regalia was awe-inspiring. Their tall, round, jeweled and glittering headpieces looked like something out of the Arabian Nights.

Mary and Carol arrived Monday morning and we all went up to the lovely house of the Prins. Sally Prins had offered to put us all up and we accepted with pleasure. Captain Paul Prins, USCG, was off with his ship getting repairs done in a nearby Greek shipyard.

At Rhodes we had little official entertaining and we had time to enjoy the beach and play tennis and go sightseeing. We all love Rhodes - it has great charm and the weather was perfect. Mary and Carol took a trip to Lindos and saw the Acropolis there that precedes the one in Athens by forty years. We enjoyed the Ioannou's especially, he is the Nomarch (governor) of the Dodecanese Islands. They are both highly educated and charming people, one of whose enthusiasms is poetry. At a small cocktail party Sally Prins gave the last night in Rhodes the governor read some of Cavafy's poems. The reading was very well received and added an interesting and charming touch to the usual dull cocktail party routine. The next morning Mary came out to breakfast and we left for Marmaris at 1000.

Marmaris is a small and very poor Turkish village at the head of a magnificent landlocked harbor just thirty miles northeast of Rhodes. We anchored about 1430. The local sub-prefect called with the Assistant Naval Attache from Ankara, LCDR Mayo. The next day we went swimming and water skiing and then I went ashore to walk around the village. Mayo's truck drove me up into the pine covered hills and we saw the villagers returning from their big day in town. Mayo's host, Hassan, with whom he always stays (there is no hotel) asked me to dinner. First we sat in the village square and heard the local political candidates harangue the crowd. We had an excellent dinner at Hassan's house, grilled fish, salted roe, grilled liver and kidneys, fresh tomatoes, fruit, beer and wine. Hassan, Mayo and I ate alone, women and children in the kitchen and serving.

The next morning Mayo came out and reported three old pots for sale by the local sponge fishermen who had brought them up in their nets from deep water. I had asked him about the possibility of buying any antiquities. We went ashore and bought five lovely amphora, a matched pair, a tall one, and two smaller round ones. They were in perfect condition and cost $10.00 for all five. Bob Curts had asked for one too so he got the tall one.

Later I joined the Admiral in his barge for a long swim and lunch. We water skied again and before dark the Hassans all came out for a visit and refreshments.

The weather was perfect - cloudless with the temperature about 90° and the water just cool enough. Sparsely inhabited, the bay was surrounded by pine covered hills and looked quite unlike Asia Minor as we usually see it.

Sunday we were underway at 0900 to pick up mail and passengers from the INDEPENDENCE off Rhodes.

November 1961

INSTALLMENT XIII

Storm at Sea - Barcelona - Home for Thanksgiving

We left Villefranche for a week at sea, including a missile shoot, before going to Barcelona. After an ADEX (Air Defense Exercise) off Minorca, VAdm McDonald heloed over to the INDEPENDENCE to greet some arriving VIP's and we headed back to Ceres where we were to use the French target range. The missile shoot went well and we headed back to the general area of the Balearics to pick up the Admiral. A strong gale came up quickly in the Central Med and this increased unexpectedly to a major storm. At first all ships carried on with normal operations but as the wind rose and the seas built up it became evident that safety of men and ships was paramount. This was the most severe storm we had experienced in the Med. The seas were big and steep; the wind gusted to 75 kts. We finally hove to, making little more than steerageway. Amphibious ships, destroyers and the little minesweepers had already done the same and even the big carriers chose a safe course. Despite these precautions a man or two went overboard in the Fleet and all ships suffered from the buffeting.

This was my first really bad weather in the SPRINGFIELD and I was concerned, not only for topside gear such as boats and life rafts but for the hull itself. At first a great many disquieting reports were made to the bridge: "Compartment _____ is flooded, Sir", "Water on the deck of all forward living compartments", "Fuel oil on the O1 level", "Helicopter has been damaged, Sir." On a dark night, with the wind howling past the bridge doors, the ship lurching and pounding as she rises to a big sea and then bangs into the next wave, these are far from pleasant reports to hear. The Executive Officer soon had his damage control organization going and all reports went to Damage Control Central and action was taken as needed by the nearest Repair Party. As might be expected most initial reports were inaccurate or exaggerated. The ventilation ducts leaked a bit and some gear came adrift topside. The fuel oil report turned out to be oily rags blown off the 5" loading machine. The helo lost some fabric in its tail and the rotor blades were bent a little and had to be replaced. It was a thoroughly miserable forty-eight hours as we inched our way northwest towards Barcelona but no significant damage was done.

As unpleasant as it was (and terrifying to many) the storm taught us all a great deal. I learned how the ship handled in big seas and how to ease her. We all learned how to secure some topside gear better. Many of the crew learned that being actively seasick was no disgrace - as long as he used a bucket and did not spray the vicinity of his duty station. We all regained our respect for that usually quiescent monster, the sea.

Barcelona was a welcome sight as we picked up the pilot inside the new section of breakwater. He was an old friend from ALTAIR days and took us in promptly to our berth near Barconoletta.

Barcelona was heart warming. We all stayed with Myles Morris who normally lives alone in a large flat. The Consul General gave a reception at the Ritz the first night and we saw dozens of old friends and met many new people. The next day I squeezed in some tennis with my old pro, Antonio, at the tennis club we enjoyed so much when we lived in Barcelona. Then an official stag lunch aboard ship with the Admiral. The days went quickly, with luncheons aboard ship for our Spanish friends, shopping and tennis ashore, dinners with Spanish friends, etc. Mary and Felix, Los Marqueses de Castelldosrius, gave a dinner for us and the McDonald's at the Equestria. Saturday and Sunday we went out in the country for lunch with friends. Saturday we bought a small painting of our neighborhood, Puente Vallcarca, showing our old house. It was by a man named Villa whose work Mary had admired for a long time. We sent boxes of old clothes, candy and toys to a poor orphanage we had known before. The clothes and toys came from Norfolk, collected there in a worthwhile project called HANDCLASP by Navy wives for distribution abroad. This particular orphanage is operated by a very impoverished order of nuns who take in abandoned girl children, some from the streets and some badly abused and diseased. We also had most of them down to the ship for ice cream, movies, etc. Carol rode with her friends the cavalry and was greeted with enthusiasm by all who remembered her as the queen of the Valentine Ball. From Les Marqueses to Pilar, our former maid, we had a grand home coming.

It was encouraging to observe and to hear about the economic improvement of Spain. A flood of tourists is helping greatly, accompanied, of course, by the inevitable rise in food, lodging and land along the sea. Business in general has improved and the gamble Spain had to take when it joined the OEEC has paid off. Despite an archaic central government in Madrid Spain is pulling itself up gradually into the 20th century. This is no mean feat considering that the Marshal Plan did not apply to Spain.

The following Monday, November 13, we put to sea again in the face of gloomy storm warnings. It was only a gale this time and moved east before we felt the full force of it. As we headed southeast for our operating area south of Sicily we were grateful for only a night of moderate rolling.

A week of routine exercises followed in calm seas and sunny skies until we headed north again and Villefranche for Thanksgiving. Snow capped Mt. Aetna as we passed through Messina Straits and we knew it would be cool in France.

There was one incident I can't forget. We were about to leave the hotel at Cos. I had been talking to the woman at the desk.

Sofia, in her falsetto melancholy voice said casually, "Madame, the boat will come between 5:30 and 7:30."

Suddenly the enchantment of this particular little Greek island was broken and the mechanics of getting ourselves packed must be recognized. The poor choice of the bag that would "hold everything" must be dealt with. The bag that had been carried on a strong back four blocks from the dory to the hotel, must now be returned again to the dock.

"Can I arrange for someone to care for your bag?"

"Your bag will be at the dock, Madame, don't worry. Everything will be arrange."

In this moment with this kindly sympathetic middle aged woman I find that I can comfortably ask "Just how much shall I tip the man?" She laughed gently. "I cannot say, Madame."

"But, Sofia, it is heavy and must be carried all the way; the circumstances are so different, please give me an idea."

"Usually the fee is 10 or 15 drachs but give a few drachs extra. It would mean so much to the man and so little to you. These people have so little, almost not enough to eat. You Americans are so fortunate; you have so freedom from want. These people are so poor."

"This is what I wanted to know. Sofia, in this barren land the war must have been dreadful."

"Yes, Madame, I didn't live here during the war. I was in the south of Greece. War was declared at six o'clock one morning, at eight o'clock there were ten thousand people in the town dead, Italians."

"But how is this possible, the Italians were victorious."

"They choose to bomb a section of the city that had been occupied by Italians who'd settled in Greece. The city was in rubble so everyone moved away from the city into anything they could find. A year after the war started old people and children roamed the streets crying "Help me, help me, I'm starving, I'm starving. This I remember. An old woman reach down into a stagnant pool of water that had been used for washing clothes and waste, for a black mouldy lemon rind which she hungrily ate like an animal. I said, "Stop, Stop" but it was too late and I realized that I still had my olive pits in my mouth. Each morning I would put ten olives into my mouth (this I can laugh about now). There they would stay all morning. At noon I would eat the meat from them then hold them in my mouth for the rest of the day. By nite they would be white when I spit them out. They were so bitter it would dull my appetite. I chewed eucalyptus leaves for their bitterness, too. We lived like animals."

"Madame, it has been a long time and the time helps heal the wounds. I've lost an uncle, a brother, nieces and nephews with great sadness but I've gotten used to these ideas and adjusted. But, Madame, this I remember, as tho it had just happened and I must relive over and over the moment of the death of my daughter of only ten years."

On 17 October we arrived off Bomba on the coast of Libya where a small amphibious landing was to take place. We stayed there all day, departing at dusk to meet the CANISTEO and refuel. I took a few officers ashore for a quick swim at noon. The golden sands of Libya are splendid but full of camel dung. We had a glimpse of the desert where so much bloody fighting took place in WW II.

So home to Villefranche, fueling again enroute and feeling the tag ends of the first big winter storm.

Villefranche wore its new autumn dress: rain washed and green, with few yachts, no tourists. It was great to be home. We drove to Cannes to pick up Joy and to see her school. An old villa with a lovely self supporting staircase and a warm and charming headmistress, Mme Bly. Sunday we all went sailing after church on board. Joy returned to school on Monday and Mary and I played golf. The week went quickly: up at 0630, at work by seven, home for lunch, then tennis, sailing or golf. Some sort of a party about every other day. Thursday we took a picnic lunch and, picking up Joy at school, headed for the mountains. We went up the valley of the Var. The trees were turning and the scenery was spectacular. Saturday we attended the Homage to Picasso, a gala, very high class vaudeville with world famous singers, actors, dancers, and musicians performing for a huge crowd in the Nice auditorium. Picasso himself was there. Highlight was Antonio the classic flamenco dancer of Spain.

On Wednesday we went to sea, leaving our homeport basking in its Indian summer.

December 1961

INSTALLMENT XIV

Naples - Livorno - Sea and Storm - Home to Villefranche for Christmas

    Naples for a long weekend was routine, as was a week of operating at sea in cool, mild weather. We had our last major replenishment with the INDEPENDENCE and it came off very well except for a destroyer that got underfoot. No one really blamed the DD since it was a head on approach of one formation upon another at high speed at night with very little warning to the screen.

    We went in behind the breakwater at Livorno in a mild westerly gale. It was a bit tight in there for a cruiser but the pilot and tugs were waiting to help. We moored amidst a good deal of shouted broken English, arm waving and blowing of whistle on the part of the pilot and clouds of black smoke issued by the tugs. The pilot, despite his novel use of English, which convulsed the men standing in ranks nearby, knew his job and we finally made fast aft to the mole after dropping our two anchors. The DD PERRY, obviously conned by another ebullient Italian, insisted on passing between our stern and the mole while we were backing down, but all went well, if a trifle close. I find Italian pilots to be very able seamen and shiphandlers indeed but they operate with an elan and gusto that does not seem to recognize the possibility of a misunderstanding of signals or a mechanical failure.

    Although the weather was miserable (INDEPENDENCE, anchored outside, had no liberty the first day) Mary and I enjoyed Livorno. We stayed with my cousin, Contessa di Sergardi, a charming widow who, despite her seventy plus years, helps her daughter Fulvia take care of her nine children.

    We went to Florence for a day and did some Christmas shopping. The morning we left Mary woke me at Caterina's at about 0430 and said she heard ships' whistles blowing, in groups of five or seven blasts. Since this is our emergency recall signal and Caterina's house had no phone, there was nothing to do but go to the landing. The driver of my Navy car was at his hotel and I was not sure the beach guard could reach him. We had to wake up another guest at Caterina's, Herb Wichern and borrow his car. Caterina got up and looked thoroughly bewildered. With a good deal of confusion and much advice from the upstairs windows we got the car started and went off. It turned out to be a false alarm - there was no emergency recall. "A good drill for the Captain", said Mary.

We left Livorno in calm, gray weather but found another winter storm a few days later. We were west of the southern end of Sardinia - where the fetch is longest for a northwest storm, and again we ran for a lee as long as we could without smashing gear on deck and then finally hove to at eight knots, heading directly into the seas. We rolled up to 40°, which made the Admiral unhappy, but the ship rode well, taking no green water aboard. No damage done but time wasted and an uneasy time for me. Two days later we put into a small bay for the turnover between two big carriers and the carrier division staffs (CTF 60) who exercise operational command during our routine operations. The INDEPENDENCE headed back home for Xmas and the SARATOGA reported in for duty.

We spent the day anchored and having conferences. All the Task Force skippers had lunch with Pete Aurand in the INDEPENDENCE while ComSixthFlt entertained the Admirals and their Chiefs of Staff at a resort hotel he spotted on the beach. At dusk we sortied in formation and then broke off to go to Barcelona where we transferred ComSixthFlt by helo to the INTREPID. We lay off Barcelona for twenty-four hours, recovered the Admiral, who had entertained some Spanish VIP's in the INTREPID, and then returned to the waters south of Sardinia for some shooting.

One night we observed unusual light effects in connection with the stars. Sirius and Procyon appeared to be flashing red and green as well as showing their usual white light. Some sort of atmospheric optical illusion but not one I can easily explain. A recent Notice to Mariners, published by the Hydrographic Office, described the same phenomenon.

A surprise administrative inspection Saturday morning by Commander Cruiser Division TWO, assisted by the USS BOSTON, was most welcome. The ship and the crew looked outstanding and our paper work was in good order. We received a high mark and it was a pleasure to see old friends. The purpose behind this drill is to inspect a ship just as she is, in her everyday dress, as it were, with no time to rush over to the beauty shop. We _were_ surprised; at 0500 a message came in telling us to put at Aranci Bay where the BOSTON would also anchor. At the time we were cruising off the east coast of Sardinia. We held reveille a bit early in order to clear the mess decks and at 0900, with all hands not on watch paraded in their dress blues we received RAdm Brooks and his inspecting party. As we had been polishing up everything before the early liberty days of the holidays, the ship looked great. A short critique was held at 1130 in the Wardroom, we had lunch with Commander Sixth Fleet at 1330, and then got underway and stood out into the Tyrrhenian Sea, looking for the oiler MISSISSINEWA. We found her before dark and went alongside for fuel, passengers and freight and our Fleet Wine Mess consignment.

The next day was Sunday, blowing forty knots and temperature in the low forties. We headed for Villefranche in a gale, hugging the Coast of Italy for a lee and a smooth ride into our own smug harbor. Merry Christmas!

As we steamed past Corsica the Admiral suggested getting in early, using only the men on watch to pick up our mooring at 0530. This we did with pleasure; it was a dark clear night and we surprised many people, ashore and aboard, by being moored before daylight.

Joy was at home with a bad ear which was a great break for me since I miss not having her home when I'm in Villefranche. We were all together for Thanksgiving except Jackson whom we phoned on Tuesday. Thanksgiving was rainy and cool - a good day to stay indoors. Friday, 24 November we put to sea - next stop Naples for the weekend and then to Livorno after a week of operating.

December-January 1962

INSTALLMENT XV

Xmas at Villefranche - At Sea - Casablanca

We moored in Villefranche harbor on a bright, cold day and liberty call was sounded instanter. Jackson was at home, down from his school at Dreux, with his roommate whose family (Foreign Service) was in Ethiopia. We went down to Cannes in the afternoon and picked up Joy who was also en vacance.

The next two weeks were a most pleasant combination of family holiday gatherings, private and official parties and golf and tennis. On Xmas Eve we asked visiting ship skippers and bachelor officers to dinner. Afterwards we met the Chaplain and a few of his Carol Singers and sang carols in a local old people's home and around the old town of Villefranche. Our group grew as stray sailors and civilians, in various stages of exuberance, joined in. It was something unique for the "O2 level" and was written up in the Nice papers as an interesting and attractive American folk custom. So was the three minute blast of the ship's whistle at midnight - a distinctly unofficial incident whose instigators escaped detection and retribution.

After Christmas there was Mrs. Florence Gould's fabulous New Year's Eve dinner party at her villa in Cannes. The people, a cross section of Riviera VIP's, Navy, and the wealthy international set, were interesting as were the paintings from El Greco to Rembrandt. The collection of portraits in the long, panelled dining room (Ramsey, Gainsborough, etc.) must have been worth $2,000,000.00. Dinner lasted until after midnight and dancing until about 5 A.M.

Despite much cloudiness and considerable rain, golf and tennis were possible most of the time. Mary and I played several times at Mont Angel and I played in the Christmas tennis tournament at the Monte Carlo Country Club. This was for seniors only (over 45) and was a local affair except for half a dozen Italians. Had lots of exercise and met the top local senior players. Lost in the semifinals to the number one seeded player and was in the finals of the doubles when rained out and I had to go to sea.

Jackson and Carol did some sailing and even entered one race but our boat is too slow to be a racer, we have concluded.

My orders came in on Xmas Eve, Naval Attaché in Paris. Mary and I are delighted and are working hard on our French.

One curious incident in the Small World department. Months ago at the Tennis Club at Monte Carlo I had wandered around looking for a game and had met an old Englishman, Herbert Milne, and played a set with him. He said he was 74 and did not play much anymore. During Xmas Mary met him while watching some tennis and they talked for awhile. It turned out that he had been born and raised in Lima, Peru and had played polo with my father in Lima about the time I was born, 50 years ago.

On 3 January I held mast for the holiday sinners. There were not many, nine all told, and some of these quite trivial. The others were all variations on the same unhappy theme - too much alcohol. A small but persistent number of men can't handle the stuff. They become obstreperous, belligerent, disrespectful. Most of these are beyond our help and, despite every effort on our part to help them, continue to get in trouble ashore and must be discharged from the Service. A few respond to probation and learn their lesson. We spare no pain and patience to save a man who is useful to the ship. Some of the men really go ape. One seaman, a good lad aboard ship, became drunk and unmanageable ashore and was escorted to the landing. There he broke away from the Patrol and started swimming out to the ship. Before a boat could pick him up he disappeared. A report was received a short time later that a man was running around Villefranche in his underwear. Our boy was corralled and put in a straight jacket. Going up the accommodation ladder he jumped into the water again, still in the straight jacket, and two men had to jump in and pull him out. Everything got back to normal when he was safely locked in the brig.

After mast I had the pleasure of presenting a plaque which SPRINGFIELD received as the outstanding cruiser of fiscal 1961 in Refresher Training. We gave it to those of the crew who had been in SPRINGFIELD at Guantanamo. All hands not on watch fell in aft, old hands forward, and I gave the plaque to Cdr Faubion, the senior officer aboard who had been through refresher training. We also had our Sailor-of-the-Month presentation at that time.

Off to sea on 4 January - next port Casablanca. We fueled that afternoon - uneventful except for a man falling overboard. The helicopter was airborne within minutes and picked him up (from under the bow of a destroyer) four minutes after he fell in. No harm done, water temperature was a mild 62°, and a well done from ComSixthFlt for the smart rescue.

Our days at sea were routine, the weather was fairly good, and the ship did all her assigned tasks smoothly. On the 10th we headed west for the Straits of Gibraltar and reached Casablanca on schedule. A long, moderately big swell from the northwest was running and we rolled a bit until we got in behind the breakwater. Mary was there, having driven down with Joyce Douglas the day before from Tangier. We had the usual calls and ceremonies and went to Rabat for a luncheon with Ambassador Bonsal. While the Admiral made his calls, John Chaisson and I were shown about the city by Mr. Johnson, a First Secretary at the Embassy. The narrow streets, lined with tiny shops where things were being made by hand, looked almost medieval.

That evening Consul General Tomlinson gave a reception and afterwards we had a typical Moroccan dinner. After dinner we went to a large dance for the crew that had been arranged by the American Community in Casablanca. There were many girls, lots of beer and food, the excellent Sixth Fleet dance band and a belly dancer who really shook things up. Mary and I danced the Bunny Hop and in general had a grand time. Mary was the belle of the ball and danced for hours with many of the men.

The next day, Sunday, we played golf at an attractive course nearby, Fedala. The sun came out and we had a grand game. That afternoon late we had a reception aboard SPRINGFIELD for several hundred Moroccans, among them the governor and several prominent left wing politicians.

Monday I was involved in much official entertainment, most of it stag, and Mary flew to Marrakech with Clay Lindus. They went in a small Comanche, owned by the Air Force Flying Club and piloted by a very able sergeant. This expedition was arranged for through the courtesy of Col Thornton, an AF officer we had met on Saturday, who was president of the flying club. It was a great adventure for Mary, who had never flown in a small plane and Marrakech lived up to its advance billing. It was colorful, interesting and beautiful; on the edge of the desert at the foot of snow covered mountains. Here is her account of seeing Marrakech and Fez.

These past two days of our trip to Morocco have been a journey into the ancient past in both the real and in an imagined sense. For the first time, I rode in a small Comanche Aircraft. Our pilot was a serious, intelligent, charming young Air Force Sergeant. Soon we were running down the field, in the air, thru the clouds, and into the sun and heading toward a ridge of snow topped mountains. Our plane, I'd not realized until this moment, had been transferred into a flying carpet and we were on our way into "the Arabian Nights."

We took a cab from the airport to the hotel and then hired a Berber Guide and a horse drawn carriage. The street into this ancient city is wide and attractive, the vegetation that I'd always imagined in an oasis: sub-tropical and quite familiar. Here it is unusual to have rain more than three times a year but the water table is high due to the snow on the mountains. Our guide pointed out the two tallest mosques. These were so like the towers on the Stanford Campus and entirely different from those we'd seen in Istanbul.

Our first stop was the Mausoleum of the Sultans. The magnificence of these buildings is for me in the proportions. The detail, in plaster, of the passages from the Koran and the beautifully carved ceilings and arches in the most fragrant cedar contribute to the over-all effect. Surprisingly, the effect is one of simplicity. Many herbs are planted in the gardens. Our guide picked sprigs of various herbs along the way which we put in our pockets. We added to these fragrances bits of cedar shavings. Having done no shopping, these wads of wilted leaves and wood were our only material rememberances of Marrakech; the perfect touch to recapture the atmosphere of the whole day.

Our next stop was an old sultan's place - unfortunately in a comparatively extensive state of decay. We climbed to the top of the outer wall of the center portion of the building where we got the general effect of the plan of various gardens and the public patios. There were three of these huge patios, each we were told, served a different purpose in the old days. One was for the dancers, one musicians and the other miscellaneous kinds of entertainment. The museum a few blocks away proved to be most interesting and helpful in distinguishing the crafts from each section of the country and various tribes.

We had luncheon in a beautifully restored old place that has become a restaurant. The tables were low; the walls were lined with couches, and hassocks. The waiter appeared with a large covered basin with a deep sill in which there were many holes. Soap and a towel were provided. As we held out our hands over the basin he poured the warm water with which we washed our hands. We had many tall glasses of sweetened orange juice and a chicken cous-cous. This is the most typical dish of the country; a great quantity of a farina type cereal which has the consistancy of barley after hours of cooking is served on a large platter. Over it is poured a stew. This cous-cous was made of chicken, raisins and grabansos beans. A very hot sauce was served which reminded me of Mexico. The pigeon stuffed with almonds and other nuts was marvelous. The sauce in which the bird was roasted was made of butter and lemon juice and seasoned with cummin and saffron. We ate from a common dish with wooden spoons carved by hand from a single piece of orange wood.

After luncheon we walked thru the Medina where on each little street various artisans were busy at their trades. One young man was turning out various spool designs with a razor sharp chisel, and a hand-powered lathe, turned by a bow. The artisans use their feet as deftly as they do their hands and neither seemed calloused or hard. On this same street were the rug makers under a great canopy of dripping, drying multi-colored bands of wool.

From there we went to the city square and to the terrace of a coffee shop where we watched the circus performers. Groups of people formed circles around each of these persons. Some were telling stories, one reading from Koran, another had trained pigeons, and others were dancers. The dancers clapped large metal instruments, one in each hand, that had much the same effect as castanets. They accompanied themselves by singing and beating a drum. Here, too, were the colorful water carriers; the goat-skins slung over their shoulders were complete with hair. I thought their hats most interesting as they seemed to be exact duplicates of those worn by some of the native dancers in Cuernavaco, Mexico. It was here that we felt the culmination of all our impressions, the mountains in the background, the warm dry air, the fragrances of cedar, spice, and the noises.

On our way back to the plane we wandered through a private garden composed of bamboo and cactus, begonias and geraniums. The profusion with which these things were growing in this soil is unbelievable.

Back again into our little plane, up into the air, half an hour later down through the clouds and we'd returned from our chapter of Arabian Nights.

If our trip to Marrakech was a trip into the Arabian Nights, the trip to Fez was a journey back through time. We left Casablanca in the morning by car arriving at eleven at the U.S. Naval Communication Station at Kinetra where we were served a most magnificent luncheon by our friends the Weirs.

After driving through rather symmetrical farming country that is at this moment beautifully green and also through rather low foot hills we arrived at the outskirts of Fez, again with the Atlas mountains as a backdrop. The ancient wall that surrounds the city is not a ruin, it contains this great mass of people apparently living in the 13th century. We stopped briefly on a low hill overhanging the city to listen. It did indeed sound like a beehive. We went directly to the hotel, the Palacio Samais, stopping only to leave our bags and to arrange for a guide. This we got but in the narrowest sense of the word, he merely directed us through the great maze of Fez. As we started out the faithful were being called to prayer by a loud speaker system. The streets, made of cobble stone, are no more than eight or ten feet wide, the buildings much higher so that little sun could shine on the city streets. Some streets were very narrow. Someone had told me that Fez was very much like London before the great fire.

Suddenly from out of the darkness of one of these little streets would appear a child. Men on horseback came galloping through the streets and donkey caravans were common, carrying anyone of a hundred items produced in this city. We saw no other tourists. The people seemed indifferent to our visit - they went about their business with great urgency. The shops were composed of artisans working in metal, weaving, dyeing and wood working. Some buildings housed pieces of cedar four or five feet wide and six or eight inches think. In another large building we saw olives being ground for oil in a great stone mortar by stone wheels. Did not we have the feeling that any of these industries were to demonstrate how things used to be done - this is how it is done. The children were dismissed from school while we were walking - they would giggle and say "Bon Jour" and dare the next to speak to us. One brave little lad of ten talked to us about school and was most manly and well mannered. They seemed well fed and happy but with far too many skin diseases, caused, I assume by the lack of sun and a great deal of dirt. Unlike Istanbul, where visitors were allowed to enter, no one was permitted in the various mosques throughout the city. In looking through the doors we had the impression of a cool, clean, quiet oasis.

The hotel was an adventure in itself. It had been a sultan's palace, with beautiful gardens and terraces. The next morning we went on to Tangier to catch the ferry to Gibraltar.

In Tangier we were sitting at a table in a sidewalk cafe feeding potato chips to a dog. A man, dressed in rags came along and started towards us when he saw food being given to the dog. He was obviously very hungry but he stopped and turned away - as if to say - "If these cursed infidels give food to dogs I'll have none of it."

January-February 1962

INSTALLMENT XVI

Gibraltar - Rota - Cadiz - Cartagena - Toulon - Villefranche

After leaving Casablanca we anchored overnight in the bay of Tangier, after debarking several Moroccan Naval Officers who had enjoyed their trip up the coast in SPRINGFIELD. The next morning we were underway before daylight - crossing the straits against the heavy traffic. We arrived off Gibraltar, fired our salutes and were escorted inside the breakwater and berthed.

It was a brief but relaxing visit. After the strain of Casablanca, where the political situation was potentially explosive and the people not all overjoyed to see us, the warm and friendly British were a balm. Mary and I stayed with the Gullettes in their immense, old and comfortable quarters. He is our liaison officer at Gibraltar. The Flag Officer, Gibraltar, RAdm Powlett, and Mrs. Powlett were most charming and their dinner was much fun. After our return dinner in SPRINGFIELD the next evening we sailed at midnight, arriving off Cadiz the next morning to fire our salute. We moored at Rota and had a pleasant weekend, staying at an attractive hotel on the beach. We met many of the local Spanish Navy and other Spanish gentry from Jerez and Cadiz. Sunday we went to Cadiz for the day.

We were shown some of the most interesting and rarely seen Spanish paintings by Sra Villar, the charming wife of Dr. Pepe Villar. First we went to the cathedral, built between 1500 and 1600, and thus one of the newest in Spain, since others are built on Moorish ruins which usually cover Roman and pre-Roman buildings. The gold, silver and jewels in the cathedral are fabulous - one item of silver weighs 3000 lbs - and must be worth millions. Here is a part of the wealth of the Indies - the small part that remained in Spain. What a waste when this fortune could be used to endow a clinic or a school! We went next to an old chapel filled with paintings by Murillo. One was his last and it was from the scaffolding in front of this painting, high above the altar, that he fell to his death, aged 60 odd and, according to local gossip, a bit tipsy at the time. His St. Francis of Assisi is in this chapel.

The most unusual and most attractive pictures, however, were three Goyas in a small and dusty chapel built for men only and recently opened to visitors. The chapel was a gem, built by a rich priest who could afford to hire Goya and Haydn. The latter wrote his <u>The Last Seven Words of Jesus</u> especially for the chapel. Goya was hired to do five paintings while he was visiting the Duchess of Alba nearby but only stayed to do three. These are The Last Supper, The Bread and the Fishes and the Parable of the Badly Dressed Wedding Guest. The first two are outstanding. Goya shows The Last Supper as it probably happened, Jesus and his disciples not seated at a banquet table but lolling informally on the ground.

From Rota to Cartagena was a short run and we approached this ancient harbor at dawn, firing our salute at a castle shrouded in a heavy smog. The small harbor was really socked in and, to make things lively, Spanish submarines and destroyers kept darting out of the fog, outbound as we were inbound. Since the entrance is only about 300 yards wide and requires a 130° turn it was a bit difficult. Two pilots came aboard, one for the outside harbor and one for berthing. We finally were berthed and the usual calls began. Mary was driving down from Granada that morning.

We had a most enjoyable visit, due to the charming Spanish Navy. We met many people, played tennis every day, and walked about the rather uninteresting town. Here Hannibal started his march on Rome but there are few impressive sights.

Our scuba divers struck pay dirt here and brought up two lovely Roman amphora. The Spanish Navy (whose officers train with our UDT at Little Creek, Virginia) showed them the wreck of a Roman ship, in about 90 feet of water. The men gave one of the jugs to Mary and the other to the Admiral.

On the 27th we sailed for the Western Basin - the sea area between the Balearics and Corsica - Sardinia - where we play at Big Game, an exercise with the French. The first day and night at sea was pleasant; then we ran into one of the gales that seem to persist in the Western Basin. The first day we took on missiles and ammo from the NITRO while heading into a heavy sea. The NITRO's forefoot (stem) was coming clean out of the water as she pitched; this made station keeping somewhat difficult. Everyone on the forecastle was thoroughly drenched with spray - we even had some up on the wing of the bridge. That night with the wind at 40 kts we fueled from a tanker. It was a dark, rough night - the kind that make you grateful for moonlight and calm seas.

Unusually rough weather persisted for the remainder of the week. Rain, sleet and snow squalls accompanied by high winds, lightning and thunder were common. On Saturday night we anchored at Porto Scudo, on the SW end of Sardinia where the Marines were putting on a landing. The only incident worthy of note was a fiasco about baggage that was funny to everyone but the victim. An Italian General had been staying overnight in my in-port cabin. As he left Sunday morning to observe the landing the steward assigned to pick up his baggage also picked up two other bags, one of mine and one of Mary's - both plainly tagged.

These bags were taken ashore before the loss was discovered. In Mary's bag was her jewelry, left on board because it was safer there than being carried around in the car. After many messages and several days both bags were located and returned.

Toulon was pleasant and near enough to Villefranche so that everyone with a family either had them down or could get home. Mary drove down with Joy and Carol. The two girls spent the day and went back the same day. Mary and I enjoyed seeing our old French friends again and met many new people.

Underway Wednesday for a missile shoot off Hyeres and then home. The missiles fired well and after replenishing from the Service Force on Friday we put into our favorite harbor for a ten-day stay.

Official U. S. Navy Photograph
USS ROCHESTER—A GOOD WILL AMBASSADOR TO SOUTHEAST ASIA

SHOWING THE FLAG IN SOUTHEAST ASIA

By COMMANDER JOHN V. NOEL, JR., *U. S. Navy*

IT WAS a few days after Christmas, 1953, that our sailing orders came by radio message. The USS *Rochester* (CA 124) was to be deployed to the Western Pacific, departing from Long Beach, California, for Japan on January 5 via Pearl Harbor, Manila, Singapore, Bangkok and Saigon. Of course we had known that we were going west early in January, but the itinerary en route had been the subject of much scuttlebutt and long speculation during the quiet night watches underway off Southern California.

This news was what we had hoped for; the *Rochester* was ready now. A long shipyard overhaul had been successfully completed during the summer, followed by rigorous refresher training in the Long Beach-San Diego area in October, November, and part of December. The first Christmas at home in four years had been a welcome reward for months of operating and for the accomplishment of thorough training. We were ready to see the world, as promised by the recruiting posters.

The desire to persuade all hands that an interesting cruise was ahead of them inspired a poster campaign. The Commanding Officer was concerned about that irresponsible five per cent who might be tempted by homesickness or by some bewitching feminine companionship to miss sailing with the ship upon her final departure. To convert these potential miscreants and to arouse the interest of all the crew in the forthcoming voyage, we had gambled in November that the ship would go somewhere in the south Pacific and had acted accordingly. The mess halls and passageways had been plastered with large, gaudy, tropical travel posters obtained from Cooks and from the Matson Line office in Los Angeles. Thinly veiled references to the delights of tropical cruising were made regularly in the Plan of the Day. Of course, the old hands aboard knew that there were few dusky maidens yearning for romance

Official U. S. Navy Photograph
ROCHESTER'S SHELLBACKS AFTER ANNIHILATION OF ALL POLLYWOGS

under waving palm trees, but we believed that most young men were romantic and susceptible to suggestion. The gamble paid off, the tropical cruise was announced as a reality, and all but three men of a total crew of 1400 sailed with the ship on January 5. As an added proof of the efficacy of our propaganda campaign, several reserve officers requested extensions of their active duty in order to make the cruise. Unusual as it may sound, an appreciable number of men eligible for class A schools ashore declined those much desired assignments in favor of staying on sea duty in the ship that was going to visit the South Pacific.

The *Rochester* seemed a happy choice for

GRADUATED from the U. S. Naval Academy in the Class of 1936, Commander Noel spent World War II in destroyers and has since served at sea as an amphibious-planning officer and as executive officer, USS *Rochester*. His shore duty has been in the Office of Naval Operations, at Stanford University, and at the Naval Academy. He is the author of the *Division Officer's Guide* and *Naval Terms Dictionary*, a co-author of *Shiphandling* and the *Watch Officer's Guide*, and assisted in the current revision of Knight's *Modern Seamanship*. Commander Noel is now at the Industrial College of the Armed Forces.

---

this duty of showing the Flag in foreign ports. She was just about the right size for a visiting man-of-war; large enough to be able to entertain distinguished visitors on board and small enough to enter most major ports and be berthed alongside a pier. Her outstanding appearance, with symmetrical superstructure arranged around a single stack, was also an asset. Her Commanding Officer had just completed a course at the National War College where his indoctrination in Asia and our foreign policy there had been extensive. Captain, crew, and ship were an ideal combination to promote good will and respect for the United States.

In addition to the routine preparations for extended cruising away from the mainland, two extraordinary although minor steps were taken to prepare for the southern cruise. A quantity of the excellent National Geographic Society maps of Asia and the Western Pacific was obtained. These were posted in living spaces and passageways. A quartermaster was detailed to maintain a rough track and daily ship's position record on these charts during the cruise. Special short essays on the geography and history of the area the ship was traversing were included in the Plan of the Day, available to all hands. The second special step was to obtain a shelf

Official U. S. Navy Photograph
PENULTIMATE STAGE OF A POLLYWOG'S INITIATION

of books on southeast Asia, including the specific ports which the *Rochester* would visit. These books not only proved popular for general reading but were invaluable as sources of information for the Plan of the Day stories mentioned above.

The first leg of the voyage, to Pearl Harbor, was made without incident. Most of our time was devoted to removing the Long Beach dust which covered the ship from bow to stern. Dirt had also permeated into every storeroom and stateroom; into drawers, desks, and clothes closets. A series of December Santa Anas and a big forest fire on the slopes of Mt. Wilson, back of Los Angeles, had caused an unusual amount of dirt, dust, and smoke in the atmosphere, even for the Los Angeles area. It was not until the ship encountered the northeast trades, several days out of Pearl Harbor, that the men succeeded in cleaning the topsides. This was accomplished by having the ship chase rain squalls in the hope of getting a thorough freshwater washdown of the masts, stack, and other parts of the superstructure that are inaccessible underway. It was amusing to see the Boatswain, standing on the forecastle, scanning the horizon forward of the beam for a good dark rain squall that the officer of the deck could head for without getting too far away from his prescribed track. It was not so many years ago that rain squalls served naval ships in a more serious way; as a refuge when Japanese planes buzzed overhead.

For the many new men aboard Pearl Harbor was a famous and a historical battle site. It was hard to realize that most of the young sailors learned about the Day of Infamy, December 7, 1941, in their grade school history classes. For the old timers, however, who remembered how it looked during the war, Pearl Harbor seemed to be a ghost harbor. Few ships were in sight along the wharves and none were in the channel, while Ford Island had the door closed and the blinds pulled down. The green hills back of the base seemed to be covered with many more new houses, but the mountains to the north were still filled with purple shadows as the tradewind clouds spilled over the ridges. For many of us who had lived out here and passed in and out during the war it was almost a homecoming; to the many *malahinis* aboard it was their first taste of the tropics and the Orient. Waikiki seemed to have developed into an expensive Coney Island, with Polynesian curios for sale (made in Japan), but for those who love the surf and the inimitable climate the magic was still there.

After an enjoyable five days we left Hawaii on the long leg to Manila. We passed into the Philippine Sea between the tiny volcanic island peaks of Agrihan and Asuncion of the Marianas group, both in sight as the sun rose on the 27th of January. A note on the chart that Agrihan was suspected to be north of the charted position was confirmed and a detailed report was made to the Hydrographic Office. Another small contribution that the *Rochester* made to scientific knowledge in this stage of the cruise was the discovery of a seamount which, as far as we knew, had not been reported. The ocean in many places is still uncharted and it is not too difficult to play explorer with a sonic depth finder and look for new mountains and deeps under the sea while making routine passages.

Landfall in the Philippines was made off San Bernardino Straits and passage was made through these historic waters in excellent weather. Here the last desperate lunge of Japanese sea power failed in October, 1944, as Admiral Kurita led his big ships, battered by Halsey's airmen, back into the Philippine Sea to fall upon the small carriers off Leyte Gulf. It was a bold stroke, not the least hazardous being the transit of these narrow swift moving waters at night.

The following morning we entered Manila Bay, picked up the pilot, and moored port side to a commercial pier. As soon as pesos could be obtained for dollars (at the somewhat depressed, official, rate of two pesos for one dollar) the liberty party was ashore, and, as far as could be determined, having a fine time. Manila has made a tremendous recovery from its wartime devastation, but many scars remain. The hulks lying half submerged in the harbor have been the subject of a good deal of haggling while their scrap value oxidizes away at the rate of about five percent a year.

In 1946 the Japanese reportedly offered the Philippine government several million dollars for salvage rights. This was considered insufficient and no agreement on price was reached. It now appears that the government will have to pay to have the wrecks removed. Unofficial and small-scale scrap collectors are steadily whittling away at the most accessible parts of the wrecks; soon there will be little remaining above water. Most of the wrecks can be credited to the Third Fleet airmen whose activities were cheered by a large part of the population of Manila who had assembled along Dewey Boulevard as if to witness a boat race. At least that is the tale now told around the bar at the Army-Navy Club.

The important story in Manila was the new President, Ramon Magsaysay. His dynamic leadership and unusual accomplishments have impressed the American officials and business men as much as they have inflamed the enthusiasm of the ebullient Filipinos. The young boarding officer from the staff of Commander Naval Forces, Philippines, reported the improved efficiency of the commercial port of Manila under Magsaysay's clean-up and speed-up directives. Another popular account of recent improvements concerned civilians ashore who were able to pay their telephone bills on time without paying a "tip." The former practice had been to temporarily "lose" telephone bills unless a few pesos were produced. If the telephone bill remained lost the victim became eligible for an overdue penalty. President Magsaysay was using his Army to dig wells and repair roads. His Navy, in addition to controlling "pirates" and smugglers in the Subic Sea, was employed to transport freight and produce. A naval LST saved the potato crop by transporting potatoes, for example, when a bumper crop on Mindanao overtaxed the road facilities. The new President has taken positive and vigorous action against the Communist outlaws by offering them a homestead if they turn themselves in and stand trial for any crimes they may be charged with. This enlightened approach, together with vigorous military action, has achieved considerable success. Much of the bitterness of the peasants in the Philippines and their consequent interest in Communism stems from the occasional monopolistic control of the land by disinterested and even absentee landlords.

The *Rochester* left Manila behind with less regrets than anticipation for Singapore and the experience of Crossing the Line. A slight departure from a direct track to Singapore was needed to cross the Equator, which passes a few miles south of the tip of the

CREWMEN OF THE *ROCHESTER* ENJOY LIFE IN SINGAPORE

Malay Peninsula. This detour had been arranged for in advance and was included in our sailing orders. The 1200 pollywogs quite outnumbered the 200 hardworking shellbacks, and some concern was felt about the whole ceremony getting out of hand. As it turned out, there were no serious revolts on the part of the landlubbers; the traditional show was put on with complete good humor. No injuries worth reporting to sick bay were logged, which was a matter of some relief to the Commanding Officer. Over twelve hundred men earned their shellback certificates in about four hours by running the gauntlet, serving a short sentence in the Royal Stocks, being sentenced (while grasping an electrically charged rod) by the Royal Judge, kissing the Royal Baby, receiving the attentions of the Royal Dentist, Doctor, Photographer, and Barber, in that order, and finally being flipped out of the barber's chair into a tank of water

Singapore was big and busy and clean and hot; more impressive as a monument to world shipping and British colonialism than picturesque. There was a new, beautifully equipped enlisted men's club opposite the famous Raffles Hotel. The British sailors, however, were reported to object to its being so big and glossy; they claimed it looked too much like an officer's club. At any rate, our people had no such inhibitions and thoroughly enjoyed it. For most of the men Singapore was the first opportunity to shop in an Asiatic city but it had little appeal as a liberty port. For officers, however, the hospitable English tennis, swimming, and golf clubs made the visit most enjoyable. The tennis players aboard particularly enjoyed the unusual opportunity of playing on grass courts. The golfers enjoyed the efficient and inexpensive caddies.

Official social affairs in Singapore commenced upon our arrival and slacked off very little during the visit. The U. S. Naval Attache gave a large reception for ship's officers and Singapore military and diplomatic persons. The Governor of the Crown Colony of Singapore, Sir John Nicoll, honored the Commanding Officer with a luncheon that was a most splendid and impressive affair. The executive officer was fortunate enough to be invited as well. Government House, about the size of the White House in Washington,

WEST MEETS EAST BEFORE A TEMPLE IN BANGKOK, THAILAND

had grounds so spacious that a nine hole golf course was lost in the front garden. Pink gins and gimlets were served before lunch, a Singapore custom among the British that *Rochester* personnel found somewhat enervating. The pomp and splendor of this luncheon was matched by the cordiality of Sir John Nicoll and his guests who were senior British Naval Officers The whole affair seemed straight out of Kipling: the British officers looking very fit and sunburned, and the costumed servants providing an air of oriental luxury. There seemed to be four servants assigned to each guest as we stood about before luncheon, one to provide a drink. one to offer a cigarette. a third to light the cigarette, and still another to hold an ashtray conveniently at hand. The Empire seemed as strong as ever in Singapore that afternoon.

Another luncheon was given for the Commanding Officer and three ship's officers by the acting American Consul General, Mr. Richard Hawkins. Guests from Paris and from Jakarta and superb Chinese food were highlights of this occasion. A call on Sir Charles and Lady Lambe was another outstanding event. The Admiral is the Commander in Chief, Far East Station. They are both talented and interesting people; Sir Charles is a painter and an accomplished pianist, Lady Lambe is an art collector.

On the last day in port the *Rochester* gave a reception which set the pattern for those to follow in Bangkok and Saigon. The forecastle was draped in bunting and tables were set up for refreshments. The lack of alcoholic beverages seemed to disturb no one; on the contrary, the cold boiled shrimp dipped in hot sauce, turkey sandwiches, and good American ice cream proved very popular. Parents were urged to bring their children and this turned out to be a most distinctive and popular feature. Under the salty and kindly leadership of the ship's Chief Boatswain's Mate a group of whitehats was organized as guides and escorts for the children. The small guests were met on the quarter-deck and taken on a special tour of the ship, then stuffed with ice cream and cookies. The lads who stole the show were a troop of tiny Malayan Cub Scouts who saluted gravely upon arrival and departure and never broke ranks all the time they were aboard. The sight of our burly, genial Captain gravely saluting and shaking hands with each of these tiny military tots as they departed was one that few who saw it will ever forget. From the hundreds of children who boarded the *Rochester* in Asian ports the United States should someday gain many important friends.

One other incident is worth relating. Among the officers assigned Shore Patrol duty from the *Rochester* were a Chinese-American lad and a young Negro officer. The former was able to exchange a few pleasantries in Cantonese with the Chinese who thronged on the pier The comment and interest aroused in the local Chinese press by this routine evidence of American non-discrimination was astonishing. It seems to reveal the acceptance by many foreigners of the familiar false Communist propaganda concerning minorities in the United States.

The big story in Singapore was the slow improvement in the Communist guerrilla situation "up country" in Malaya. The British claim to have this problem under control. There is no large scale popular support of the guerrillas and they seem to be running out of arms. Their objective since World War II has been to murder or scare away all the rubber planters (British), thus stopping the harvest of rubber and destroying the economy of Malaya. If this economic paralysis was accomplished with resultant poverty, misery and general disorder would provide the Communist core with a large following and probably give them the strength to take over Malaya. The Communists have been defeated by the skill and courage not only of the British troops (in a large part, Ghurkas), but particularly by the courage of the planters and their wives who have stuck it out under the most terrifying conditions. Many have been killed; all live behind barbed wire and go about their daily living armed to the teeth. A trip by automobile is always made at very high speed with guns loaded and hand grenades on the seat. Most of the planters have special armored cars and they roll up the armor when approaching possible ambush points much as we roll up the glass when it starts to rain. Their wives and children in most cases live on the planta-

Official U. S. Navy Photograph

A FORMAL RECEPTION FOR CIVIC VIP'S WHILE AT SAIGON, VIETNAM

tions too. With characteristic British tenacity the planters are holding on to a way of life that is important to the free world. It is also, in normal times, a pleasant life for them; the country is beautiful, the climate healthy, and the Malayan people are easy-going, charming, and helpful.

Bangkok was the next stop—a few days northward up the calm Gulf of Siam. The last major U. S. naval ship to visit Bangkok had been the heavy cruiser U.S.S. *Augusta* before World War II. There was just about time during the short passage from Singapore to have everyone's whites laundered and get the ship cleaned and polished. The *Rochester* was required, because of her draft and length, to anchor off the bar, a position which resulted in a long boatride (about thirty miles) to the city of Bangkok. LSMs were provided by the Thai Navy but liberty trips were not very pleasant, particularly the return to the ship, leaving Bangkok at 0100 and arriving alongside the *Rochester* about 0400.

Bangkok was to many of us the high point of the cruise. Thailand is one of the few large countries of Asia that has never been conquered or colonized by Europeans. In the 18th and 19th centuries the Siamese maintained their independence by playing off the British against the French, and vice versa. When it is realized that Thailand is a major part of the "rice bowl" of Asia, one of the largest rice exporting areas, it is all the more remarkable that the Siamese have not been conquered. Their tradition of independence has given them a friendly and cheerful character—they have no repressed feelings of inferiority and they meet Europeans as equals. They seem to like Americans and our relations with all the citizens of Bangkok could not have been more pleasant. No American sailor has ever been mugged or rolled in Bangkok, according to a local dignitary; a far better record than most of our own coastal cities can claim.

The names of Thailand and Siam are often confused, actually they are almost synonymous, although Thailand is now the official term. The people have always called themselves Thai and their country the Land of Thai (*Muang Thai* meaning: the land of the free). The most common name for their country was, however, Siam. In 1937 they decided to establish the name of their country as Thailand, but in 1945, to avoid confusing the peace negotiators after World War II, they officially reverted to Siam. In 1949 the name of Thailand was officially resumed.

The Thai people are Buddhists, an en-

Official U. S. Navy Photograph
CAMBODIA'S MYSTICAL, DESERTED CITY OF ANGKOR WAT ATTRACTED *ROCHESTER* TOURISTS

lightened and particularly tolerant variety, whose tenets seem very well suited to these warm and friendly people.

The city is laid out on the flat, marshy delta of the Bangkok River. Canals are used as much as streets and none of the land is more than a few feet above sea level. To build a house in the suburbs you must dig a large hole to obtain dirt for the foundation. The hole then becomes your pond. The mosquito problem is not as acute as it might be because those that carry malaria breed in fast running water, not stagnant water. Malaria is thus much more prevalent in the uplands than along the coast. With the assistance of the United States Foreign Operations Administration there is considerable large scale spraying done to discourage insects. The FOA has also introduced a small food fish in the canals that is reproducing rapidly and is helping to provide the much needed protein for this rice eating population.

The Royal Thai Navy gave a formal dinner for the Commanding Officer and fifteen officers on the spacious verandah of their officer's club overlooking the river. It was a tremendous affair; magnificent appointments, superb food and wines, and elaborate service. An excellent band played during dinner and after dinner a troupe of dancers performed their graceful and stylized classic dances. For this dancing there was rhythm furnished only by an exotic assortment of percussion instruments. The high point of the evening were the toasts, accompanied by patriotic music and short speeches. A huge Thai silver cup or goblet was presented to the *Rochester* and, after being filled with several quarts of champagne, was passed around as a loving cup. The officers of the *Rochester*, particularly the junior ones, were most impressed by the whole affair; even Ambassador "Wild Bill" Donovan declared it was one of the finest dinners he had ever attended. Most of us older officers felt that this was the sort of thing that could happen to officers whose ships showed the Flag around the world and would make up, in large part, for some of the rigors of the naval service that seem to be discouraging young officers from making the Navy a career.

There was much to see in Bangkok; native art and architecture as well as the mode of living of the people themselves. Silver and silk are the two tourist attractions. The silver is perhaps better known throughout the world; Thai silk is a relatively new industry as revived by an enterprising American. The silk is the product of small private looms and uses much gold and silver thread as

Official U. S. Navy Photograph

THE *ROCHESTER* TOOK PART IN OPERATION FLAGHOIST OFF IWO JIMA

decoration. The number and size of the temples was noticeable, most of them elaborately decorated. But of all the things to see the most fascinating was the way the people lived along the many canals that crisscrossed the city. An early ride in a small shallow draft motor boat in the cool of the morning was most revealing. Along the banks and in the sampans moored to the shore people were rising, washing, bathing, brushing their teeth, making their breakfast. Swarms of friendly little brown children waved to us as they were being fed and bathed. The filthy river and canal water was used for everything. Siamese are very clean, they bathe several times a day, but sanitation in our Western sense of the word does not exist. A colorful inhabitant of the canals was the saffron-robed priest, paddling his little wooden canoe among the other small boats that were either selling food or fuel or ferrying commuters into the heart of town. School children and business men stood on the shore as if they were waiting for a bus. They were waiting for a canal passenger boat to take them into town.

Saigon was the last port of call in southeast Asia and in some respects the most unusual. There was a war going on in French Indochina and there was no doubt whose side we were on. Special precautions were taken against sabotage and a sneak attack while moored to the wharf at Saigon, but there was no outward evidence of hostilities. The approach to Saigon is up a narrow, winding, tidal river with turns as great as 120 degrees. The French had swept it well as a precaution against mines and a plane overhead was used to observe possible guerrilla action. The ship was buttoned up and kept at a modified general quarters with the 3/50 battery manned and riflemen stationed along the deck. There was something incongruous about this huge grey ship steaming up the slim brown river at fifteen knots, swinging her great broad stern rapidly around the bends, seeming to brush the mangrove roots in passing. The French civilian pilot knew his business and never misjudged either the current or the shape of the bottom. The shore along the river was flat delta land, covered with low shrubs. At frequent bends in the stream the undergrowth had been cleared from a point of land and a barren, wooden outpost surrounded by barbed wire flew the tricolor as evidence that French Colonial troops were guarding one of Viet Nam's major logistic lifelines.

The *Rochester* passed Saigon to find a broad enough part of the river in which to

Official U. S. Navy Photograph
R.O.K. MIDSHIPMEN'S GRADUATION EXERCISES WERE ON THE *ROCHESTER'S* ITINERARY

turn around. Above the city a diminutive French naval pilot took charge. There was a great scurrying around in the vicinity of the bridge to find him something to stand on so he could see through the bridge windows; finally an overturned bucket had to suffice. But, size notwithstanding, this second pilot knew his business too. The *Rochester's* bow was stuck into the mud of the river bank and tugs pushed the stern around upstream. There was not much clearance aft and all river traffic ceased. Mooring was then accomplished along the waterfront of Saigon, heading downstream.

The political aspects of the visit soon became of absorbing interest. The three semi-autonomous states of French Indochina—Viet Nam, Laos, and Cambodia—were joined in a loose federation, to which our Ambassador, the Honorable Donald Heath, was accredited. In addition, the United States maintained diplomatic relations with each of the three independently. These states are somewhat different in their culture, language, and customs, although there are enough factors common to all to make eventual union possible. Their strongest bond is a desire to be rid of their masters, the French. It was necessary for us to recognize the fact that while the French were our allies the *Rochester* was visiting the Viet Namese.

The most unusual feature of the *Rochester's* visit was a reception given by the Mayor of Saigon, a Viet Namese, for the ship's officers. This was the first time such an honor had been given to a visiting man of war. The Viet Namese were shy but extremely cordial. All of them spoke French, a fact which helped a little to overcome the language barrier. Their own language is a most difficult one for an Occidental—most words have dozens of meanings depending on the inflection and intonation one uses. As a mark of special courtesy the wives and daughters of our Viet Namese hosts served refreshments at the reception. A most colorful, exotic, and attractive group of ladies they were.

Saigon, known as the Paris of the East, is a busy, prosperous metropolis. Men and officers enjoyed the many fine shops and cafes. For those with guest memberships the Club Çercle Sportif is one of the most attractive with an open-air restaurant and bar. It was noted with some interest by our alert young officers that while the men and women both wore the scantiest of swimming costumes, on the adjoining tennis courts it was forbidden to remove one's shirt, although the heat is normally so intense that playing is done early in the morning or late in the evening.

Official U. S. Navy Photograph

JUNKS AND SAMPANS AT ABERDEEN, HONG KONG ISLAND

The *Rochester* served as flagship for the Commander, Seventh Fleet, during visits to Korea and Hong Kong during April and May, 1954. These assignments came after the flag-showing cruise to Southeast Asia.

The sailors, of course, enjoyed the unusual alcoholic beverages available in a French port. Absinthe and many varieties of wine were reportedly experimented with. Despite these temptations, however, the men behaved very well, as they did in all the ports we visited, and no altercations with the police or shore patrol were noted. No one was missing upon departure either, although one young whitehat made a last minute arrival as all lines were cast off and had to make a pier head jump. Overcome during the night by languor (induced, according to his story, by the fatigue of intensive sight seeing) this young man had spent the night sleeping on the grass in the park. Awakened by the distant testing of the *Rochester* whistle and siren, he found himself without funds. A benevolent Chinese, dressed in a robe and carrying a Bible, came along and paid his fare down to the waterfront in a pedicab.

These man-powered taxis were a source of endless pleasure and amusement to our sailors. It was not uncommon to see the driver in the back seat with a whitehat pedalling rapidly through traffic, weaving in and out to the very evident discomfiture of the pedicab's driver who was torn between concern for his own safety and the large number of piastres he was going to get for this venture. The most amusing spectacle, visible from the quarter-deck late one afternoon, was a pedicab that was pedalled rapidly down the avenue past the ship's berth, the "driver" sitting at his ease in the back seat with his legs crossed, smoking a large cigar, a sailor pumping the pedals with great energy. The Communist propagandists who make so much out of the yellow-man white-man relationship must have a difficult time persuading people who actually see Americans that we are imperialists who wish to exploit them.

A most enjoyable reception by Ambassador and Mrs. Heath and a reception aboard the *Rochester* our final day in port marked the end of our short visit. Again the children received a warm welcome aboard the cruiser, which seemed to greatly please both the children and their parents. An uneventful passage down the river was completed and the *Rochester* headed north through the South China Sea for Japan and more mundane assignments.

The complex problems presented by Asia in tumult are very difficult for the casual visitor to understand, much less propose solutions for. There are, however, certain impressions, certainly not original, that strike even the passing visitor. One is that, for good or for evil, the old order has changed, the days of colonialism in Asia are definitely over. Economic logic must surrender to the fierce and long suppressed forces of nationalism and racism. The starving and impoverished brown masses have seen a glimpse of power and plenty; they want it for themselves and in their own name. The west can help them or fight them; it will perhaps make little difference in the flow of history, but it is a vital factor in the struggle of the United States against Communism. For survival in an unfriendly world our country needs friends and allies, and these we have and can keep by understanding the forces that motivate the people whose culture and state of political development is so far different from ours.

The value of short foreign cruises, similar to the one described briefly above, to both the Navy and to the interests of the United States is believed to be considerable. First of all, foreign visits are instructive, educational, and interesting for ship's personnel. An immediate benefit here to the Navy should be an increase in reenlistments and an inducement for young men to make the Navy a career. The appeal of travel and adventure to young men is a real and strong one that should be exploited to the full to attract the men we need. The dull drudgery of training exercises, both from home ports and when deployed abroad, can well be broken by foreign visits without loss of fighting efficiency. Secondly, the visits are good public relations for the Navy. The men send back gifts and relate experiences which arouse the interest of the home town folks as well as their pride in our Navy as a symbol of strength and freedom throughout the world.

The interests of the United States are advanced in several ways. Our men and officers present a fine appearance; they make friends with their good humor, generosity, and good conduct. Just as the big grey ships are impressive as symbols of the power of the United States that can reach any corner of the world and help our friends no matter how remote, so do our people stand as living arguments for our way of life. One has only to note the contrast between our own men, spotless in appearance, shining with good health, energy and friendly exuberance, and the populace of almost any city in the world to see what a powerful argument their appearance alone presents for the American spirit.

The Navy and the Department of Defense

By
Captain J. V. NOEL, JR., U. S. Navy

One of the facts of our times is that unification of the Armed Services is under way. Even a cursory review of the growth of the Office of the Secretary of Defense during the last 10 years confirms this. Every few months a new joint agency is established or another "single manager" is appointed. These organizations perform for the entire defense establishment certain services, and are staffed by all Services under the direction, or policy guidance, at least, of the Office of the Secretary of Defense.

Moreover, there is plainly visible in Washington a constant intrusion by the Office of the Secretary of Defense into the routine administrative activities of all the Services; first a demand for reports and data, then policy direction, and finally, in some cases, detailed supervision. All the forces at work, often stimulated by Congressional or Bureau of the Budget interest, are centripetal in nature, never centrifugal.

This is happening at a time when control of the sea is more important to the security of the United States than it has been since the early 19th century. A new dimension of submarine warfare within the ocean depths now provides a significant deterrent in the form of Polaris. There is, as well, a concurrent threat to our security in Soviet missile-carrying nuclear submarines. Meanwhile, the Fleet must still perform its historic—and growing—role of extending the nation's power to all distant shores where smolders, and at times bursts into flame, the fire of world revolution.

It is one of the great ironies of our time that, as its mission is enlarged and its responsibilities grow, the Navy itself, as a recognizable, distinct official entity, is threatened with eclipse by a burgeoning, all-powerful Department of Defense.

It would serve no purpose here to attack or defend the process of integration taking place. Whether or not it should be happening is entirely academic; the fact remains that it is underway. It might then be useful to consider the matter objectively, to learn something about the people of that hydra-headed bureaucracy, the Office of the Secretary of Defense, and to determine what attitudes should be encouraged and what techniques might be adopted by naval officers on duty in Washington to assist them in performing their duties more effectively.

The Office of the Secretary of Defense has quadrupled in terms of personnel since its inception in 1947. During this rapid expansion it was inevitable that many men of limited background, experience, and ability would rise quickly to supergrade level. Some of these were people who had formerly been employed by the Services and moved over because of the greater promotion opportunities offered by an expanding organization. Some of these men were not entirely happy and successful in their former employment and their performance of duty in the Office of the Secretary of Defense reflects this bias.

It is also true, of course, that many first rate people have been hired by the Office of the Secretary of Defense. Across the board it would be fair to assume that the working level of civilian officials in the Office of the Secretary of Defense is a representative cross section of Washington bureaucracy, not very different from the officer corps of the Armed Services. In fact, 80 per cent of the OSD Grade 11 and above civilians have had military experience.

More significant than the quality of its people is the attitude of the men in the OSD. Here we find the key to many problems officers encounter in dealing with them. By the very nature of their duties and responsibilities, few men in the OSD have a real and personal identification with anything more concrete than the "defense effort." This unhappy state of affairs, a lack of personal involvement with a group or a cause, is responsible for one of the most frustrating phenomena encountered in Washington—the tendency of OSD officials to ally themselves with the Bureau of the Budget or the General Accounting Office instead of with the Services.

Quite the reverse, however, happened. The Services found themselves lined up against BuBud *and* OSD. Similar cases are on record in such areas as substandard housing, air conditioning of buildings, and other matters related to health, comfort, morale, and habitability. At one time, for example, the Office of the Assistant Secretary of the Defense (Properties and Installations) would not approve the air conditioning of military family housing in certain parts of Texas where the Federal Housing Authority would not underwrite a building mortgage unless the house *was* air-conditioned.

This apparently anti-military bias of some OSD officials does not, of course, represent all OSD activities. There are a great many able and dedicated men in OSD who make a tremendous contribution to the efficiency of the Services. But it happens often enough to reveal a baffling problem in human relations and one that serves to disrupt the relationship of many officers with the offices in OSD with whom they must work on a day-to-day basis.

It can be assumed, of course, that a similar unwarranted prejudice against civilians exists on the part of some officers who resent the intrusion of any outsider into matters they conceive to be purely military. When this sort of an officer becomes *persona non grata* in OSD, it is not too difficult to accomplish his transfer. Conversely, however, the removal of a civil service employee who offends the military is rarely feasible.

There is one major block to a sympathetic understanding by OSD people of military needs and requirements and that is the well established stereotype that all the military services, aside from certain obvious and superficial differences, are essentially alike. This delusion results in a naïve clamor for uniformity of administration which, according to the second Hoover Commission and the more recent Symington Report, would be the key to tremendous economies in national defense. Several Congressmen are addicted to this theory and thump for a single service, single uniform, *etc*. Less extreme views are held by most responsible civilian officials in Washington, but enough of the idea of uniformity has rubbed off on the OSD to provide the Armed Services with endless headaches.

We who have spent most of our lives in uniform know that forcing all military people into the same mold would not be practicable, but we fail to realize that our civilian associates naturally have no such perception. Even our brothers-in-arms in the other Services are often ignorant of the essential differences. It sometimes surprises those outside of the Navy to realize that the Navy and Marine Corps have a major task in supporting the Fleet, and that roughly half of all Navy personnel are serving in this Fleet. In contrast, the Army between wars has normally been shrunk to relatively small forces in the field and is prepared to expand enormously and quickly by calling up the reserves.

A typical Air Force or Army enlisted man lives with his family on a post, provided with the housing, schools, and recreational facilities that compensate for his modest take-home pay. This is in sharp contrast to the typical Navy man who serves at sea in a ship or aircraft squadron, finding his own housing among civilians ashore. The Navy does, of course, have a shore establishment where men live on the station, but for the average sailor, this is the exception, not the rule. Among junior officers of the Services the contrast is even more acute; almost all newly commissioned naval officers report to the Fleet where they face at least four years of continuous deployment—which means a severe deprivation of home life for those youngsters who marry early. They can plan on getting home at night only 25 per cent of the time, or one year out of four. Compare this with the situation facing a newly commissioned Air Force or Army second lieutenant who reports to a base or post ashore and it is apparent why retention rates of junior officers are so much lower in the Navy.

A directive some years ago from the White House concerning joint or combined staff duty as a prerequisite for flag or general officer rank illustrates the confusion that can arise when the actual differences in structure, mission, and operation of the Services is not appreciated. Superficially, especially from an Army point of view, it seemed logical to ensure that all flag and general officers have joint or combined staff duty sometime in their career before promotion. Traditionally, the Army has always put its brightest and most promising officers in the General Staff Corps and grooms them for high command by repeated staff assignments. Operational duty with troops in the field for these selected officers is important, but is relatively infrequent due to the relatively small size of the standing regular Army.

The Navy, however, has had quite a different philosophy because most of the top officers were needed in the Fleet or to fill important posts related to Fleet support in the Navy Department. Hence, a flat dictum that joint or combined staff duty is necessary for promotion, inspired by the best of motives, is impossible for the Navy and the Marine Corps to implement sensibly. In the Marine Corps, for example, if all available joint or combined staff billets for colonels were filled for a year's tour of duty only about 25 per cent of all colonels could be accommodated. The Marines then, to obey the order, would have to drastically increase their staff billets or resign themselves to preselecting their general officers at the junior colonel level. Both of these solutions are, of course, too harmful to combat readiness and morale to be considered seriously. The Navy's situation in this regard is similar to that of the Marine Corps.

Another dramatic example of the incongruity of lumping all the Services together in implementing a White House directive is the recent order reducing the number of military dependents living abroad. No responsible official in the OSD—including Army and Air Force policy planners whose job it was to advise the Secretary of Defense—apparently had a clear understanding of the difference between the Army and Air Force on one hand and the Navy and the Marine Corps on the other in regard to their dependents living abroad.

The Army and Air Force normally send their people abroad accompanied by dependents except for a few thousand men in Korea, Okinawa, and Iceland. On most of the really isolated posts, such as early warning radar sites in the Arctic, civilian contractor personnel are hired at high salaries. The Navy and Marine Corps, in contrast, normally deploy their men abroad without dependents. The Sixth and Seventh Fleets, with only a very few exceptions, leave their dependents home and this deprivation of home life is one of the major causes of the Navy's severe problems in the retention of junior officers and critical enlisted ratings.

Despite these radical differences, however, the return-of-dependents directive was initially implemented by assessing each of the services a pro rata reduction based on the actual number of dependents abroad. Whatever justification there might be for returning some of the thousands of Army and Air Force dependents from their large concentrations in hard currency countries abroad, it was illogical and extremely damaging to morale to apply the same rules to the very small numbers of Navy and Marine Corps dependents, most of them in soft currency areas.

Here, again, the stereotype of uniformity served as blinders for the OSD officials whose administrative decisions can have such a marked effect on the combat readiness of the Armed Services.

It is a common fallacy, even among the general public, to believe that all military aviators are essentially the same and that great economies could be achieved by organizing all aviators in one group or service. Some civilian officials in the OSD, supported by Air Force officers, often subscribe to this doctrine. The facts are, of course, that Naval and Marine aviators are first and foremost seagoing naval officers and combat infantrymen respectively, not as a matter of tradition or pride alone, but because this basic qualification is vital in order for them to perform their highly specialized duties efficiently. Similarly, an Army aviator is first and foremost a soldier. These essential differences, well known to most Naval, Marine and Army officers, are quite commonly unappreciated on the policy-making level of officials in the OSD.

The diffusion of authority not accompanied by responsibility is another phenomenon of the OSD which poses a problem to officers of the Armed Services assigned to duty in Washington. A professional military man is accustomed to a close link between authority and responsibility—a division officer, a company officer, the commanding officer of a ship or station, all wield great power and authority over their men but are held strictly accountable in terms of efficiency, safety, and combat readiness.

In the world of business, this same sound principle of management is considered optimum. The local manager of a chain food store or bank is given much independent authority, but is held strictly accountable for making a profit. In the higher echelons of the defense establishment, however, it is apparent that a marked separation has occurred. The Chief of Naval Operations, for example, faces a growing and increasingly formidable array of civilian officials who assume no responsibility for the combat readiness of the Fleet yet who have the authority not only to say yes or no, but, increasingly, to say how.

The rationale for this proliferation of irresponsible supervision has traditionally been civilian control, accentuated by the budgetary process and the stupendous cost of modern armaments. Many thoughtful officials, however, both military and civilian, are viewing this matter with growing concern. Even the routine administrative operations of the Services are becoming, in the OSD, subject to more and more layers of co-ordination, policy direction, and detailed supervision. The *Wall Street Journal* of 7 December 1960, makes the following editorial statement: "The trouble is not merely that there are staffs upon staffs, secretaries upon secretaries, or committees upon committees; more vital is the fact that command responsibilities have been diffused and almost destroyed."

As responsibility in the OSD seems to be obscured by bureaucratic growth so does the assumption of more and more authority by lower and lower echelons proceed apace. Fourth and fifth echelons of administrative authority in the office of an Assistant Secretary of Defense now grandly direct the Service Secretaries to take appropriate action or to submit a new series of reports. Often these reports appear to accomplish no real purpose and may cost thousands of dollars to produce —dollars not available in current budgets.

This is perhaps the best argument against the kind of extreme unification advocated by the Symington Report. A huge monolithic structure would so diffuse responsibility that necessary changes and innovations would be difficult to make and the responsibility for major delays or mistakes would be impossible to fix.

Big business has found a means of avoiding much of this process of proliferation by subdividing large corporations into manageable segments. The Buick, Chevrolet, and Pontiac Divisions of General Motors are good examples. There is a reasonable relationship between authority and responsibility—Buick may be almost independent, but unless the operation is successful in terms of profits, there might be a new set of Buick executives in office next year.

Whatever may be the shape of the DOD in the years to come—quite apart from the theoretical arguments for or against a particular plan for reorganization—the professional officer today on duty in Washington faces several dilemmas. Some of them are suggested by the discussion above, while others are more subtle. For example, how can he reconcile his early allegiance to a particular weapon, such as carrier aircraft, destroyers or submarines, and his Service devotion as a sailor or Marine, with the larger views and broader horizons expected of an officer who must, to be useful in working with the OSD, identify himself with the total defense effort?

It is a matter of the first importance for an officer coming to Washington to understand the great changes that are taking place in the over-all defense effort and particularly the Navy. The historic mission of the Navy, control of the seas, is the same, yet in the Polaris submarine the Navy has brought into being a new dimension of warfare, the optimum deterrent which is playing such a vital role in filling the missile gap. The agony being suffered by the Navy in getting money for men, ships, and conventional arms is a reflection of this great pioneering into undersea operations while maintaining an adequate limited war and ASW capability.

Thus the Navy, in the course of events and not because of any greater inherent virtue than the other Services, has been drained of excess personnel and materials. It operates on a lean and austere basis and is, unfortunately, much more vulnerable to budget cuts "across the board."

A more obvious major development in the nation's defense effort is the transition from manned aircraft to missiles as the major offensive, deterrent weapon. This, of course, does not portend the demise of air forces, as some

The Navy and the Department of Defense

ALL MILITARY PEOPLE SIMPLY WILL NOT FIT INTO THE SAME MOLD

Men who have spent most of their lives in uniform realize this, but many civilians in the Defense Department do not, says the author. The White House order that Joint Staff duty be a prerequisite for flag rank was fine for the Army, but would have eliminated three out of four Marine colonels from consideration, as well as many outstanding naval officers from serving in vital billets at sea.

of our Sunday supplement military critics seem to imply, but it does mean that the Air Force, for example, as the number of bombers decreases, will be able to concentrate on some of its less glamorous missions, such as the transportation and close air-support of troops. While the Marines have historically been the brushfire fighters, the world, in its current social and political revolution, now promises the possibility of too many brushfires for the Marines to handle alone. The Army's role in limited war must be fully supported by the Air Force in order to give this country the limited war protection it needs. President Kennedy's recent directive increasing our troop-lift capability is a timely recognition of this need.

The two examples mentioned above of changes underway in the large defense picture are relatively obvious because they are military and deal with familiar facts and forces known to even the casual student of military matters. There are other significant changes underway, however, that are based on social

> A 1936 GRADUATE of the U. S. Naval Academy, Captain Noel served in destroyers in World War II, most of the time in command, and as an amphibious planner during the first part of the Korean War. He has written extensively on professional subjects. His best known work is the *Division Officers Guide* published by the Naval Institute. He also edited the 13th edition of Knight's *Modern Seamanship*.
>
> Captain Noel's current assignment is commanding the guided missile cruiser USS *Springfield* (CLG-7).

and economic forces at work in our society. One of these changes involves the profession of arms. Military men have historically been detached, as a profession, from the main stream of American life. They lived between wars in small numbers on their posts or manned a tiny Fleet and came into prominence only when mobilization for war brought them a major role in world events. Since World War II, however, there has been a marked change. A large defense effort, costing the nation a major share of its tax revenues, seems destined to be with us for the foreseeable future. This has made the profession of arms an integral part of American life, responsive to the interest, curiosity, and criticism exercised by our citizens upon all major institutions. This explains, of course, the pressure from citizen's groups and the Congress for economy, consolidation, and the introduction of economical management and business practices into every facet of defense.

This is the rationale for the Office of the Secretary of Defense—a vital, legal instrument designed to administer the defense effort as economically and as efficiently as humanly possible. If this administration falls short at times, it is important to remember that the men who staff the OSD are well motivated and sincere people who have a duty to eliminate the waste that has, does, and inevitably will exist to some degree in all large enterprises, such as the military services.

The importance and expense of national defense portend a marked change in the conduct of foreign affairs. It is no longer possible to separate foreign relations and defense; every aspect of our intercourse with the world affects our over-all strength in some respect. There must be the closest rapport between State and Defense, and this is underway on many levels. One example is the recently inaugurated program of exchanging senior Foreign Service officers and military officers between the Departments, not as liaison men, but as full fledged participants in their new assignments.

An officer ordered to Washington must prepare himself for a professional environment that may be foreign to any of his previous experience. Perhaps the first requirement on his part should be the assumption of a positive attitude, receptive to the acquisition of unsuspected information, new impressions, unexpected stimuli. Most of us are victims to some degree of our prejudices; too many of these can make duty in Washington frustrating and disappointing. Our allegiance to carrier aircraft, submarines or destroyers, for example, can provide useful operational knowledge where this rare commodity is most needed, but it can also serve to foment discord and dispute. A successful man in any profession must grow, must broaden his horizons, increase his knowledge and understanding. A naval officer must, even as a junior officer, identify himself with the whole Navy, not just the weapon of his choice. As a senior officer he must similarly identify himself not only with the Navy but with the whole defense effort of his country.

This does not imply that fighting vigorously for a Navy point of view is not often necessary; it does mean, however, that this effort is more effective if all aspects of the controversy are understood, including the rationale of your opponents. It is always wiser to build your case on the over-all national interest rather than on a seemingly narrow partisan approach.

In reacting to an OSD interest in matters that might appear to be purely a military or operational function, it is important to be objective. If the OSD (and certain committees of the Congress) seem to have an insatiable appetite for data on personnel utilization it is well to look at our own Navy with an open and enquiring, not to say critical, mind. Can we justify the thousands of sailors who perform permanent mess duties ashore? Could not a few minor technological advances reduce appreciably the number of men in the Fleet who perform the dull, repetitious tasks of chipping and painting, scrubbing paintwork, *etc?* Can it make any sense to a civilian to observe some of our naval bases composed of several independent commands all jealously guarding their minor prerogatives, functions and components? Answers to these and countless other questions are rarely clear cut and simple to obtain, but the important point is that they must be asked. If we do not ask them of ourselves, then we cannot justifiably resent others doing so.

There are times and occasions, of course, when sincere efforts on the part of OSD to coordinate efforts and save money are exceedingly ill-advised and a positive menace to national defense. Most of these concern the civilianization of logistics or support operations such as the procurement of weapons or the organization of communications. What appears to be good business practice may be very poor defense practice. Somewhere in between the newly mined iron ore and the steel missile in flight the military man must have control. The exact location of this control is the subject of considerably controversy.

A naval officer's major contribution, in addition to his operational knowledge, can be the courage to stand up and, when he considers it necessary, to remind his civilian associates and superiors that the object of the ball game is not saving money or achieving efficiency, but is deterring and defeating the enemy in total or limited war.

A naval officer reporting to Washington for duty with or in the OSD must be, of course, a good seaman or a good airman, but he must, in fact, be much more besides. He must have some knowledge of good management, not only as reflected by effective naval leadership in the Fleet, but as needed by a successful business administrator. This includes some knowledge of accounting, budget procedures, and Civil Service regulations, for example. The Dean of the Navy Management School at Monterey has reported the initial resistance of many of his students to learning about such unfamiliar procedures, for example, as those outlined in the Navy Civilian Personnel Instructions. Yet these young officers, who have spent their time flying planes or operating ships, are eventually persuaded that their future holds quite a different life as they become more senior—more of it ashore than at sea and most of it concerned with all aspects of efficient management.

We should face here, and accept gracefully, the dissolution of one of the Navy's most cherished traditions—that skill in going to sea in the Fleet is the only really important goal of a naval officer. There is no doubt, of course, that an officer is nothing if he is not an able seaman, highly skilled in Fleet operations. But for senior officers, many of the most difficult and challenging assignments will be ashore.

It is in working with the OSD that the critical importance of many duties seemingly unrelated to the Fleet will become evident. There are few quick rewards, as there can be for superior performance at sea—no heart-warming "well dones" from a Fleet Commander for winning the "E" or completing a successful foreign cruise. But the stakes can be higher in the OSD for a job well done; the long range effect on the Navy of seemingly minor decisions and rulings can be immense.

The Pentagon paper mills, like those of the gods, grind exceedingly fine, but the results can be an important weapon for the Fleet or a substantial personal benefit for Navy people. In the jungles of Washington bureaucracy there are many strange pitfalls which are as real a hazard as rocks and shoals are to mariners. Both the rewards and the hazards are welcome stimuli and can make duty with the OSD a professionally profitable and personally enjoyable experience.

www.ingramcontent.com/pod-product-compliance
Lightning Source LLC
Chambersburg PA
CBHW080619170426
43209CB00007B/1463